Small Cities USA

Small Cities USA

Growth, Diversity, and Inequality

JON R. NORMAN

RUTGERS UNIVERSITY PRESS
NEW BRUNSWICK, NEW JERSEY, AND LONDON

Library of Congress Cataloging-in-Publication Data

Norman, Jon R.
　　Small cities USA : growth, diversity, and inequality / Jon R. Norman.
　　　p. cm.
　　Includes bibliographical references and index.
　　ISBN 978–0–8135–5277–4 (hardcover : alk. paper) — ISBN 978–0–8135–5278–1 (pbk. : alk. paper) — ISBN 978–0–8135–5332–0 (e-book)
　　　Small cities—United States. 2. Small cities—United States—Growth. 3. Emigration and immigration—United States. I. Title.
　　HT123.N654 2012
　　307.76'20973—dc23　　　　　　　　　　　　　　　　　　　　　　　　　2011028835

A British Cataloging-in-Publication record for this book is available from the British Library.

Copyright © 2013 by Jon R. Norman
All rights reserved
No part of this book may be reproduced or utilized in any form or by any means, electronic or mechanical, or by any information storage and retrieval system, without written permission from the publisher. Please contact Rutgers University Press, 106 Somerset Street, New Brunswick, NJ 08901. The only exception to this prohibition is "fair use" as defined by U.S. copyright law.

Visit our website: http://rutgerspress.rutgers.edu

Manufactured in the United States of America

Dedicated to the memory of my father, Jack C. Norman,
who inspired my love of scholarship and learning

CONTENTS

Maps, Figures, and Tables   ix
Acknowledgments   xiii

1. Introduction: Small Cities in a Big Nation   1
2. The Divergent Fates of Small Cities   27
3. Putting Out the Welcome Mat: How People Affect Small Cities   71
4. Diversify, Don't Specialize   91
5. Balancing It All: Paths of Success or Failure for Small Metro Areas   116
6. Small Cities Matter!   132
7. Epilogue: Small Cities after 2000   148

Appendix: Technical Information on Data Sources and Statistical Analyses   155
Notes   165
Bibliography   171
Index   179

MAPS, FIGURES, AND TABLES

Maps

1.1.	Eighty Small Metro Areas, United States	18–19
2.1.	Providence, Rhode Island	38
2.2	Green Bay, Wisconsin	48
2.3	Salinas, California	58
2.4	Laredo, Texas	67

Figures

2.1	Median Population for Entire Metro Area, Eighty Small Metro Areas, 1970–2000	33
2.2	Median Central City Population of Eighty Small Metro Areas, 1970–2000	35
2.3	Median Suburban Population of Eighty Small Metro Areas, 1970–2000	36
2.4	Median Percentage Population Identified as White in Eighty Small Metro Areas, 1970–2000	43
2.5	Median Percentage Foreign-Born Population in Eighty Small Metro Areas, 1970–2000	44
2.6	Median Percentage of Population with College Degree in Eighty Small Metro Areas, 1970–2000	46
2.7	Median Percentage of Population Employed in Manufacturing Sector in Eighty Small Metro Areas, 1970–2000	54
2.8	Median Percentage of Population Employed in Professional Services Sector in Eighty Small Metro Areas, 1970–2000	55

2.9	Median Values on the 90:10 Economic Inequality Index in Eighty Small Metro Areas, 1970–2000	64
2.10	Median Unemployment Rate in Eighty Small Metro Areas, 1970–2000	65
3.1	Median Percentage of Population with a College Degree by Income Growth Group, Eighty Small Metro Areas, 1970–2000	84
3.2	Median Percentage Foreign Born by Income Growth Group, Eighty Small Metro Areas, 1970–2000	86
4.1	Median Percentage of Workforce Employed by Sector for Eighty Small Metro Areas, 1970–2000	97
4.2	Median Percentage of Firms by Sector for Eighty Small Metro Areas, 1970–2000	98
4.3	Median of Average Wages by Sector for Eighty Small Metro Areas, 1970–2000	99
4.4	Median Location Quotient for Employment by Sector for Eighty Small Metro Areas, 1970–2000	100
4.5	Median Location Quotient for Number of Firms within Sectors for Eighty Small Metro Areas, 1970–2000	101
4.6	Median Location Quotient for Wages by Sector for Eighty Small Metro Areas, 1970–2000	102
4.7	Percentage Change in Level of Employment by Sector by Level of Change in Median Household Income in Eighty Small Metro Areas, 1970–2000	107
4.8	Average Wages by Sector by Level of Income Change in Eighty Small Metro Areas, 1970–2000	108
4.9	Changes in Employment by Sector by Change in Economic Inequality Levels in Eighty Small Metro Areas, 1970–2000	110
4.10	Median Percentage Change in Average Wages by Sector by Change in Economic Inequality Levels in Eighty Small Metro Areas, 1970–2000	111

Tables

1.1	Changing Numbers of Cities in the United States, 1970–2000	15
1.2	Small Metro Areas by Region	17
1.3	Median Population, Population Range, and Largest MSA, Eighty Small Metro Areas, 1970–2000	21
1.4	Median Growth Rates for Eighty Small Study Metro Areas, Percentage of Metro Areas That Shrank by Decade, and List of Metro Areas That Shrank by Decade, 1970–2000	22
2.1	Eighty Small Metro Areas Grouped by Rate of Population Growth for the Period 1970–2000	31
2.2	Median Percentage of Workforce Employed in Various Economic Sectors, Eighty Small Metro Areas, 1970–2000	52
2.3	Average Median Household Income by Decade by Rate of Population Growth, Eighty Small Metro Areas, 1970–2000	62
3.1	Eighty Small Metro Areas Grouped by Percentage Change in 90:10 Economic Inequality Index, 1970–2000	88
4.1	Increase in Median Household Income by Quartile, Eighty Small MSAs, 1970–2000	105
4.2	Median Household Income Levels by Growth Quartile, Eighty Small Metro Areas, 1970–2000	106
5.1	Success Index Rank of the Eighty Small Metro Areas in 2000	122
5.2	Small Metro Areas That Experienced the Biggest Change in Success Index Rank, 1980–2000	125
5.3	Success Index Rankings of Case Study Metro Areas, 1980–2000	127
6.1	Median Location Quotients by Success Index Quartiles in 2000	140

ACKNOWLEDGMENTS

Green Bay, Wisconsin, according to many, is not much to look at. Yet as someone interested in the built environment, in the development of urban places, and in how people solve collective problems, particularly in relation to the two preceding concerns, I have continually been fascinated by my hometown. While I could not wait to escape what I considered to be the mundane and provincial atmosphere of Green Bay when I was a teenager, in retrospect I see that it provided many wonderful opportunities and experiences to me as a young person. Once I left Green Bay, I began to see what was unique about it—though perhaps this perspective was viewed through rose-colored glasses, since I have not lived there in nearly twenty years. Green Bay is a big city in its own neck of the woods, but it has a small-town feeling as you drive its streets. Smaller cities, as I write in this book, present an alternative urban experience from larger ones. This particular small city shaped me into the person I am today. And nearly as important, the peculiarities of Green Bay, which I began to take note of once I left the city, fueled a research agenda that culminated in this project.

This book is about small cities. Urban sociologists and others interested in urban change have generally ignored smaller places, and I view this book as a step toward ameliorating that blind spot. Small cities such as Green Bay may lack the glamour of New York City and Los Angeles, but that does not mean that they are not worthwhile objects of study. But in addition to putting these places on scholars' maps, this book is also an argument for expanding how we do urban sociology. This book examines eighty small metro areas across time, starting in 1970. Much urban sociology these days focuses on small numbers of places that are studied in-depth, often synchronically. Studies of that nature are incredibly useful for helping us understand the details of how large- and small-scale changes affect particular places. But we also need to pay attention to how classes of places change, particularly over time. This book is, I hope, an opening salvo in a campaign to enrich the study of urban areas by studying places according to common characteristics.

This book was written while I had the privilege of teaching at Loyola University Chicago. The sociology department there was a wonderful place to be as I expanded upon the original research of this project, and course releases offered me valuable time for working on the book manuscript. Funding from the College of Arts and Sciences at Loyola University Chicago also assisted in completion of this project. Japonica Brown-Saracino, a dear friend and colleague who is now at Boston University, read early versions of various chapters and provided useful critiques and suggestions that have improved the text. I also thank her for the times when we simply talked over coffee about my project, her book, our classes, and the other miscellany that contribute to life. Jennifer Barrett, now at the Wageningen University in the Netherlands, perked me up repeatedly when I was overwhelmed by this project. Mary Byrnes, now at Marygrove College, was always available with a smile and an infectious laugh that helped me through writer's block and moved me forward to getting my work done. I thank them for being gracious colleagues and friends.

I benefited from conversations with other colleagues at Loyola in a variety of ways. Kelly Moore, Anne Figert, Judy Wittner, Rhys Williams, and Marilyn Krogh all helped me in various ways, often by simply being good colleagues who buoyed me through the many unknowns that young scholars encounter in their early years. Kelly Moore was a particularly strong supporter of my endeavors, and I thank her for her unwavering support. I thank my research assistant, Robin Bartram, for her excellent help with preparing this manuscript. Robin demonstrated the intellect, tenacity, and attention to detail that ensures that she will be a highly productive scholar, and I look forward to helping her along in that process. Research assistant Bill Byrnes also provided help with formatting the tables and text.

At the University of California, Berkeley, Claude Fischer, an outstanding scholar and mentor, provided timely and useful feedback, sage advice, and support as I stumbled through the initial phases of constructing this project. Mike Hout generously spent much time discussing the complex statistics I used in the analysis and offered support about the importance of studying small cities. Margaret Weir helped me think through many of the problems I encountered in trying to explain how smaller cities end up on paths of success or stagnation and encouraged me to discover the punch line of my project. Margaret also encouraged me to see this project as a book rather than a series of articles. Paul Groth, a longtime mentor, advisor, and friend, was an unfailing supporter of my academic endeavors and offered a thoughtful perspective about generating meaning beyond the tables and charts. His influence can be seen throughout these pages.

I also thank Dawne Moon, now at Marquette University, for unwavering support, a wry smile when I was overwhelmed, and a genuine sense of continued intellectual curiosity even as my own work wandered far afield from her areas of expertise. Dawne is truly a magnificent scholar and an amazing friend, a rare combination of attributes. My friend Patrick Phelan generated the maps in this book as well as others that were set aside along the way. Patrick eagerly created beautiful maps on his own time, offering them to me freely. He is also one of my best friends and has steadfastly been there for me throughout my long and circuitous academic career, listening to me complain about saving my wrists for typing while we did gymnastics. Kipp McMichael and Jean-Claude Breach, his partners, took me on hikes, invited me over for dinner, hosted movie nights, and helped create the web pages that contain ancillary tables and information that could not be accommodated in the main text. I owe them considerable thanks as well.

Finally, I offer personal thanks to the many important people in my life who have believed in me during my meandering sojourns in Massachusetts, California, and Illinois. My friends from the University of California—Jonathan Bean, Jodi Short, Jennifer Sherman, Jessica Vasquez, Cinzia Solari, Anna Wetterberg, Damon Maryl, Nalini Kotamraju, Youyenn Teo, Christine Carter, and Fareen Parvez—all offered companionship and advice as I embarked on the start of my journey toward becoming a scholar. My old friends from Boston, Sharon O'Toole and Chris Dore, provided long-distance support and sympathetic ears during the challenging periods. Ming Lee, Brandon McCormick, Becky Long, and Justin Anderson, gymnastics compatriots both in Chicago and Berkeley, listened to me as I complained about working on the project and rambled on about sociological issues of no relevance to anyone and just plain cheered me up when I was down. My brother, Jeff, and his partner, Jolee, have been wonderful about keeping me going. My mother and father, Carol and Jack Norman, offered all sorts of support, although my father did not live to see the publication of this book. My father was a professor for over thirty years at the University of Wisconsin, Green Bay, and I dedicate this book to his memory. He was an outstanding scholar, teacher, and human being whose legacy I seek to uphold.

Small Cities USA

1

Introduction

Small Cities in a Big Nation

On a busy street, the sounds of Hmong and Spanish fill the air as people wander about. People talk about attending a professional football game, going to see a touring Broadway musical, visiting the local Native American heritage museum, or driving north to watch the leaves change color. Head east to New England, a freshly revitalized downtown features an expansive riverwalk where one can view fire sculptures on the water that burst into life on summer nights. There, amid ivy-covered colleges, brick warehouses being converted into lofts, and thriving neighborhoods with residents from around the world—from the Azores to Zimbabwe—city streets teem with life. Far to the south, along the border with Mexico, the largest import-export center between the two countries offers a different vision of urban life. Spanish and English commingle on the streets as people literally walk back and forth between the two countries on their way to work. Finally, on the West Coast, an area steeped in both agriculture and literary tradition attracts tourists as well as agribusiness professionals. The city—the heart of the "Salad Bowl of the World"—offers close proximity to the beach and exclusive, high-end communities populated by people fleeing the hustle and bustle of the nearby San Francisco Bay Area.

Where are all these places? They easily sound as though they could be major metropolitan areas in the United States, and in some ways they are. However, each city described above—Green Bay, Wisconsin; Providence, Rhode Island; Laredo, Texas; and Salinas, California, respectively—is small by most people's standards. Each city contains between roughly 100,000 and 200,000 people but represents a vibrant slice of urban life in America. Yet in reading contemporary scholarship on urban issues, it would likely never be mentioned that these places are where many Americans live and that the ways these places are faring in the wake of the demographic and economic changes of the last forty years greatly affects many people.

Smaller cities in the United States present an alternative vision of urban life compared to large cities, which have been the locus of most social scientific research over the past 100 years. Analysts argue over the causes of growth and stagnation in American cities. Indeed, the very existence of cities appears to be in peril in the early twenty-first century; city dwellers have been leaving for suburbs and exurbs since the 1970s at rates that have transformed the nation from majority urban to minority urban. Yet researchers' analyses almost exclusively center on the fates of the nation's historically largest cities such as New York, Los Angeles, and Chicago or on up-and-coming larger cities such as Phoenix, Houston, and Miami (Garreau 1991; Mollenkopf and Castells 1991; Portes and Stepick 1993; Scott and Soja 1996; Abu-Lughod 1999; Sassen 2001). Much has been written and said about those places, but few analysts have focused on smaller cities—those with 200,000 residents or fewer—which, combined, contain nearly 34 million people and are continuing to grow.[1]

Smaller cities and their metro areas present a different story of urban life. The changes seen in larger places have also been taking place in smaller ones, but in different ways and to a different extent. If growth and stagnation are measured as a combination of population change, economic well-being, and other quality-of-life indicators, smaller cities are not identical to their larger cousins. Scholars have not sufficiently documented or theorized changes in smaller cities. This book addresses both the changes that have occurred and theoretical explanations for these changes. I argue not only that is there insufficient research on what has actually happened in smaller urban places over the last thirty years but also that the theories scholars have developed do not adequately account for growth or stagnation among smaller urban areas.

The eighty small places examined throughout the text will be referred to as "cities," "urban areas," and "metro areas" interchangeably. This is not meant to confuse. In order to refer to places easily, I use the name of the primary city of the metro areas. However, metro area data—that is, data for both the central city and its suburbs or other adjacent communities—is important. Cities do not exist in isolation from their nearby communities, and metro area level data are important for understanding how places have changed given the movement of people from cities to suburbs over the last century (Jackson 1985; Rusk 2003). Generally, I refer to the places primarily as "cities" even though much of the data will be at the metropolitan statistical areas level. Metropolitan statistical areas (MSAs) are geographic areas composed of multiple incorporated and unincorporated areas centered on a historically recognized central city designated by the U.S. Census Bureau. Data at this level captures the dynamic relationship that characterizes cities and their nearby communities.

The goal of this study is to produce a better understanding of the nuances of urban life in the contemporary United States by focusing on smaller urban areas. In part, this effort is directed toward understanding how the smaller urban areas of the United States have changed and what factors most directly influence those changes. At the same time that I hope to explain some of the differences among smaller places, I also hope to provide some insights that will be useful in ongoing debates about urban public policy. Smaller cities represent a wide diversity of experiences, and "sizing down" policy solutions will not necessarily lead to brighter futures for them. Policy solutions for small places need to be based on research done on smaller urban areas.

Small cities are qualitatively and quantitatively different than the larger cities of the United States. They differ qualitatively in several ways. First, smaller cities like those studied here combine the elements traditionally defined as "urban"—being comparatively larger in size, denser in population, and with a greater mixture in types of residents than their hinterlands—with a small-town feeling not found in New York, Chicago, or Los Angeles (Wirth 1938/1969). Smaller cities also frequently function as centers for vast hinterlands, particularly in the Midwest and West. In addition, there are more small cities than large ones, they continue to grow over time, and they contain different groups of people, economic activities, and social worlds than larger places do.

But why have smaller places not been studied much? A variety of factors appear to be at work. First, American scholars who study urban areas trace their intellectual roots to the sociologists of the early part of the twentieth century who were at the University of Chicago. This "Chicago School" of urban sociology used Chicago as a laboratory for studying urban phenomena and then extrapolated outward. In part, this made sense. Scholars at this time were concerned with the rapid urbanization of the United States as the nation drew immigrants from abroad, migrants from rural areas, and African Americans from the South to the North, all in search of greater personal and economic freedom. These movements of people were further tied to the emergence of large cities in the United States that grew because of increased industrial production. Chicago served as an ideal example of these trends, and other researchers who were influenced by the Chicago School strove to examine how such changes played out in other large cities and to compare such places to Chicago, the archetypical American city.

The period of time, however, when even Chicago exemplified these trends was short, as patterns of settlement in the United States changed and continue to change. Not long after native and foreign-born individuals and families entered the largest cities in waves, they started moving out of them. Historical events such as the world wars, public policies such as those involved in stabilizing the real estate market after the Great Depression, and social attitudes such as racism influenced the movement of people from central cities to suburbs. Together, these factors created a shift of population and economic activity from central cities to suburbs.

While suburbs of large cities grew because of these factors, small cities outside the orbit of the largest cities in the United States also grew. As the historian Thomas Gardner (2001) has shown, cities of different sizes have experienced different growth cycles. Gardner documents the changing growth patterns of small cities in the nineteenth century that have become some of the larger cities of the twentieth. While the largest cities of the United States such as New York and Boston experienced early and continual growth from the eighteenth century on, cities such as Milwaukee and Cleveland did not experience growth until the end of the nineteenth century. Indeed, many of the cities Gardner studies in the nineteenth century were similar in size and position to the cities included in this book.

Some smaller places experienced increasing levels of urbanization, or at least metropolitan growth in the latter part of the twentieth century, just as smaller cities did toward the end of the preceding century. While many of the largest places in the country have seen declines in both central city and metropolitan area population, smaller places have not necessarily followed suit. In fact, around the world, more people live in small and medium-sized cities today than in large metro areas, and smaller places are expected to experience far greater population growth than large cities between now and 2050 (United Nations 2007).

Yet small cities are worth studying for more than the reason that they continue to grow. Because small places are more numerous, they offer the opportunity to explore how changes affect many places at once. While they may be "off the global map" (Robinson 2002) and neither the beating heart nor the brains behind the vast changes that have occurred during the twentieth century, small cities are an important part of the central nervous system of the nation. By examining how changes have occurred in smaller places, we are able to get a sense of how large-scale changes have affected America writ large.

The Central Question: How Have Smaller Places Changed?

This study examines eighty smaller metro areas across the United States to investigate the effects of local, national, and international forces on smaller cities and suburbs. This requires thinking about how and why cities change as the effects on metro areas of internal forces (such as local government and economic activity) and external forces (such as changes in migration patterns and national economic shifts) on metro areas. This book focuses on the period 1970 to 2000 not only because is it characterized by large-scale changes in the economy, such as the shift from an industrially based to a service-based economy, and demographic changes, such as the influx of non-European immigrants, but also because public policy debates shifted during this period to emphasize less state action and more market-driven solutions to public policy problems. These same issues arise in scholarly debates about how cities are doing and what sorts of policy solutions might be useful. While the main focus is on this thirty-year period, data from 2000 through 2010 are used when possible to assess how places have changed.

Assessing change over this period allows an examination of theories of urban change related to the biggest socioeconomic transformations of the latter part of the twentieth century. I center this analysis on several key issues. The first is the shift toward greater integration of local economies into the global economy.[2] Second, I concentrate on internal changes in the U.S. economy related to changes in the global economy. Over the past half-century, the United States has shifted from an economy based chiefly on manufacturing to one based mainly on services. This post-industrial shift changed the economic, social, and physical landscape of the country. I also include in my analysis place-specific attributes that may account for change in a metro area's well-being. Including change at the global, U.S., and local levels generates a better understanding of how and why small places change in the United States over time.

Cities in the United States have followed many paths. Although the United States experienced increasing urbanization in the early twentieth century, out-migration from cities to suburbs characterized the latter half of the century (Jackson 1985). But not all cities shared the same fate. Some small cities, such as Youngstown, Ohio, have faced many problems, including declining population, lower median incomes for the remaining residents, and fewer jobs overall, especially high-paying jobs. Other cities, such as Boise, Idaho, have had the opposite experience: increasing population in both the central city and suburbs, rising incomes, and more economic opportunities for residents. Scholars offer competing arguments for why cities suffer different fates. Some scholars emphasize public policy decisions, while others focus on private business decisions, changes in the way the economy works such as the shift from manufacturing to services, or even the local weather, to name a few. Even though these understandings of why cities are doing better or worse are based primarily on evidence from large cities, the theories that are derived from large cities provide the tools, or at least the framework, for studying small cities.

Local Connectedness to National and Global Economies

During the last thirty years, small cities have been buffeted by changes in the global and national economies. Cities change with the ebb and flow of the national and international currents of economic expansion and contraction. In addition, the economies of the United States and other developed nations have changed in fundamental ways: manufacturing has declined in importance as services have increased in importance. Little is known about the fate of small cities in the "global economy" other than that many smaller cities have lost industrial jobs. Urban geographers such as James Vance (1971) and Brian Berry (1967) contributed influential studies on how small cities and towns exist within networks of urban areas in the 1950s through the 1970s. However, since then the national economy has changed considerably, and the connections between smaller places and between smaller places and larger ones need a thoroughly new investigation (Christaller 1933/1966; Berry 1967; Vance 1971).[3] Scholars posit that small cities may become specialists in providing tertiary or ancillary services to the major "global cities" of the United States. Such services include call centers for banks and credit card companies or claims-processing centers for insurers. These types of centers provide essential support to a primary business but do not generally provide high-paying jobs with good benefits, and they are not thought to generate much economic growth for an area. In addition, there is little evidence to show that these jobs now predominate in small metro areas (Negrey and Zickel 1994; Sassen 2001; Savitch and Kantor 2003).

While media reports tell us about the death of the smallest towns in the Midwest because of isolation and out-migration, the fate of smaller but truly urban areas remains undocumented (Egan 2002). The global cities theory posits that small cities located outside the orbits of larger metropolises will die out because they will be unable to take part in the new global economy. But while smaller cities have seen significant economic changes—influxes of "big box" national retailers at the expense of local retailers, for example—the details of the how the greater interconnectedness of economies has affected them has not been studied.

The original world cities hypothesis, which was put forth by John Friedmann in 1987, contained several key ideas that have been greatly expanded upon by subsequent scholars. Friedmann (1995) argues that world cities serve as the centers of global capital, are highly interconnected and are heavily influenced by changes in the international economy. Saskia Sassen expands upon these ideas by showing that, global cities, as she refers to them, have high employment in the high-end services sector and in the finance, insurance, and real estate (FIRE) sector; are the centers of both their local areas and their hinterlands; and are more closely tied to other global cities than to the nation-state in which they are located.

Other scholars have taken up the challenge of determining which cities are truly "global" or "world" cities. Some argue that particular cities should be added to such lists, while others have evaluated the accuracy of the global cities theory by assessing change in world cities such as New York (Knox and Taylor 1995; Abu-Lughod 1999). In this book, I reframe the question from "Is place X a world city?" to "How do the processes presumed to illustrate greater globalization affect smaller cities?"

According to Sassen and others, global cities are assumed to have large populations in order to carry out these functions and partake in their assigned economic activities. By definition, then, small cities cannot be global. In addition, smaller urban areas are seen as completely subservient to larger ones, and it is thought that only those located near global cities benefit as they become the outposts of back offices or provide tertiary services that can be provided off site. Finally, these scholars posit that only a few cities can be "global" because part of the definition of the term is that a global city is the center of tremendous economic and social power. Global cities supposedly rule over other large cities, over smaller cities, and over their hinterlands in the post-industrial economy centered on finance, law, and other high-end services. As I will show later on, small cities located outside the direct influence of larger metro areas are not literally off the map, and many have managed to accommodate the newer forms of economic relations that global cities theorists discuss.

The global cities hypothesis ignores many urban areas in both the developed and developing worlds. Eugene McCann argues that the polarization between research on "global cities" and "presumably 'non-global' cities" is problematic because it obscures the ways that smaller cities are part of national and international economies (McCann 2004b). But other scholars argue (particularly in relation to the developing world) that the global cities perspective cannot adequately account for urban change and growth because it focuses only on the largest cities of the developed world (Robinson 2002). The hypothesis accounts for only those cities that it describes (cities that generate as well as fulfill its presumptions), thus preventing it from being a truly "global" hypothesis capable of explaining urban change in most places. Both McCann's and Robinson's critiques provide an opening for thinking about smaller urban places in relation to the global cities hypothesis.

The evidence from the eighty places analyzed in this book suggests that instead of functioning as the back offices or dumping grounds of large cities, smaller cities potentially fill roles akin to those of global cities, just at a much smaller scale. Smaller places have some of the same economic characteristics that global cities possess, and they also function as the centers of local regional areas. However, smaller cities are generally not significant players in the international arena. Instead, these smaller places are perhaps best thought of as "glocal cities," to borrow a recently coined term. I use the term "glocal cities" to describe those places that are most successful because they look like global cities in terms of economic diversity and activities but operate on a much more local level, be it regional or national. Many of these cities are tied to the international marketplace as well. For example, from 20 to 40 percent of the cities in this study were home to a Fortune 500 firm at some point during the thirty-year period of this study.[4]

Creativity, Human Capital, and Growth

While some scholars emphasize the role of firms and market forces, others turn to the role of people within these institutions to explain the success or failure of an urban area. Richard Florida (2001, 2005) theorizes that levels of human capital in cities best explains urban growth. Human capital can be thought of as the levels of education and the skill sets people have. The concept has become more important in sociological and economic analysis as the nation's economy has shifted from an emphasis on Fordist manufacturing work to the high- and low-end services sectors, which provide jobs in fields that range from law and medicine (high-end services) to food preparation and retail sales (low-end services). Florida argues that the cities that best foster human capital by offering a diverse, "bohemian," tech-savvy, and hip environment are succeeding economically compared to cities that lack those qualities. The shift to an economy oriented to the service sector underlies this argument. While there has been some debate about whether or not Florida's assertions are correct, the basic premise that cities face a new economic reality that requires a different work force seems clear (Clark 2004).

Florida (2001) offers a compelling theory of why certain cities remain strong and vibrant while others stagnate. He argues that cities that have capitalized on the "creative class" have done better in the last thirty years than have cities without large creative classes. The "creative class" consists of highly educated professionals who work in a wide variety of areas; the commonality is that these professionals are called upon to provide creative or imaginative thinking on a regular basis as part of their jobs. Florida shows that the cities with the largest number of people in the "creative class" tend to be the most diverse and tolerant; such cities are more likely to welcome gays and lesbians and "bohemians," value racial and ethnic minorities, and be safe places for women. Places that have these characteristics score well on his "tolerance index," a ranking system based on these concepts. Florida argues that diverse places are attractive to liberal-minded creative class workers who then fuel the high end of the service economy, thus making a given place wealthier.

Some scholars have questioned how well Florida's perspective explains urban change and growth. Cynthia Rausch and Mary Beth Negrey (1994) note that a concentration of the creative class appears to be only somewhat related to the economic strength of a metro area as measured by the area's total economic output. Allen Scott (2006) cautions against seeing the creative class as the engine for change in all urban areas; the creative class theory ignores the striking inequalities that continue to grow in the wake of the move toward a creative economy that focuses on the high-end services sector, such as jobs in the fields of research and high-tech. The results of fostering a creative class seem helpful for metro areas, but the mechanisms for achieving those results seem to be situated in traditional economic development programs rather than in newer ones designed to capture the creative class specifically (Jenkins, Leicht, and Jaynes 2006).

My assessment of the performance of metro areas takes into account Florida's perspective and the recent critiques of it. According to Florida (2005), smaller cities did not do very well at the end of the twentieth century because they were unable to attract the professionals that constitute the creative class. Because some of the small cities included in this study are "glocal cities," they cater to the creative class, mainly through the mixture of employment opportunities found in glocal cities. Other cities, however, have succeeded in ways that do not seem to be related to the creative class. Green Bay, Wisconsin, for example, is firmly "glocal" without being overly "creative," although it does have some creative jobs in higher education and health care. Green Bay has had continued economic success more because of its mix of firms and industries than because of the emergence of an economy focused on the creative class. While the creative class theory works well for larger places, smaller cities such as those examined here appear to travel a wider variety of paths to success. Because of this, policy solutions aimed at attracting the creative class may not be the best for all small places.

Place-Specific Attributes

While both the global cities and the creative class hypotheses speak to external forces that act on places, such as changes in the economy and accompanying changes in the education levels of workers, many scholars point to place-specific attributes of urban areas in explaining why a city is doing well or not. Many place-specific attributes influence how well a metro area fares, but I focus on the few key factors that have appeared in scholarship over time. And while I refer to these attributes as "place-specific," they often have gained notice primarily because they are part of a general trend across places, such as climate. I examine key institutions, such as the presence or absence of Fortune 500 companies, the number of colleges and universities, or whether or not a city is a state capital. These elements link my analysis to other investigations of urban change that point to place-specific features as determinative of growth (Carroll and Meyer 1983; McCann 2002; Pack 2002).

Over the past fifty years, the geographical distribution of U.S. residents within metro areas has been the subject of much research and debate. Scholars and others identify two key processes at work: the suburbanization of households and the movement of people from the Northeast and Midwest regions to the South and West regions of the United States. These two phenomena radically changed the face of America from 1950 to 2000. Prior to the 1950s, America was becoming increasingly urban; people were moving out of rural areas to cities in search of jobs in the new industrial economy (Jackson 1985). The two world wars hastened this movement considerably, as did the movement of African Americans from the South to the North at the end of the nineteenth and the beginning of the twentieth centuries. By 1920, the majority of people in the United States lived in urban areas. However, this trend reversed in the second half of the century: by 1990, nearly half the nation's population lived in suburbs (Glaeser and Shapiro 2003b).

People not only left central cities in general, they specifically left the large central cities of the Northeast and Midwest during the latter part of the twentieth century. The U.S. Census Bureau calculates the mean population center of the United States every ten years; this is the geographic center of the distribution of population in the country. In 1900, the population center was in Indiana. In 1950, it had migrated slightly west to Illinois, and by 2000, it had moved to the west and south to Missouri (U.S. Census Bureau 1990). The movement of the mean population center charts the movement of the population in a general way from the Northeast and Midwest. Southern and western cities and suburbs experienced unparalleled growth from 1970 to 2000, generally at the expense of cities and suburbs in the north and east.

These two trends have generated considerable scholarly research. Much has been written about why people moved to the suburbs and why they moved to the South and the West. Scholars theorize that this movement is due to a variety of factors, including lax labor laws, zoning laws, average temperatures, and other factors (Pack 1980; Jackson 1985; Garreau 1991; Hayden 2003). My analysis focuses on the ramifications of this mass movement of people on smaller urban and suburban areas, a topic that has generally not received much scholarly attention. Interestingly, the data I examine show that a location in the West or South does not appear to guarantee success for a smaller places. Many of the small cities in Texas have not fared well. Laredo, for example, has seen considerable population growth. However, while income levels there have increased over time, they remain well below the national average, and economic inequality levels in these places are strikingly high. The differences among small cities can be learned only by comparing a wide variety of cities across the nation.

The Eighty Small Cities and Their Metro Areas

The group of cities in this book includes some surprises. While places such as Erie, Pennsylvania; Madison, Wisconsin; Little Rock, Arkansas; and Boise, Idaho, are obvious specimens of smaller cities, others such as Providence,

Rhode Island; Grand Rapids, Michigan; Orlando, Florida; and Las Vegas, Nevada appear to be fundamentally different because of their much larger populations. But the difference appears only if we look at these cities from today's standpoint. These four cities (and the other handful of comparatively larger places) were small cities in 1970. Las Vegas, for example, had a metro-area population in 1970 of roughly 300,000 people, and the city of Las Vegas itself had only 125,000 residents. Orlando was even smaller in 1970. The population of Orlando proper then was 98,000, even though nearly 500,000 people lived in the metro area. So while including these places may seem odd given their current size, at the outset of the period of this study, they clearly fit the criteria for small cities.

The eighty places I study in this volume are all small center cities that are distant from larger places at any point in time. Cities have trajectories of growth along multiple lines (demographic, social, and economic) that converge and diverge across time. Some cities' trajectories are like straight lines, for these places, the metro area has a steady rate of population change across time. Other places grow or shrink over time. Thus, it is not important for this study that all cities look completely alike across time. Rather, what is important is that these eighty places share some commonalities (were on similar paths) during the thirty-year period of this study because that allows us to see how changes affect different types of small places. This allows us to examine how and why some metro areas stay on one path and others forge ahead into new territories. By including a variety of places, we are better able to explain both empirically and theoretically how different places experience large-scale changes such as globalization, post-industrialization, and immigration.

Small cities are as varied as the locales they occupy. The small cities included here capture the diversity of smaller urban areas in the United States. The group includes very small places—such as San Angelo, Texas; Pueblo, Colorado; and Sioux City, Iowa, all with populations of less than 150,000 residents—as well as larger places such as Fresno, California; and Salt Lake City, Utah, whose metropolitan populations (central city and suburbs together) reached nearly one million residents in 2000. However, the cities selected for this study met two criteria. Each of them has a central city or had, at some point between 1970 and 2000, a population of between

100,000 and 200,000. In addition, all of these cities are the centers of their local region; they serve as the "big city" for a hinterland.

The center cities of smaller metro areas are the focus of this book. Center cities are the historic centers of local regions and generally grew in size and economic activity before their adjacent (suburban) or outlying communities did. While local regions—metro areas—are increasingly important in people's lives because of the dispersal patterns of jobs and retail centers, in most small places, the center city is still often the local center of social, cultural, and economic activity. However, I use metropolitan statistical area–level data for much of my analysis, which includes data about areas outside the city center, for several reasons. First, "suburbs" of smaller cities are often more fully integrated into the urban fabric of a nearby small city than is the case with areas located just outside larger metropolises. People who live in Woonsocket, Rhode Island, fill many of their needs in Providence, just as residents of De Pere, Wisconsin, head to Green Bay regularly. Second, the relationship between the central city and its adjacent municipalities must be examined to understand how places have grown or stagnated in the wake of the intense de-urbanization the United States has experienced.

What Is a "Small City"?

For the purposes of this study, a small city is the central municipality (of a metropolitan area) with a population of between 100,000 and 200,000. I use this population-derived definition for several reasons. First, the U.S. Census Bureau categorizes cities by size, and the smallest metropolitan areas the bureau provides aggregate data for are cities in this population range. Second, other researchers use this population range for the category of "small city" or "small metro area" (Mitchell-Weaver, Miller, and Deal 2000; Pack 2002; Stanback 2002). Finally, this population span captures cities of a certain type and flavor; these cities are large enough to be truly urban yet have (or had) a small-town feel in many respects. For example, Green Bay, Wisconsin, still has cornfields within the city limits, something far less common among larger cities in the United States.

As table 1.1 indicates, the number of cities with populations greater than 100,000 has increased in the last thirty years, as has the number of cities with populations of between 100,000 and 200,000. And although there

TABLE 1.1
Changing Numbers of Cities in the United States, 1970–2000

In 1970:

- 157 cities had populations above 100,000
- The population of 92 cities (59 percent of all cities) was between 100,000 and 200,000
- 75 cities (82 percent of smaller cities) were the center city of a metro area as defined by the U.S. Census

In 1980:

- 174 cities had populations above 100,000 (11 percent growth in number of cities from 1970)
- The population of 101 cities (58 percent of all cities) was between 100,000 and 200,000 (10 percent growth in the number of smaller cities from 1970)
- 76 cities (75 percent of smaller cities) were the center city of a metro area as defined by the U.S. Census (1 percent growth in number of smaller cities from 1970 that were the center cities of metro areas)

In 1990:

- 201 cities had populations above 100,000 (16 percent growth in number of cities from 1980)
- The population of 124 cities (62 percent of all cities) was between 100,000 and 200,000 (23 percent growth in number of smaller cities from 1980)
- 81 cities (65 percent of smaller cities) were the center city of a metro area as defined by the U.S. Census (7 percent growth in number of smaller cities from 1970 that were the center cities of metro areas)

In 2000:

- 246 cities had populations above 100,000 (22 percent growth in number of cities from 1990)
- The population of 157 cities (64 percent of all cities) was between 100,000 and 200,000 (27 percent growth in number of smaller cities from 1990)
- 96 cities (61 percent of smaller cities) were the center city of a metro area as defined by the U.S. Census (19 percent growth in number of smaller cities from 1990 that were the center cities of metro areas)

Source: U.S. Census Bureau data from the 1970, 1980, 1990, and 2000 censuses.

has been a larger proportional increase in the number of smaller cities that are part of larger metro areas (due primarily to people either moving to suburbs from other central cities or instead of moving to central cities) compared to the rate of increase in nonsatellite smaller cities, the net number of small cities that are the centers of their own metro areas has increased—from seventy-five in 1970 to ninety-six in 2000.[5]

To determine the universe smaller urban places that could be included in this study, I looked at urbanized areas within metropolitan statistical areas of cities that are the primary economic and social center for a MSA. The relationship between large urban centers and their suburbs is different than the relationship between smaller central cities and their suburbs. Thus, for example, Cambridge, Massachusetts, and Berkeley, California, are excluded since they are part of larger metro areas of which they are not the economic center. Other scholars have studied larger suburbs in large metro areas and have documented the dynamic of growth and decline in these places (Jackson 1985; Garreau 1991; Hayden 2003).

Because I examine how places that are small grow into large places (or how they stagnate or even shrink), I use the population of the central city as opposed to the population of the total metro area. While total metro area population is important, using the center city population better captures the centrality of smaller cities within their local areas. In addition to limiting central city population to from 100,000 to 200,000 people, I also limited the cities that could be included to metro areas that are the center of their local area. To be included, a city had to be more than thirty miles away from another city with a population that is greater than 50 percent of the target city's population. This criteria removed larger suburbs from the study.[6] Finally, the analysis in the study includes all MSAs with center cities with populations from 100,000 to 200,000 at any point during the 1970 to 2000 time period. (The thirty-year period is used because the data is more comprehensive for all places for that time frame, but data from after 2000 are also used when available throughout the book and in the epilogue.) Including those cities that "sized out" (i.e., shrank below 100,000 or grew above 200,000) allows for speculations about how different forces affect different cities.

Using these two limiting conditions, I collected data on eighty metro areas for the thirty-year period from 1970 to 2000. Table 1.2 lists (and map 1.1 illustrates) the cities by region in the study. Reflecting the history of

TABLE 1.2
Small Metro Areas by Region

Northeast	Midwest	South	West
Erie, PA	Ann Arbor, MI	Abilene, TX	Bakersfield, CA
Providence, RI	Cedar Rapids, IA	Amarillo, TX	Billings, MT
Reading, PA	Columbia, MO	Baton Rouge, LA	Boise City, ID
Springfield, MA	Decatur, IL	Beaumont, TX	Colorado Springs, CO
Syracuse, NY	Des Moines, IA	Chattanooga, TN	Eugene, OR
Trenton, NJ	Duluth, MN	Columbia, SC	Fresno, CA
	Evansville, IN	Columbus, GA-AL	Las Vegas, NV
	Fargo, ND	Fayetteville, NC	Modesto, CA
	Flint, MI	Fort Smith, AR	Pueblo, CO
	Fort Wayne, IN	Gainesville, FL	Reno, NV
	Grand Rapids, MI	Huntsville, AL	Salem, OR
	Green Bay, WI	Jackson, MS	Salinas, CA
	Kalamazoo, MI	Knoxville, TN	Salt Lake City, UT
	Lansing, MI	Lafayette, LA	Spokane, WA
	Lincoln, NE	Laredo, TX	Stockton, CA
	Madison, WI	Lawton, OK	
	Peoria, IL	Lexington, KY	
	Rochester, MN	Little Rock, AR	
	Rockford, IL	Lubbock, TX	
	Sioux City, IA	Macon, GA	
	Sioux Falls, SD	McAllen, TX	
	South Bend, IN	Mobile, AL	
	Springfield, IL	Montgomery, AL	
	Springfield, MO	Orlando, FL	
	Topeka, KS	Richmond, VA	
	Youngstown, OH	Roanoke, VA	
		San Angelo, TX	
		Savannah, GA	
		Shreveport, LA	
		Tallahassee, FL	
		Tyler, TX	
		Waco, TX	
		Wichita Falls, TX	

MAP 1.1. Eighty Small Metro Areas, United States

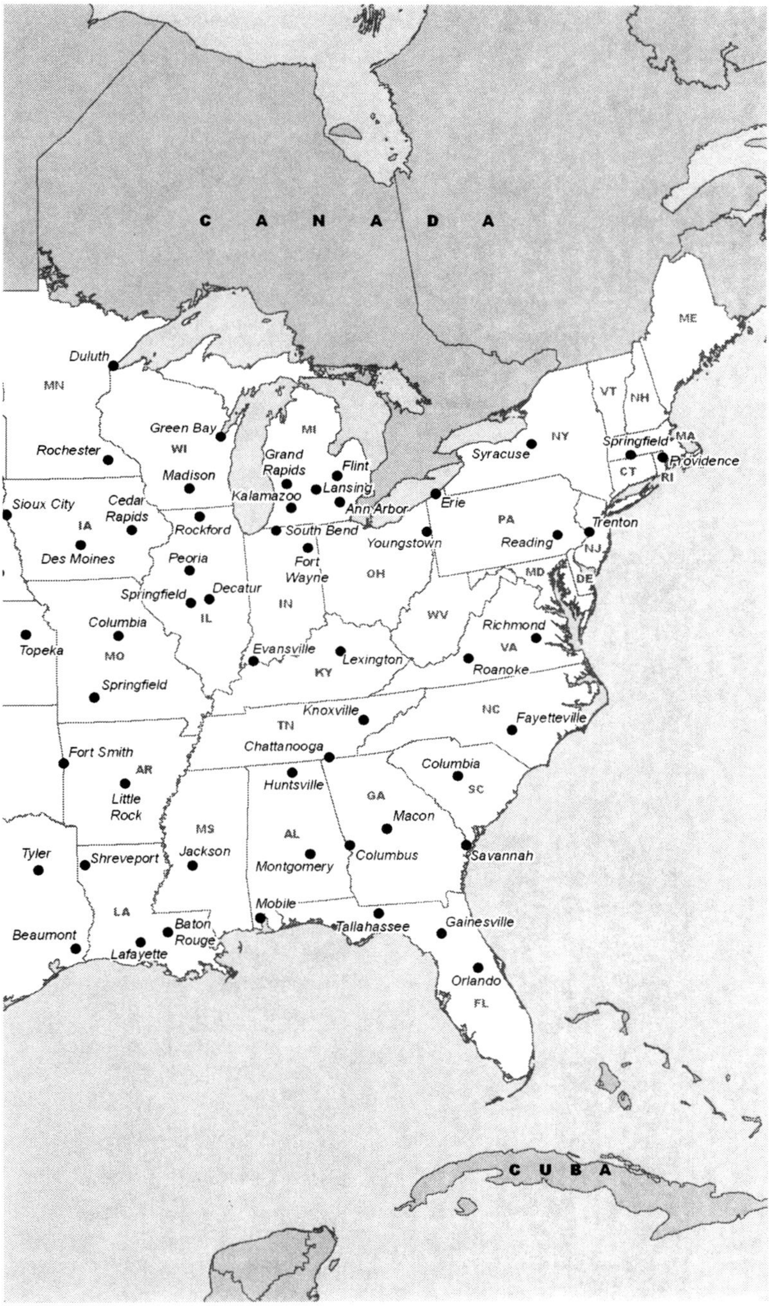

CANADA
Duluth
MN
ME
VT
NH
Green Bay
MI
NY
Springfield
MA
Rochester
WI
Syracuse
Providence
Grand Rapids
Flint
CT
RI
Madison
Lansing
Kalamazoo
Erie
Sioux City
Cedar Rapids
Ann Arbor
IA
Rockford
South Bend
PA
Trenton
Youngstown
Reading
Des Moines
Peoria
Fort Wayne
NJ
MD
OH
DE
Springfield
Decatur
IN
IL
WV
Richmond
Columbia
Topeka
MO
Evansville
Lexington
VA
KY
Roanoke
Springfield
Knoxville
NC
Fayetteville
TN
Fort Smith
Chattanooga
AR
Columbia
Huntsville
SC
Little Rock
GA
Macon
MS
AL
Tyler
Jackson
Shreveport
Columbus
Savannah
Montgomery
LA
Mobile
Baton Rouge
Gainesville
Tallahassee
Beaumont
Lafayette
Orlando
FL
CUBA

urbanization in the United States, the dataset includes more cities in the Midwest, South, and West in this study than in the Northeast. About one-third of the cities in the study are in the Midwest, while slightly over 40 percent are in the South. Because the Northeast is characterized by larger, physically contiguous metro regions with very large central cities (e.g., Boston or New York) that have substantial suburbs and the countryside of the region has many outlying small villages and towns that nearly run together, most places from that region do not fit the criteria specified for being included in this study. The states with the largest number of places in the book are Texas (ten), California (five), and Michigan (five). Although these states appear to be overrepresented, these are three of the most populous states in the nation. It is therefore not surprising that they would have more small cities.

This group of cities captures the vastly differing experiences of small places. One key way of illustrating the different experiences is to examine population levels over time in these eighty places. Most cities averaged a thirty-year rate of growth in population of between 11 percent and 49 percent. However, some cities such as Decatur, Illinois, and Flint, Michigan, experienced a decline in population over the thirty-year period. Other cities such as Boise, Idaho, and Las Vegas, Nevada, experienced well over 200 percent growth during that time. The diversity of experiences of small cities belies the dominant theoretical explanations. Small places have not all shrunk into husks of their former selves, and factors such as region do not successfully explain population trajectories.

While the fastest growers are in the South and West, the slowest-growing places are found disproportionately in the Midwest. The distribution of growth rates by region is not surprising given national trends. Researchers have noted for years that the cities of the Northeast and Midwest have been growing very slowly (or actually shrinking) as both businesses and citizens have moved to the South and West (Pack 2002). What is interesting is that some cities in the South and the West have not benefited from these changes. Places such as Laredo that grew over this period remained economically behind the rest of the nation in terms of income even as their regions prospered. Fresno, California, for example, nearly doubled its metro area population between 1970 and 2000, but it experienced only modest income growth. The median income level in Fresno also stayed well below the national level over time. For small places, population growth is no guarantee of economic growth.

And while Las Vegas, Nevada, experienced the fastest population growth over the thirty-year period, it was not the largest metro area during any of the decennial censuses. The largest metro area of the sample changed over time, shifting from the Northeast to the West to the South over the course of thirty years (table 1.3). While the decade of the 1970s was a period of great population growth among the MSAs, the opposite was the case in the next decade. Indeed, the 1980s yielded more net losses of population than the decade before or after (table 1.4). In the 1980s, some cities in every region lost population, in contrast to the 1970s and 1990s, when only cities in the Midwest or the Northeast lost population. Such trends capture the general trajectories of smaller places, but more detailed examinations of what these trends are like on the ground is essential for understanding success or failure among smaller places.

Case Studies

While the general trends are best shown through aggregate depictions of the eighty smaller places, concrete pictures of what different levels of growth, success, or stagnation mean are best shown through in-depth

TABLE 1.3
Median Population, Population Range, and Largest MSA, Eighty Small Metro Areas, 1970–2000

	1970	1980	1990	2000
Median Population of all MSAs	243,909	247,086	292,872	344,795
Population Range (MSAs)	71,047–854,286	84,784–910,222	98,458–1,224,852	104,010–1,644,561
Largest MSA	Providence, RI	Salt Lake City, UT	Orlando, FL	Orlando, FL

Source: U.S. Census Bureau data from the 1970, 1980, 1990, and 2000 censuses.

TABLE 1.4
Median Growth Rates for Eighty Small Metro Areas, Percentage of Metro Areas That Shrank by Decade, and List of Metro Areas That Shrank by Decade, 1970–2000

	1970–1980	1980–1990	1990–2000	1970–2000
Median growth rate for all metro areas	15.1%	7.8%	13.8%	45.2%
Percentage of metro areas that shrank	4.8 (N = 4)	10.7 (N = 9)	3.5 (N = 3)	4.8 (N = 4)
List of metro areas that shrank	Akron, OH Topeka, KS Springfield, MA	Decatur, IL Duluth, MN Peoria, IL Youngstown, OH Flint, MI Beaumont, TX Pueblo, CO Sioux City, IA Erie, PA Lawton, OK Cedar Rapids, IA Akron, OH Shreveport, LA	Decatur, IL Syracuse, NY Youngstown, OH	Decatur, IL Duluth, MN Flint, MI Youngstown, OH

Source: U.S. Census Data from the 1970, 1980, 1990, and 2000 censuses.

examination of cases that illustrate what the numbers mean. The four case-study cities that appear throughout the book represent many types of diversity: diversity of region, economic activity, demographic characteristics, and success and failure over time. While these places cannot be considered to be completely representative of the rest of the MSAs in the study, they do provide insight into how things have changed in particular places. The individual metro areas—Providence, Rhode Island; Green Bay, Wisconsin; Laredo, Texas; and Salinas, California—illustrate the types of developments that have occurred in eighty places over time. Although they differ considerably from one another, they reflect the broad patterns of urban change found in the group of cities as a whole.

These case studies illustrate the variety of paths of success or failure these eighty metro areas have taken since 1970. In the South, Laredo has seen a tremendous increase in population, income level, and immigration. In the Northeast, Providence has had stagnant income and population growth but relatively stable and high median income levels compared to other cities in the study. In the Midwest, Green Bay has experienced moderate population growth and income growth but has seen high levels of immigration. In the West, Salinas, has had sizable income growth and relatively strong population growth and represents metro areas that have seen influxes of both foreign-born immigrants and people moving from larger metro areas to smaller ones. Together, these four places provide a more nuanced view of how and why change has occurred in smaller places over the thirty-year period of the study. Throughout the book, the case-study cities provide in-depth explorations of how trends among smaller cities have played out.

I selected the case-study cities to represent the variety of changes that have occurred in smaller metro areas since 1970. Each city represents a different region of the United States; each of the four areas differed in terms of how much they grew demographically and economically over time. These areas also vary in the types of residents, the economic sectors that have thrived or died, and the ways they are tied to regional, national, and global activities. The case-study cities are introduced in chapter 2.

Outline of Chapters to Follow

This book illustrates the changes that have occurred in smaller metro areas in the United States and provides explanations for why these changes have taken place. In chapter 2, the divergent paths of smaller places are presented to establish a baseline understanding of the different trajectories of small cities. These trends show that while some smaller places have experienced population loss and moribund economies, others have seen population explosions and economic miracles. This chapter sets the stage for the next three chapters by showing general trends across places and providing a context for understanding the analysis presented in chapters 3 through 5.

Chapter 3 shows that for a small city to be successful, it needs to welcome all kinds of people. Smaller cities that have done better in terms of population, income, and economic inequality have had a steady stream of in-migration of foreign-born workers and their families. At the same time, there places have also had rising levels of educational attainment among their residents. In this chapter, the role of immigration is examined in detail through the case studies. Green Bay's ability to attract new immigrants has served it well, but Laredo's inability to increase education levels among its immigrant population has stunted economic growth. In addition, the chapter examines different levels of educational attainment, changes in opportunities for higher education, and shifts in employment for groups with different levels of education.

Economic diversity is key to the success of small cities. In chapter 4, the economic environments of small cities are examined in detail. The analysis shows that having diversity in economic sectors and sizes of firms helps small cities. Using many different types of data, this chapter shows how small cities can be economically successful even when they are located in the shadows of the largest global cities of the United States. Revisiting the case-study cities fleshes out the picture of economic health or malaise by demonstrating how places such as Providence, Rhode Island, have had a harder time maintaining a strong mix of firms even as they have successfully shifted from weaker economic sectors (textiles and manufacturing) to stronger sectors (health care and educational services) as time has passed.

While chapters 3 and 4 highlight people and jobs, respectively, chapter 5 centers on how the different pieces fit together with its discussion of how changes in population, income level, and economic inequality are intertwined. Drawing on an innovative analysis that examines the three outcome measures in combination over time, this chapter highlights the factors that affect all three concerns simultaneously and shows—particularly through the case-study cities—exactly how places fare that do not take care to ensure that population growth is accompanied by an increase in median income over time.

Chapter 6 brings together the findings from the previous chapters to illustrate the theoretical contributions and policy ideas that emerge from the analysis. While many economists, city planners, and civic boosters argue that economic specialization, pandering to a single industry, or vying for a sports team lead to success, the analysis here demonstrates that paths of success or failure are achieved through more complicated and nuanced means. Smaller cities that are more like big cities—regardless of population size—do better than other small cities. A final reexamination of the case-study cities demonstrates how Green Bay and Salinas have charted paths that have led to continued growth while Laredo and Providence have struggled. Even so, the stories of the four places are not straightforward; Salinas grew by replacing poorer people with richer people, and Providence has had a very up-and-down history and still houses several industries that may yet yield future dividends for the community. This chapter not only offers the reader an assessment of how well or how poorly smaller cities have fared but also provides ideas for the types of policies or strategies leaders and residents could use to ensure the continued fututre health of their own communities.

The epilogue offers some perspective on what has happened in smaller metro areas since 2000. Because the most comprehensive data for metro areas is available through the decennial censuses, most of the analysis in the book uses data from 1970 through 2000. But more recent data are available for some characteristics of smaller places. The epilogue examines the data available at the time of writing. Unfortunately, while the period between 1970 and 2000 was good for small places, the years since then have been rockier. Of course, the United States as a whole experienced worsening economic conditions as the decade of the 2000s progressed, so it is no wonder that data from the latter part of the decade depict a cloudy future. The picture was bleaker overall after 9/11 than it was before that tragedy.

Even so, the epilogue shows that small cities have been resilient in the face of challenging economic and social changes. While places that had done well in the period from 1970 to 2000 appeared to falter after 2000, many are poised to regain their solid positions. The economic well-being of Providence, Rhode Island, for example, fluctuated quite a bit during the thirty-year period of this study, but by the 2000s, it had begun to capitalize on some of the seeds of change that had been planted in previous decades. It is now home to a vibrant cosmopolitan population with immigrants from around the world and boasts growth in the higher education, health care, and finance sectors. In short, Providence has begun to prosper again. The resilience of smaller places will be tested as the United States struggles to move beyond the "Great Recession" of the late 2000s, but the epilogue shows that small metro areas remain an important part of metropolitan America.

2

The Divergent Fates of Small Cities

As one drives down University Avenue in Green Bay, Wisconsin, one sees history written into the very fabric of the city. The old Fort Howard paper company building changed names several times as the company went from public to private and from being locally owned to being part of an industrial giant, Georgia Pacific Corporation. Although not nearly as much paper pulping employ locals today as in 1970, there are still many high-paying mill jobs in paper production that provide a comfortable standard of living for residents with only a high school degree.

Heading out along University Avenue toward the local state school—the University of Wisconsin–Green Bay (UWGB) campus—one passes several local grocery stores. These stores used to cater to Polish, Dutch, and Scandinavian neighbors, but in the 1980s they became Asian markets selling lemon grass and durian fruit to the local Hmong community. More recently, the stores have changed again. Now they are bodegas stocking masa and tomatillos, serving the recent influx of Central and South American immigrants. These Latino men and women moved to the area eager for good jobs in meatpacking companies such as Packerland Packing. The meatpacking industry predates the national football team and is the origin of the name of the Green Bay Packers. The old Italian Mona Lisa Ristorante is now a tavern after a brief life as a Mexican bar, and the Piggly Wiggly has been replaced by a Walgreens.

As one heads further out of town, past the lesbian bar that closed after a fire in the early 1990s, past the empty furniture store in one of the many mini-malls that sprang up in the late 1980s and early 1990s, past Rivera Lanes (one of the few bowling alleys left from the days, as recently as the 1980s, when Green Bay had more bowling lanes per capita than any other city in the United States), new apartment complexes have appeared on what used to be open fields. The UWGB campus sits where University Avenue becomes Nicolet Drive (named in honor of the French explorer who first came to the area). The university has changed its look and focus considerably since it opened in 1969. Originally intended to be a magnet school for environmental studies, it has become a medium-sized general four-year college for students studying the liberal arts and sciences.

While this drive down one street in one of the eighty cities included in this study might seem prosaic, it illustrates many of the changes that have occurred in these cities over time. The buying and selling of the Fort Howard paper company illustrates how local economies have become ever more integrated into the national economy over time, and how this process affects places of all sizes. Similarly, the change from a locally owned Piggly Wiggly to a Walgreens exemplifies the increasing influence of national chain stores on local social, economic, and physical landscapes. The shifts in local stores to reflect newcomers to the community from various points of origin shows how even small cities are now home to diverse communities. Even the transformation of the local university presents the opportunity to understand large-scale changes: from a 1970s idealism concerning the environment to a 1990s emphasis on educational institutions as sources of "good jobs."

Green Bay is not unique in presenting in microcosm the many changes that have affected urban areas in the United States since 1970. Providence, Laredo, and Salinas and the other seventy-six places in this book also have stories to tell. One way to understand the divergent fates of these small cities is to examine some common questions about how small cities have fared over the last several decades.

1. Smaller cities are dying, aren't they?

    Researchers, journalists and concerned citizens are all alarmed at the disappearance of smaller places in the United States. But are all small places dying? Yes and no. Some small cities are losing people but many are not, and previous explanations for why different patterns exist prove insufficient. While change in population is not the only measure of how a place is faring, it is an important one in many respects.

2. People matter, but how?

   Richard Florida and other scholars argue that places that are able to attract certain types of people—generally a mix of liberal, well-educated people and new immigrants—are doing better economically. But are small cities whose populations are growing following this trend, or is something else going on? The answer is that small places are attracting more educated and diverse populations than ever before, but large-scale in-migration does not always yield benefits for the community as a whole.

3. Out with the old economy, in with the new one?

   Scholars such as Saskia Sassen note that the United States is now characterized by a service-sector economy and that our reliance on manufacturing jobs is a thing of the past. Yet what does the service-sector economy look like in small places, and has it benefited residents? The answer is that the new service economy indeed has arrived in small cities, but the old economy that was centered on manufacturing seems to offer as many benefits to residents as the new one, even as the old one decreases in importance.

4. If a rising tide lifts all boats, does that mean we want to be in any boat?

   For all the discussion among city leaders of the importance of growth, especially population growth, little attention is paid to what accompanies such growth. Does growth benefit everyone? In many ways, cities with the most population growth do not appear to be gaining much more than additional residents. It appears that economic benefits are tied to slow or moderate growth.

This chapter explores these questions and offers some initial answers to them. To do so, the cities are examined in aggregate over time to provide some general observations of how small cities have changed.

How Have Cities Grown?

Growth has become a mantra for cities. While some suburbs and outlying areas have, since the 1970s and 1980s, begun to question uncontrolled population expansion, most central cities, facing declining populations, continue to try to lure people to live and work within them (Davis 1992; Portney 2003; Bogart 2006). This is because permanent residents benefit the local tax base, stabilize neighborhoods, and potentially generate a sense of community. Many leaders also tie population growth to economic growth.

Economic growth is an unquestioned goal of all cities. As John Logan and Harvey Molotch noted in their important book on urban growth, *Urban Fortunes*, "The growth ethic pervades all aspects of local life, including the political system, the agenda for economic development, and even cultural organizations like baseball teams and museums" (1987, 13). They further note that while growth is often promoted as being beneficial to everyone who lives in a community, some people benefit more from it than others. The authors show how more well-off people reap rewards from growth, while people with fewer resources generally do not. Logan and Molotch are critical of growth for this reason.

How growth happens, where it happens, and what its effects are for small cities remains virtually unknown. This matters not only because so many people live in small cities but also because small cities show us how well our understanding of urban change can account for the experiences of cities of different sizes. I too am critical of growth, but my critique stems primarily from empirical examination. As we will see later, population growth and economic growth are not always tied together. And economic growth does not yield less economic inequality.

Table 2.1 lists the eighty cities in groups according to rate of population change.[1] Each group represents a particular trajectory of change. In subsequent chapters, I will examine how characteristics interact to influence changes in specific measures such as income and population levels. In this chapter, I focus on describing aspects of these cities using levels of population change as a lens to help clarify how places differ.

The cities in these four groups grew at different rates. I have divided the eighty cities into four groups based on rate of population growth quartile:

- The *slow growers* are located mostly in the Northeast and the Midwest. These cities were not very racially diverse and drew few immigrants during the three decades of this study. Although income levels in these cities remained high, unemployment was a problem; the largest employers in most cities were manufacturers, a stagnant area of the national economy. Many slow-growing cities are classic "rustbelt" cities that have seen economic decay set in.
- The *medium growers* are found mostly in the South and the Midwest. These cities were racially mixed but were not much affected by

TABLE 2.1

Eighty Small Metro Areas Grouped by Rate of Population Growth for the Period 1970–2000

Slow Growers[1]	Medium Growers[2]	Fast Growers[3]	Explosive Growers[4]
Beaumont, TX	Abilene, TX	Amarillo, TX	Bakersfield, CA
Cedar Rapids, IA	Chattanooga, TN	Ann Arbor, MI	Boise City, ID
Columbus, GA	Des Moines, IA	Baton Rouge, LA	Colorado Springs, CO
Decatur, IL	Fayetteville, NC	Billings, MT	Columbia, MO
Duluth, MN	Fort Wayne, IN	Eugene, OR	Columbia, SC
Erie, PA	Grand Rapids, MI	Fargo, ND	Fort Smith, AR
Evansville, IN	Green Bay, WI	Huntsville, AL	Fresno, CA
Flint, MI	Lafayette, LA	Jackson, MS	Gainesville, FL
Kalamazoo, MI	Lansing, MI	Knoxville, TN	Laredo, TX
Lawton, OK	Lubbock, TX	Lexington, KY	Las Vegas, NV
Peoria, IL	Macon, GA	Lincoln, NE	McAllen, TX
Providence, RI	Mobile, AL	Little Rock, AR	Modesto, CA
Sioux City, IA	Pueblo, CO	Madison, WI	Orlando, FL
South Bend, IN	Reading, PA	Montgomery, AL	Reno, NV
Springfield, MA	Roanoke, VA	Richmond, VA	Salem, OR
Syracuse, NY	Rockford, IL	Rochester, MN	Salt Lake City, UT
Topeka, KS	Savannah, GA	Salinas, CA	Springfield, MO
Trenton, NJ	Shreveport, LA	San Angelo, TX	Stockton, CA
Wichita Falls, TX	Springfield, IL	Sioux Falls, SD	Tallahassee, FL
Youngstown, OH	Waco, TX	Spokane, WA	Tyler, TX

1. Population growth from 8 to 16 percent.

2. Population growth from 17 to 43 percent.

3. Population growth from 45 to 61 percent.

4. Population growth from 61 to 413 percent.

immigration from Central or South America. The residents of these cities were generally somewhat better off economically than people in the cities in other three groups. These are southern cities that have not participated in the regional trend of growth and fairly prosperous but slow-growing midwestern places.

- The *fast growers* are scattered across the Midwest, the South, and the West. These cities had diversified and strong economies but grew more from domestic in-migration than from immigration from abroad. The cities in this group generally have adapted well to the "new economy" because they are home to universities and other service jobs. They represent the rise of the South and the West in the economy as well as the ability of some midwestern cities to buck a regional trend of stagnation.
- The *explosive growers* tend to be located in the South and the West. These cities were destinations for people from abroad, but the local economies often could not accommodate all the newcomers. The jobs that were available tended to be in the low-end service sector, not the "good jobs" that are thought to be essential for growth and prosperity. Overall, cities in this group had higher levels of unemployment and lower levels of income than other cities.

Each group of cities presents an approximate path that is fleshed out through the next sections of this chapter. The case study cities are interspersed throughout the chapter in small, detailed histories. The short social histories of the four metro areas illustrate changes to particular places in concrete terms. Although these four cities cannot stand in for all of the cities in a given group, they do present a general picture of the types of changes that the places in each group have experienced.

Smaller Cities Are Dying, Aren't They?

Conventional and scholarly wisdom holds that small places are dying throughout the United States. Sadly, there is some truth to this assertion. Small towns in rural areas are indeed on the decline in terms of population (Egan 2002; Flora, Flora, and Fey 2004; Carr and Kefalas 2009; Johnson 2009). Very small places—those with fewer than 10,000 people—seem to be disappearing at a quick rate. Small towns in America suffer from "the blues," as Richard Davies (1998) notes in his extensive exploration of change in a small Ohio town. Yet the small cities in this book present a different story. While small towns in the rural hinterland are overwhelming exporters of young people, these young people are often moving to a variety of larger, more urban locales, including the cities studied here.

Most of the small cities in this study experienced continuous growth, albeit of varying levels, from 1970 to 2000. In contrast, many larger cities in America saw population losses over the thirty-year period. Overall, seventy-six of the eighty cities grew between 1970 and 2000, and the average city grew by about 45 percent.[2] During the 1980s, however, cities grew at a slower rate than during the preceding or subsequent decades. During the 1980s, more small cities (and their adjacent communities) lost population than during the other decades combined. While about one-quarter of the population losses were quite small (less than 1 percent), four of the metro areas (Decatur, Duluth, Flint, and Youngstown) lost over 5 percent of their population during that period and have not recovered from this loss.

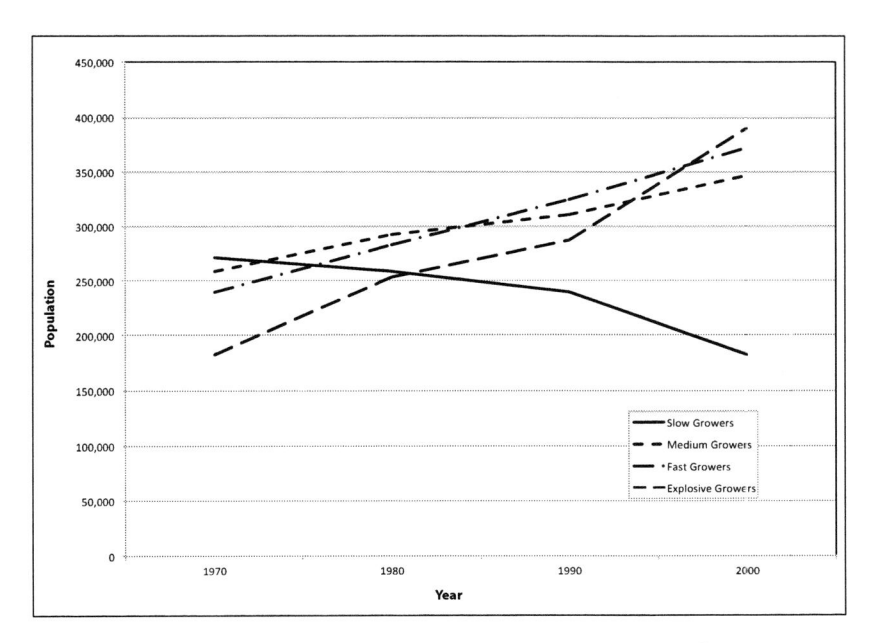

FIGURE 2.1. Median Population for Entire Metro Area, Eighty Small Metro Areas, 1970–2000

Source: U.S. Census Bureau data from 1970, 1980, 1990, and 2000.

I use the median rate of population change as one way to examine change. The median is the 50th percentile, or middle number, in a list of numbers. Thus, in any group, half of the group is less than the median and half of the group is greater than the median. For example, if there are three cities with populations of 100,000, 150,000, and 200,000, the median population would be 150,000. The median is a useful measure because unlike simple arithmetic averages, it is not influenced by extreme cases. This is especially helpful when looking at rates of population change. To take one example, Las Vegas grew by over 400 percent between 1970 and 2000. If that growth rate were used in an average, it would make all of the fastest-growing cities appear to have grown much faster than they really did, since Las Vegas grew so much more over time than all the other places in the study.

Losing population during the 1980s did not necessarily resign a city to a net loss of population over the entire period. The 1980s was a particularly hard period economically for many cities as the national economy continued to shift from manufacturing toward services. Places that relied on manufacturing jobs had to adjust to fewer manufacturing firms. Other places found it easier to attract or create new service-sector jobs. Both of these trends contributed to population declines in smaller places, but larger places generally had more resilient economies over time. Because of these trends, some metro areas such as Cedar Rapids, Iowa, and Pueblo, Colorado, saw double-digit increases in population in the next decade, more than compensating for any losses from the previous ten years. During the 1990s and 2000s, many small cities regrouped and offset their population losses.

Interestingly, the size of a city in 1970 is not a very good predictor of how much it would grow over the next thirty years. Some of the largest cities in 1970—such as Providence, Youngstown, and Syracuse—drew few newcomers in the next three decades. Instead, the smallest cities of the 80 places examined here, which often had a population in 1970 below 150,000 people for the entire metro area, such as Laredo, experienced rapid growth over time. Figure 2.1 illustrates that on average, the fastest-growing places tended to start off smaller than did the slower-growing places. (Unless otherwise noted, all graphs show data for the entire metro area of a city; refer to the appendix for details on how data were compiled.)

In hindsight, it is not surprising that the slow-growing areas were all "rustbelt" cities: places in the Northeast and Midwest whose economies relied on heavy industry and manufacturing for the majority of jobs. These economic sectors have been on the decline in the United States. Yet in 1970, these places seemed to be better bets in terms of predicting which cities would grow in the future. Rustbelt cities had strong economies before the 1970s and were historically good destinations for people (both from within the United States and from abroad) looking for high-paying jobs that did not require advanced levels of formal education.

The trend of slow growth or even population decline among northeastern and midwestern small places matches trends in the largest metro areas of the nation (Pack 2002). But the center-city growth in faster-growing small cities runs counter to dominant trends among large places. Most large places that grew in population since 1970 did so because their suburbs grew. Surprisingly, the small places that grew the most from 1970 to 2000 did so because people moved to both the central city and its suburbs or nearby communities.

As figure 2.2 shows, the populations of central cities in slower-growing places changed very little. In contrast, central cities in faster-growing

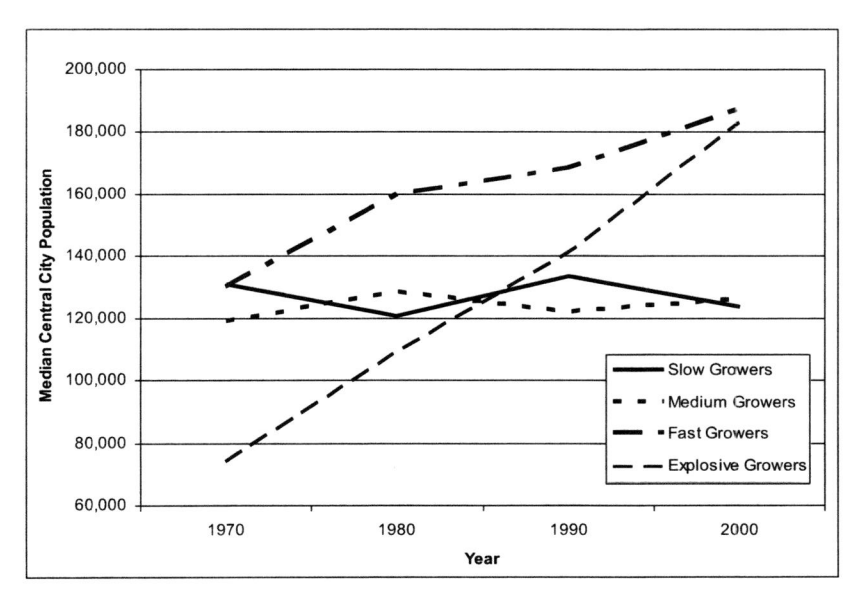

FIGURE 2.2. Median Central City Population of Eighty Small Metro Areas, 1970–2000
Source: U.S. Census Bureau data from 1970, 1980, 1990, and 2000.

places grew phenomenally. While much of the United States experienced *suburbanization* between 1970 and 2000 (in most metro areas, people moved from central cities to suburbs), fast-growing small places often experienced *urbanization* (people moving from outlying areas to center cities) as well (Furdell, Wolman, and Hill 2005).

Boise, Idaho, presents a great example of growth led by people moving into a central city rather than to suburban or nearby communities. As the biggest city in Idaho, Boise is a natural destination for many people from rural parts of the state looking for employment opportunities beyond the agriculture and natural resource extraction industries. In 1970, Boise's center city had a population of about 96,000 and a metro region population of about 174,000. By 2000, the metro area of Boise had more than doubled, but the center city still accounted for more than 55 percent of the area's population. Other, slower-growing places such as Beaumont, Texas, had nearly level central city populations over time, even as their suburbs and outlying areas grew.

Figure 2.3 shows that the suburbs (and outlying but nearby communities) of fast-growing small cities grew as well. Even so, the cities that grew

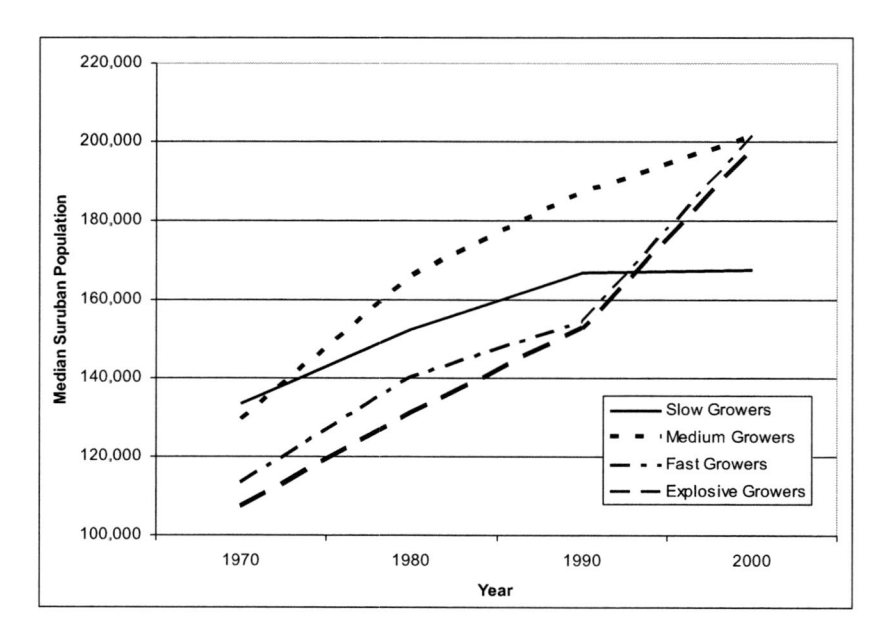

FIGURE 2.3. Median Suburban Population of Eighty Small Metro Areas, 1970–2000
Source: U.S. Census Bureau data from 1970, 1980, 1990, and 2000.

most rapidly did so because people moved to the center city. In fact, thirty-four of the eighty cities in this study had larger central cities than suburbs in 2000, and twenty of these cities were among the fastest-growing cities. In contrast, slower-growing metro areas grew only because of gains in suburban or metro area population (see figures 2.2 and 2.3). Providence, Rhode Island, is a good example of how smaller cities that experienced little growth fared and how they experienced more suburban growth than urban growth.

Providence, Rhode Island: Slow Growth but Poised for the Future

Some smaller metro areas grew considerably between 1970 and 2000, while others, like Providence, Rhode Island, did not. Although in 1970 Providence was the largest metro area of all eighty cities in this study with a metro area population of 854, 286, it grew by only about 13 percent over the next thirty years (U.S. Census Bureau 1970, 1982, 1993, 2003–2004). The Providence metropolitan area includes many suburbs, and what population growth the area experienced occurred in the suburbs. Providence illustrates many of the changes that occurred in cities that did not grow significantly during the last part of the twentieth century.

As the oldest city included in this study, Providence has experienced many ups and downs over its 350-year history. The late part of the nineteenth century has been described as Providence's "golden age," but unfortunately, that era of unheralded prosperity and growth disappeared quickly. In the early part of the twentieth century, cotton textile mill owners began to relocate their facilities to the South to take advantage of cheaper non-union labor, lower energy costs, tax incentives, and newer facilities. Manufacturers of machinery for mills also began to move away. Although World War II provided some reprieve by creating war-related manufacturing jobs, by the 1950s Providence had only one major manufacturing industry left—jewelry. After the war there was mass out-migration from the city to suburbs, nearby towns, and larger metro areas.

The 1970s were a rough time for Providence. One of its two major department stores, Shepard's, closed in 1974 (and the second, the Outlet, lasted only until 1982), Uniroyal left in 1975, and the city's premier local hotel, the Biltmore, closed from 1975 to 1979. During that decade,

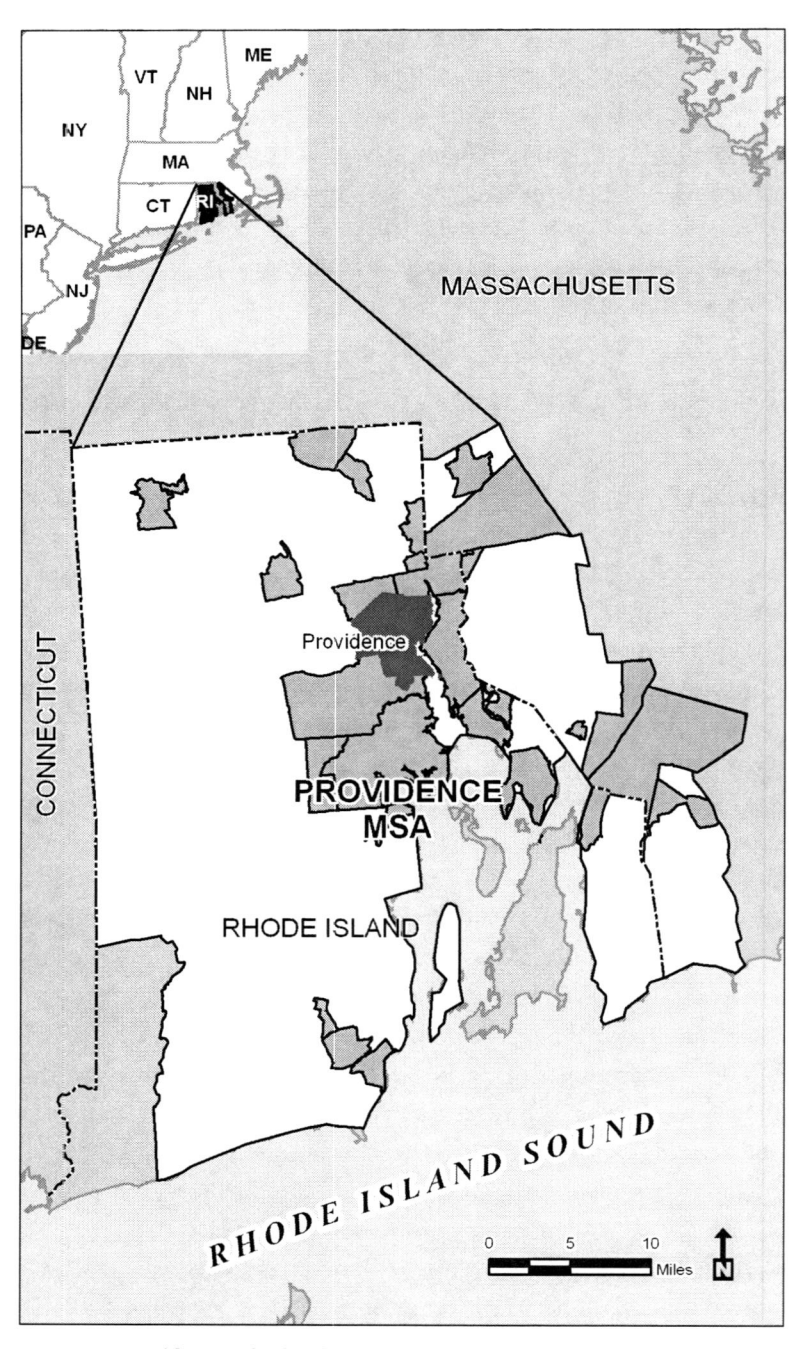

MAP 2.1. Providence, Rhode Island

unemployment grew from a little under 5 percent to 7 percent. Still, in 1974, 44 percent of all employees in the metro area worked in manufacturing, although both retail trade and services employed about 17 percent each. Over the next several decades, the percentage of people working in manufacturing declined to roughly half that number, while the percentage working in the service sector doubled.[3]

Much of the increase in service-sector jobs stemmed from the growth of institutions of higher education in the Providence area. Only one other metro area in this study is home to a larger number of colleges and universities (Springfield, Massachusetts, has eleven). In addition to the nationally renowned Brown University and Rhode Island School of Design, Providence and its environs also contain Providence College, the University of Rhode Island, Rhode Island College, Bryant College and Johnson and Wales University. Not only do these institutions create jobs at a variety of levels, they also foster a strong cultural fabric in the city. Providence hosts a philharmonic orchestra, the Rhode Island School of Design Art Museum, an opera company, several playhouses, and an active historic preservation association.

In addition to the important educational sector in Providence—Brown University is one of the largest employers in the area—insurance, health care–related services, and banking have become cornerstones of the local economy. While most manufacturing of textiles and jewelry had left the state by mid-century, as late as 1980 several manufacturers were still among the largest employers in the area: Imperial Knife Company, Cherry Semiconductor Corporation, and Eastern Wire Products employed considerable numbers of people. The largest long-standing employer engaged in manufacturing (as well as in research and design) is Textron Inc., a defense contractor. Although its employment figures have decreased since its heyday in the late 1970s and early 1980s, when it employed nearly 70,000 in New England (with the majority in the Providence area), it still employs roughly 37,000 people. Hasbro, Inc., a large toy company, has also been a large employer in the local area historically (OneSource Database 2006; Dun & Bradstreet 1980, 1990, 2000).

Providence remains an important financial center as well, even if it is overshadowed by the nearby metropolises of New York City and Boston. Throughout the period of this study, banks and financial services firms have been important businesses in the metro region, although mergers and acquisitions have decreased the number of independent banks in the area considerably since 1970. In addition, several banks, such as Old Stone Bank, were involved in scandals in the late 1980s that led to their closure.

Through this mix of employment opportunities, residents in Providence have maintained a relatively high standard of living. The median household income in Providence in 1970 was $35,700; in 2000, it was $41,500 (in constant 2000 dollars). However, although income grew about 16 percent over the thirty-year period, median home prices climbed at a considerably faster pace, increasing 56 percent between 1970 and 2000 (U.S. Census Bureau 1970, 1982, 1993, 2003–2004). Providence residents experienced a more extreme disparity between increase in income and increase in real estate prices than the eighty metro areas on average. Based on a simple cost-of-living index calculated from median household income in relation to median home values over the thirty-year period, Providence was 25 percent more expensive to live in than the average smaller city. Many residents of Providence who did not already own property faced a steep barrier to purchasing a house, which in the latter part of the twentieth century has become the main investment for families.

Since the early 1990s, civic leaders in Providence have taken many steps to revitalize the city. In the early 1990s, the city uncovered parts of the Providence, Moshassuck, and Woonasquatucket Rivers, which had been paved over during the middle of the century, to create Watercity Park. In the newly uncovered Providence River, an art installation (called WaterFire) and gondoliers attract tourists. Providence also boasts the largest mall in New England, Providence Place, built in a rundown area near the historic downtown. Civic leaders worked hard to have the mall built, believing it would be an important source of jobs and tax revenues.

Demographically, Providence represents the path of many older northeastern and midwestern cities that have grown slowly. In 1970, Providence was over 97 percent white and about 3 percent black or other race/ethnicity. Like many other slower-growing cities, Providence was home to a slightly higher percentage of foreign-born residents (7 percent) in 1970 than the average for cities in this study (2 percent). Unlike many other cities that experienced slow growth, however, by 2000, the percentage of the population born outside the United States had increased to about

12 percent. This is higher than the overall average among all study cities (about 7 percent) and even higher than the median rate of the fastest-growing places (8 percent). What makes Providence slightly different is that it remains a destination for immigrants from Europe, Central America, South America, and Asia. While the demographics of the area had changed considerably by the year 2000—the metro area was 81 percent white, 4 percent black, 9 percent Hispanic, and about 6 percent Asian, Pacific Islander, or Native American by that year—the biggest sending countries are still Portuguese speaking: Brazil and Portugal, including the Azores (U.S. Census Bureau 1970, 1982, 1993, 2003–2004).

Providence has experienced tremendous change—much of it challenging—over the past half-century. The central city population declined slightly over this period and the metro area grew only modestly. Because the city has a mix of service industries, the standard of living has not suffered as much as might be expected. But compared with the fastest-growing areas, it does not appear to be on a road to growth, and as the national and international economics continue to change, it may face tough times in the future. As with many of the slow growers, Providence's population change has occurred in the suburbs, while faster-growing cities have tended to have central city growth. Slow growers that, like Providence, offer employment in the higher-end service sector may fare better over the next several decades, but those that do not may continue to experience declining fortunes.

People Matter, But How?

Who lives where matters. Leaders in cities work hard to attract people to their locales, and boosters of all sorts suggest both sensible and outlandish schemes to attract people. Recent scholarship has focused on what makes some places more attractive to people than others. Richard Florida (2001, 2005) claims that local areas that are diverse, that welcome immigrants and gays and lesbians, that are safe for women, and that are home to artists and bohemians are thriving because they attract educated people who work in or—better yet—start high-end services companies. Florida's main point is that who lives in a particular city influences how well a city does over time.

When thinking about how knowing who lives somewhere affects a place it is important to consider the characteristics of the people who live in the community. The distribution of people of different ages, the mixture of different races and ethnicities, the number of immigrants, and the amount of education people have are particularly important. Sociologists often think of these characteristics as important for understanding the human capital of a place. The concept of human capital refers to the attributes that people have that enable or constrain the opportunities they are able to take advantage of. By examining the characteristics that compose human capital, we can study how differing constellations of people are related to different outcomes for various places.

To start with, the number of young people and old people in a community matters. Places with many older adults who are no longer active (or only partially active) in the work force, as is common in Sunbelt communities in Florida and Arizona, offer a different set of employment opportunities, such as jobs in health care or in retirement communities, than places with more young people. Conversely, places with many young people, particularly those under eighteen, may need to spend more on costly services and institutions that provide services for children and adolescents.

Among the cities examined here, places that experienced slow population growth tended to have slightly older populations. In the slowest-growing places in 2000, over 14 percent of the population was over sixty-five; in the places that grew at the fastest rate, only 10 percent of the population was over sixty-five. The age distribution of the slower-growing places appears to be tied to a lack of net in-migration, particularly foreign-born migrants (see figure 2.5), who tend to be younger. In addition, on average, immigrant women tend to have more children than non-immigrant women.[4]

All of the places studied here have become more ethnically diverse over time. Even cities that had very (primarily white) homogeneous populations became much more diverse (figure 2.4). A good example is Rochester, Minnesota, whose population was 99 percent white in 1970 but was only 89 percent white by 2000 (U.S. Census Bureau 1970, 2003–2004). Overall, the United States is becoming less homogeneous racially. This is in part due to immigration. In addition, native-born white women tend to have

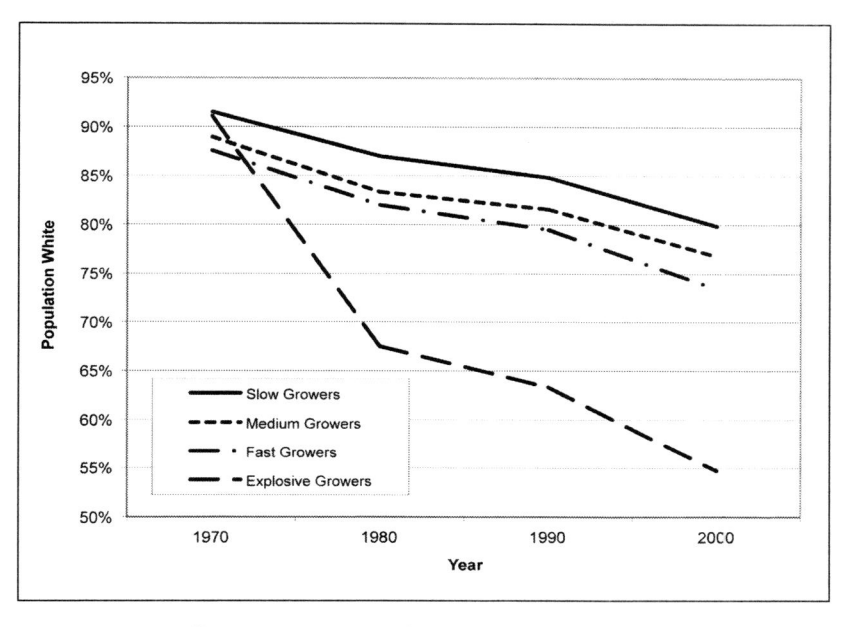

FIGURE 2.4. Median Percentage Population Identified as White in Eighty Small Metro Areas, 1970–2000

Source: U.S. Census Bureau data from 1970, 1980, 1990, and 2000.

fewer children than native-born women of color or immigrants, which may lead to decreasing white populations in these places.

Strikingly, the cities with the smallest proportion of white residents are becoming less white at a faster rate than are the other places. This holds true of places with increasing proportions of Hispanic or Latino residents and African American residents.[5] The explanations for this pattern remain speculative. One possibility is that these smaller cities are experiencing, at the urban level, something similar to what happens to neighborhoods experiencing racial change. Thomas Schelling (1971) hypothesized that when a black family moves into a predominantly white neighborhood, its presence will be enough to make a single white family move out.

Why? Survey research shows that white families generally prefer to live in areas that are predominantly white, while black families prefer areas that are racially mixed. Therefore, when a white family moves out, Schelling argues, a black family is statistically more likely to move in, because on average that family is likely to prefer to move to a racially mixed neighborhood. If this process continues, at least in theory, a neighborhood could transition from being predominantly white to predominantly African American as white families decline to move in to it. What we see in the small cities, then, may be the Schelling hypothesis at the urban level: small places are becoming racially more heterogeneous over time.

Increasing immigration is a large part of the trend toward places with fewer white residents. More people of color (both immigrant and native born) tend to have moved to faster-growing places over slower-growing ones. The fastest-growing places have fewer non-Hispanic white residents, and the percentage of the metro area population identified as Hispanic or Latino increased greatly, particularly during the 1990s.[6] Clearly immigration—and particularly immigration from Mexico and Central and South America—is driving population growth in these places (figure 2.5), as it is in all sorts of metro areas throughout the United States (Suro and Singer 2003). Changes in the proportion of African American, Asian American, and residents of other ethnic heritages have affected some metro

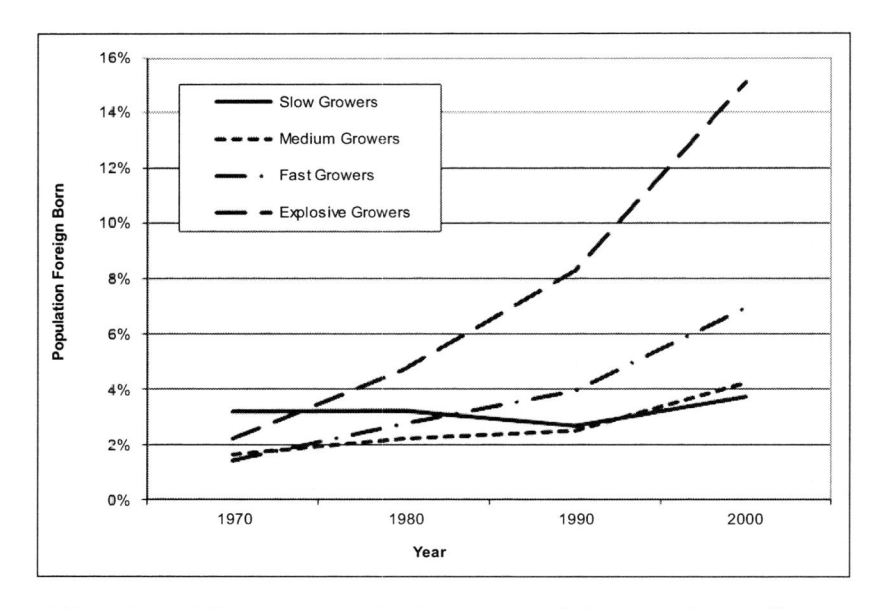

FIGURE 2.5. Median Percentage Foreign-Born Population in Eighty Small Metro Areas, 1970–2000

Source: U.S. Census Bureau data from 1970, 1980, 1990, and 2000.

areas significantly, but on an individual basis rather than as a net trend. For example, over one-third of the residents of several southern cities such as Tallahassee, Columbus (Georgia), and Fayetteville are African American, while several California cities, such as Stockton and Fresno, are over 10 percent Asian and Asian American.

The slowest-growing metro areas tend to be home to waves of immigrants who arrived before 1970 and were not replaced by more recent newcomers when they died. Youngstown and Duluth exemplify this pattern. Both cities had populations that were about 5 percent foreign born in 1970. These people were primarily immigrants from Europe, many who came as young people either before or after World War II. Such cities were attractive to immigrants in 1970. They offered employment opportunities for people of a variety of educational backgrounds, particularly manufacturing jobs for people with lower levels of schooling. But as the national economy changed and manufacturing jobs disappeared, these cities became less desirable destinations for newcomers. Immigrants began to move to places that offered jobs in the low-end service sector.

Faster-growing places fit this pattern. The fastest-growing cities were not destinations for immigrants to the United States before 1965, but they have since become home to many new immigrants from Mexico, Central and South America, and Asia.[7] Cities such as Stockton and Fresno in California, for example, attracted only moderate levels of Asian immigrants before 1970. However, during the thirty-year period from 1970 to 2000, the percentage of the population born in another country in these cities quadrupled.[8] But perhaps even more surprising is the trend in places such as Boise, Colorado Springs, and Gainesville, where in 1970 only about 1 percent of the population was foreign born. By 2000, well over 5 percent of the residents of each of these places were foreign born. While this is not high compared to the California cities and the largest cities of the United States, it represents a strong shift in the geography of immigration in the United States over the last thirty years.

Before the 1990s, most immigrants entered the United States through a handful of gateway cities such as New York, Los Angeles, or Miami. Many immigrants stayed in these cities for many years if not for their entire lives. More recently, immigrants have been skipping spending time in these large cities and moving directly to smaller places (Singer 2003; Vey and

Forman 2003). The reasons for this vary. Some immigrants seek work in the remaining manufacturing jobs for unskilled or low skilled workers that still offer relatively high wages, but these jobs have virtually disappeared from many major metropolitan areas. Others seek smaller cities because they feel they are more affordable than large cities and are better places to raise their families. This new pattern of movement is significantly changing the ethnic face of small cities across the United States.

Immigrants come with varying levels of education, from agricultural workers who did not complete elementary school to workers in high-tech industries with graduate degrees. While there are still many jobs open to individuals with a high school diploma or less, most "good jobs"—ones with benefits such as health insurance—are open primarily to people who have attended at least some college. Because of the turn toward a service-oriented economy, people increasingly need to have higher levels of education in order to obtain a decent standard of living in the United States.

Like all of the United States, the number of people who went to college in the cities examined here increased tremendously (Figure 2.7), and

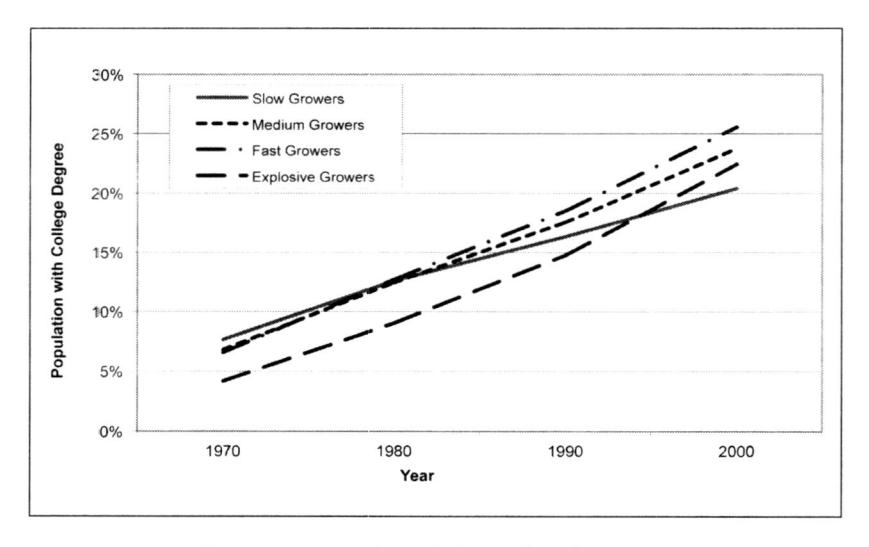

FIGURE 2.6. Median Percentage of Population with College Degree in Eighty Small Metro Areas, 1970–2000

Source: U.S. Census Bureau data from 1970, 1980, 1990, and 2000.

the number of people who did not finish high school decreased. Regardless of how fast a place grew, each started out with less than 10 percent of their populations having completed college in 1970, although the slowest-growing places started with slightly more college graduates on average. By 2000, the fast-growing cities (those in the third group) had more college graduates on average than the other cities. About 28 percent of people in these cities had a college degree. The cities that grow the most over the thirty years, however, still had much higher levels of people who had not finished high school (on average, 22 percent of their populations had not completed high school) even as they had increasing numbers of college graduates. This is primarily due to the large number of immigrants from Central and South America who came to the United States with limited formal education.

The experience of Green Bay, Wisconsin—a formerly very racially homogeneous community that has had a relatively recent influx of immigrants from Mexico and Southeast Asia—provides an excellent example of how smaller places are adapting to their changing populations.

Green Bay, Wisconsin: Moderate Growth but High Living Standards

Green Bay is one of only two cities in the book that has a major league sports franchise (the other being Orlando, home to the NBA Magic). People who live in other parts of the United States are likely to know something about Green Bay because of the Green Bay Packers football team and have seen at least quick video footage of the city during televised home games. Green Bay is one of the smaller metro areas in this book. In 1970, the population was 158,244; by 2000, it had grown to 226,778. Although the area where Green Bay is located was originally a fur-trading and agricultural settlement, over the course of the eighteenth and nineteenth centuries, fur trading died out and lumber, paper production, farming, and food processing became the staples of the local economy.

Because Green Bay's main industries were not in manufacturing sectors that moved offshore, the city did not face the same upheavals after World War II that Providence did. In the early part of the twentieth century, paper production, farming, and processing of agricultural products became the

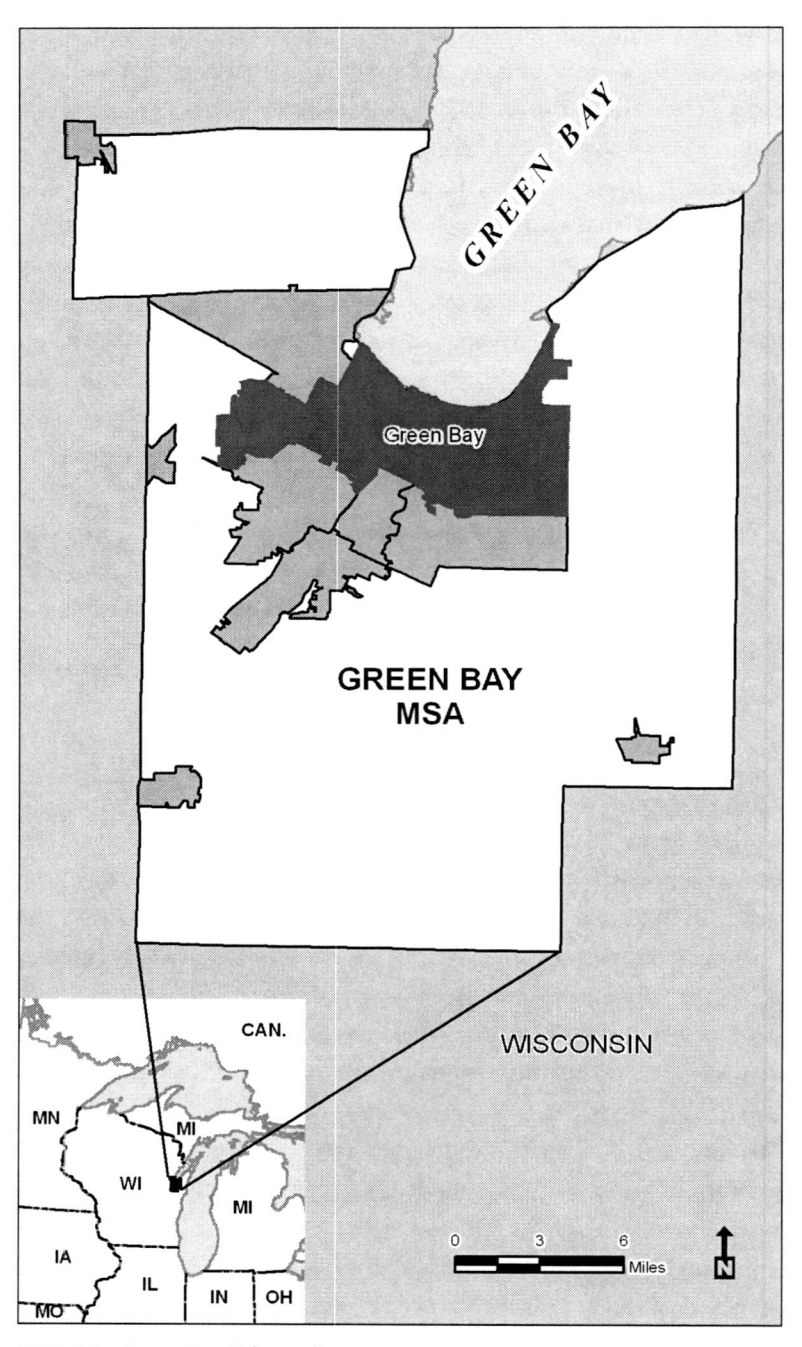

MAP 2.2. Green Bay, Wisconsin

primary industries of the metro area. During the 1970s and 1980s, paper production and processing of agricultural products were the two largest industries; paper companies such as Fort Howard Paper and Proctor & Gamble employed over 12,000 workers in the 1980s. However, the paper industry consolidated during the 1990s, and some of the manufacturing moved south when Georgia Pacific purchased Fort James (the name of the old Fort Howard company after it merged with James River, a Virginia-based paper company). Agricultural processing also became less important as companies such as FreshLike moved to other parts of the United States. However, new employment opportunities opened up in health care and related areas, and by the late 1990s, American Medical Services (an insurer) and Humana Healthcare (a managed care company) both employed several thousand in the area (OneSource Database 2006; Dun & Bradstreet 1980, 1990, 2000; U.S. Census Bureau 1970, 1982, 1993, 2003–2004).

The population of Green Bay changed significantly between 1970 and 2000. It used to be a town where people assumed that the African Americans they saw were visitors or part of the Green Bay Packers franchise, but the city changed from being nearly 99 percent white in 1970 to being 89 percent white in 2000. While this change may not seem very great compared to cities with historically high nonwhite populations, older white residents have been startled by the transformation. The Green Bay metro area has not seen the dramatic white flight of many of the other cities examined here (the white population there has decreased by only 1.5 percent), but the influx of Hmong, Vietnamese, African American, and Latino residents (primarily Mexican and Mexican American) has changed the cultural landscape considerably. Local schools have increased bilingual education, restaurants that serve the foods of these ethnic communities have sprung up, and neighborhoods have undergone transformations as different ethnic groups have moved in and out (U.S. Census Bureau 1970, 1982, 1993, 2003–2004).

Residents of Green Bay enjoy a relatively high standard of living. Median household income, which was $40,000 in 1970 (in constant 2000 dollars), grew steadily albeit slowly over the next three decades; by 2000, it was $42,000. During that same period, median home values increased 47 percent (from $77,000 to $111,000). Green Bay residents enjoyed a lower-than-average cost of living using the index of median household income and median home value; Green Bay was about 7 percent less expensive to live in than the average smaller city. Rents were even more affordable; comparing monthly median income to median rents shows that Green Bay's rents were about 15 percent cheaper compared to other cities in the book on average. Employment remained stable and high over the period as well; in 1970, unemployment was approximately 4 percent, and it remained near that level over the next thirty years (U.S. Census Bureau 1970, 1982, 1993, 2003–2004).

Nonetheless, changing national economic fortunes have significantly affected Green Bay at the local level. The cityscape of Green Bay and its environs have changed noticeably over the past thirty years. One area that illustrates these changes well is retail commerce. In the 1970s, city leaders focused on rejuvenating the moribund downtown area by building a mall around the local department store, H. C. Prange's. The mall opened in 1977 and proved successful through the 1980s. But by the mid-1990s, the H. C. Prange's Company had been bought by Younker's, an Iowa-based department store, which in turn was later bought by Saks Corporation (based in New York), which then sold it to the Bon-Ton Company (based in York, Pennsylvania). By 2000, the mall had few tenants, and it has since closed. In the meantime, a mall on the west side of the city—formerly the location of lower-end chain stores and discount stores—has successfully captured the retail sector of the city with a new, higher-end department store built by Bon-Ton and with mid-level chain stores such as Gap (which had closed its original local store housed in the downtown mall in the early 1980s). The rise of the new mall cemented the decentralized nature of Green Bay.

While much of the local economy of Green Bay changed over the period 1970 to 2000, one reassuring constant—both culturally and economically—has been the presence of the Green Bay Packers. The only publicly owned football team in the nation, the Green Bay Packers began life as a sandlot team in 1919 and became a franchise in 1921. The Packers are one of the most successful football teams in history and they are second to none in terms of fan loyalty (at least according to locals). The Packers have the smallest market in the National Football League yet manage to sell out most if not all games every season. Season tickets in Green Bay are exceedingly hard to come by because they are passed down through families, unlike in most other football cities. Lambeau Field, the Packers' home stadium, currently seats about 72,000, a figure equal to the population of nearly three-quarters of the city or about one-third of the broader metro area.

Green Bay residents benefit from the variety of industries in the local area, as is typical of other cities that experienced growth at a medium rate. In addition, the education sector is a strong presence; the Green Bay metro area houses the University of Wisconsin at Green Bay, St. Norbert's College, and the Northeast Wisconsin Technical College. Like many of the other cities in this growth group, the diversified economy has kept Green Bay from losing population and economic activity. Many of the cities in this group house several larger industries as well as several institutions of higher education. Finally, cities such as Green Bay are often more distant from larger metropolises that might feed population to them as a consequence of the rapid rise in the cost of living (primarily related to housing) in many of the largest metro areas of the United States.

Out with the Old Economy, in with the New?

The United States has experienced a shift in the distribution of job opportunities over the last thirty years. While manufacturing used to be the main economic engine for the country, jobs in the service sector now dominate. Scholars often refer to this as the shift from the "old" economy to the "new" economy. The old economy was characterized by a preponderance of manufacturing jobs that provided good wages and that did not require more than a high school diploma. The new economy, in contrast, centers on jobs in the service sectors, and jobs with good wages are generally only available to those who hold a college or graduate degree.

This transformation from old to new economy has occurred in places of all sizes. Yet it appears that larger cities often have a different mix of economic sectors than smaller cities. Saskia Sassen (2001) shows that the largest cities in the United States have more jobs in what she terms "producer services," or industries such as finance or law that generate additional employment and capital, which are often referred to as high-end service-sector jobs. More commonly, we think of the jobs that Sassen discusses (and that Richard Florida describes as key to the "creative economy" that was mentioned in chapter 1) as "good jobs" because they offer higher wages and benefits such as health insurance and retirement accounts. Jobs in the low end of the service sector, such as those in retail sales, food services, or unskilled and semi-skilled health care, are generally considered less desirable since they offer much less on all fronts. Small cities are thought to be home only to low-end service jobs that are the "back office" work for the large corporations or to manufacturing industries that are dying.

While there has been much debate about "good jobs" versus "bad jobs," I am most interested in the spatial distribution of employment opportunities. Surprisingly, the data show that in general, small cities have economies that are similar to the economies of the average metro area in the United States. The breakdown of the sectors of the economies of the cities studied here mirror the averages for all cities across the country: they have significant levels of employment in manufacturing, trade, and professional services (table 2.2). These places have slightly lower levels of employment in the finance, insurance, and real estate (FIRE) industries and in personal services than do larger cities, but otherwise they look much like the nation as a whole.

TABLE 2.2

Median Percentage of Workforce Employed in Various Economic Sectors, Eighty Small Metro Areas, 1970–2000

	1970	1980	1990	2000
Agriculture and mining	4.7	4.0	3.4	2.3
Construction	6.1	6.0	5.9	6.7
Manufacturing	21.0	19.0	16.0	14.0
Transportation and utilities	6.7	7.1	6.7	6.4
Trade (retail and wholesale)	22.0	22.0	22.0	21.0
Finance, insurance, and real estate	4.8	5.9	6.2	6.3
Business and repair services	2.8	3.8	4.4	6.7
Personal services	6.5	3.6	3.3	3.0
Professional services	20.0	22.0	25.0	25.0
Public administration	6.3	6.0	5.3	5.3

Source: U.S. Census Bureau data and County Business Patterns, various years

While the eighty small cities are not, on average, the centers of the national economy or heavily interconnected in global financial networks, they clearly are integral parts of the nation's economic nervous system. Small cities house important economic institutions such as corporate headquarters, and a surprising number of the small places examined here are important centers for national and multinational firms. These small places are indeed part of the global economy.

The small cities in this study are home to a number of Fortune 500 companies. Fortune 500 firms can be very important for local economies, not only because they directly provide jobs but also because ancillary businesses usually exist nearby that work with the firms or provide services to their employees. In 1970, sixteen metro areas (19 percent) contained headquarters of one or more Fortune 500 firms, and although the number fluctuated considerably over the thirty-year period due to changes in how *Fortune* magazine tabulated results, in 2000, eighteen metro areas (21 percent) were home to Fortune 500 firms. During the thirty-year period, over 70 Fortune 500 company headquarters called 30 small cities home. Clearly the small cities included here are places that house important, central business functions.

Small cities house a wide variety of Fortune 500 firms in a number of industries. In 2000, Columbus, Georgia, housed the insurer AFLAC, while Peoria was home to Caterpillar, the maker of construction equipment. Circuit City was headquartered in Richmond, Virginia, and American Family Insurance was based in Madison, Wisconsin (see the appendix for more information on Fortune 500 company data) (Cowle 1999). Interestingly, the faster-growing places are not attracting new Fortune 500 firms; this may be a partial reason for their more limited economic growth (as will become apparent below.)

However important Fortune 500 firms are to particular local areas, they do not form the entirety of a local economy. Their presence in small cities illustrates how small places are tied into larger economies. The local economy—the mix of jobs available in a given area—is what matters to people in their everyday lives. Good jobs now are typically associated with high-end service employment in law, medicine, or finance, since the old "good jobs" in manufacturing have disappeared. The small cities here show this to be true, but only to a certain extent.

Important Economic Sectors: Manufacturing and Professional Services

Two key areas of employment worth looking at in detail are manufacturing and professional services, which are relatively good proxies for the "old" and "new" economies. (The category of "professional services" includes jobs in fields such as law, finance, real estate, architecture, engineering, or management consulting; refer to the appendix for information about how categories were created for analysis.) The slowest-growing group of cities started out with the highest levels of employment in manufacturing in 1970 and saw the greatest relative decline in jobs in that industry, yet these cities retained a higher proportion of jobs in manufacturing even in 2000 (figure 2.7).

Conversely, the faster-growing cities had much lower levels of manufacturing in 1970. This is not surprising; few of these cities were located in the Midwest or Northeast, regions with historically higher levels of manufacturing employment. Yet with the movement of manufacturing to the South and the West (and offshore), it is surprising that these faster-growing cities did not gain manufacturing jobs from firms that had relocated.

Employment in the professional services sector increased in all cities, regardless of the rate of population growth (figure 2.8). However,

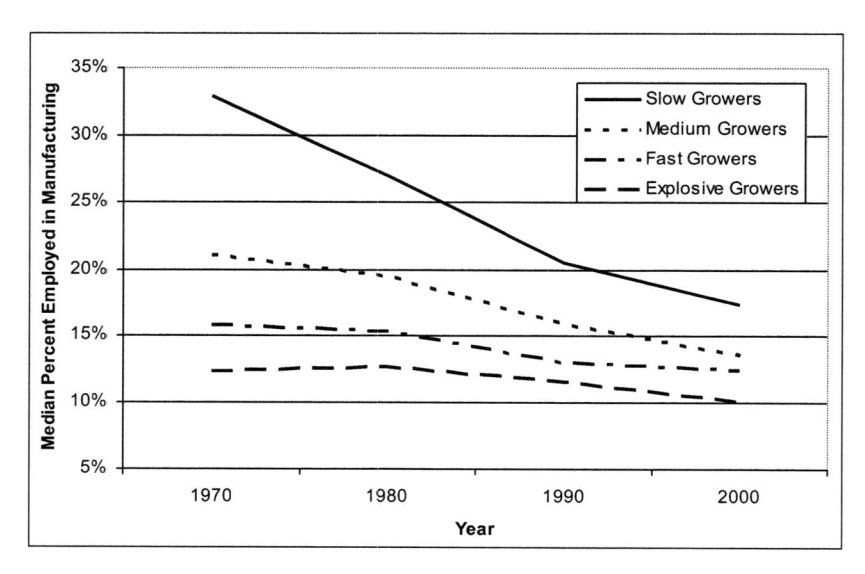

FIGURE 2.7. Median Percentage of Population Employed in Manufacturing Sector in Eighty Small Metro Areas, 1970–2000

Source: County Business Patterns data, various years.

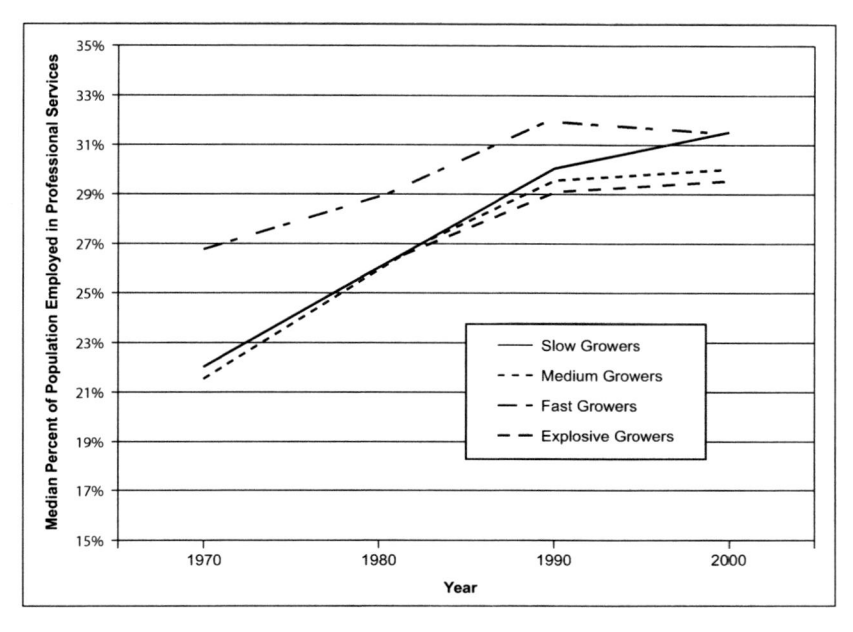

FIGURE 2.8. Median Percentage of Population Employed in Professional Services Sector in Eighty Small Metro Areas, 1970–2000

Source: County Business Patterns data, various years.

the mix of employment in the cities in this study complicates a simple tale of growth linked to employment in services (Florida 2001). While it might be expected that faster-growing places would be part of the new economy based on professional services, that is not always the case in smaller cities. As figure 2.8 shows, while cities in the fast-growing group experienced tremendous growth in professional services employment over the thirty-year period, the slowest-growing saw increased employment in that sector too. In fact, by 2000, the explosive-growing cities had the lowest level of employment in professional services among the study cities.

Population growth and growth in professional services do not necessarily go hand in hand. Faster-growing cities have added jobs in the lower tiers of the service economy, such as jobs in retail, back-office work (such as call centers for banks), and semi-skilled health services. These jobs are good in that they provide work for people, but they generally do not come with benefits or high wages. Faster-growing cities are adding people, but they are not necessarily building up "human capital." They are either not attracting people with higher levels of education or do not fit into the national (or international) economy in ways that provide openings for educated residents.

Cities stuck in the old economy are not necessarily doing worse than those in the new economy in terms of household income levels.[9] Even in cities where levels of employment in manufacturing have fallen, median household income has not fallen. The manufacturing sector offers employment with decent wages to workers without college degrees. But the continued importance of manufacturing does not diminish the increased importance of the service sector, particularly "good" service jobs. Two specialized, geographically constrained service sectors—higher education and state government—are often touted as the key to good economic growth for small cities.

Specialization in Education and Government

Over the past several decades, scholars have theorized that cities may benefit economically by specializing in higher education or government services (Carroll and Meyer 1983; Logan and Molotch 1987). Whether by design or not, many small cities have done just this. The government and education sectors offer somewhat recession-proof employment at a variety of levels, from janitorial work to administrative duties to teaching. The government sector, however, has experienced ups and downs, particularly since the 1980s and 1990s, when a move toward smaller government across levels gained momentum. Higher education, in contrast, has been an expanding industry in the United States over the last several decades.

Nearly all of the cities in this study have at least one college or university, and many of them have several. Over 40 percent have three or more four-year colleges or universities in their metro area (Owens, Melzer, and Staff of the Princeton Review 2005). A disproportionately large number of small cities are home to elite institutions of higher education. Examples include Brown University in Providence, an Ivy League school, and the flagship land grant universities of Michigan and Wisconsin in Ann Arbor and Madison, respectively. In places such as Providence, Ann Arbor, and Springfield (Massachusetts), universities and colleges are often the largest local employers.

Cities such as Madison, Wisconsin, and Lincoln, Nebraska, doubly benefit in that they are state capitals and are home to a flagship state university. Eighteen of the small cities in this study are state capitals. These cities may benefit from government jobs that are often more immune to the ups and downs of the national economy. But when viewed over the thirty-year period, it becomes clear that being a state capital is no sure bet for employment opportunities.

Twelve of the eighteen state capitals experienced declines in employment in public administration during this period—perhaps reflecting the move toward smaller government mentioned above. For example, Salt Lake City experienced a precipitous decline in public sector jobs; employment in that sector dropped by roughly half over the thirty-year period. While some scholars have seen state government as a source of economic security for localities, about two-thirds of the state capitals in this book experienced decreasing levels of employment in the government sector over time. Being a state capital might not be the panacea to economic ills that some have suggested.

Salinas, California, has ridden the wave of the new economy with high-end services, tourism, and education industries that complement the area's historically agricultural economy.

Salinas, California: Growth and Transition

Salinas, California, has often been referred to as the "Salad Bowl of the World" because of its immense and productive agricultural industry (City of Salinas 2006). The local area produces almost all of the lettuce and artichokes and the vast majority of cauliflower, mushrooms, celery, and broccoli consumed in the United States. Salinas's agricultural roots go back roughly 200 years to the early ranches of the Mexicans who settled along the California coast. During the latter part of the nineteenth century and the entire twentieth century, agriculture shaped the local economy and the landscape of Salinas. Agriculture has also shaped the demographic character of the populace. Although Salinas started out small—in 1900, the population was about 19,000—by the middle of the twentieth century it had grown to around 130,000, by 1970 to 250,000, and by 2000 to 401,000 (U.S. Census Bureau 1970, 1982, 1993, 2003–2004).

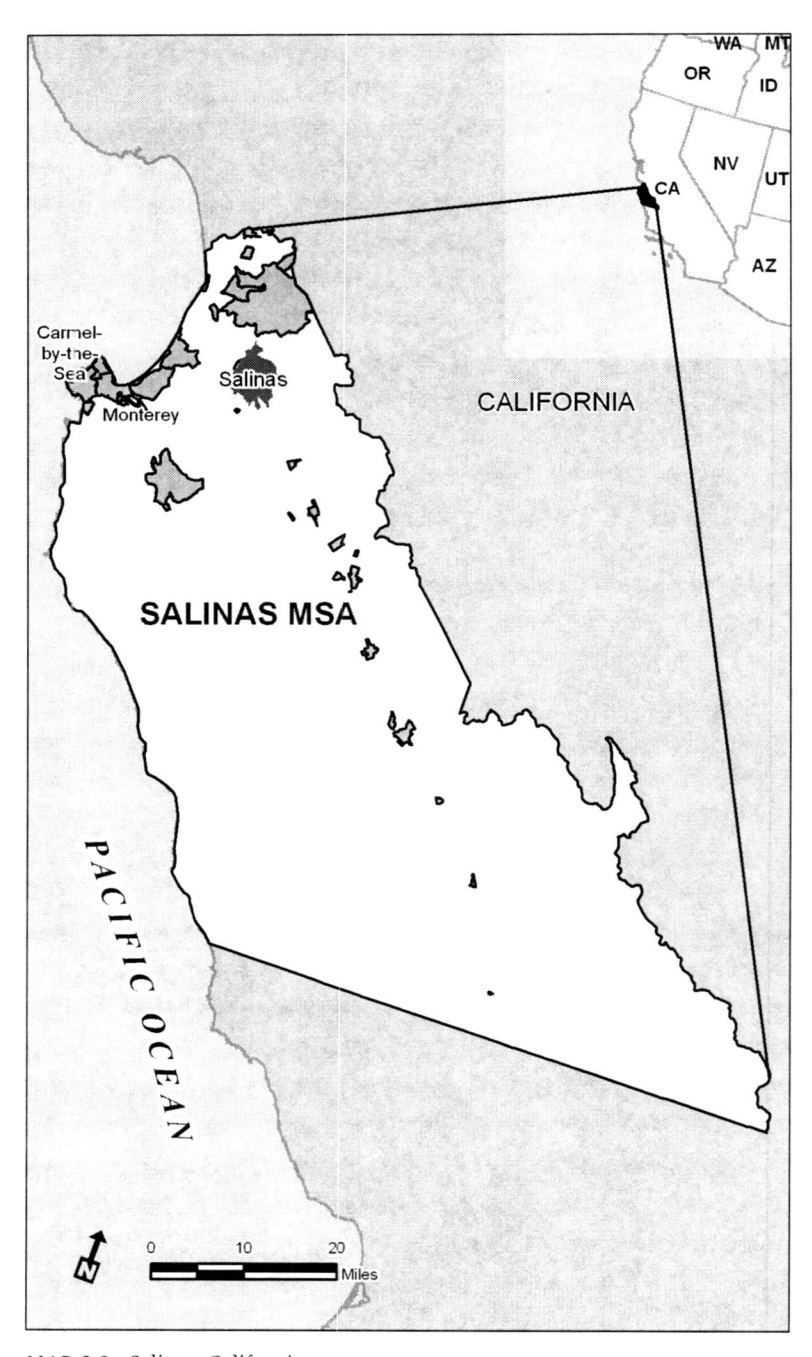

MAP 2.3. Salinas, California

During the early part of the twentieth century, farmers concentrated on sugar beets as their primary crop, employing first Chinese and then Japanese workers. After the advent of refrigerated boxcars, which made long-distance train transport of perishable produce viable, lettuce became the number one crop of the area in the 1930s. Before the mid-1980s, few large agricultural businesses existed, as much of the growing, picking, and packing was done on smaller farms and the processing was done by smaller companies. Even in 1980, only one lettuce-growing company (Salinas Lettuce Farmers Co-op Inc.) employed over 200 people and had annual revenue of over $1 million, and only eleven firms had annual revenue of over $1 million.[10]

By 1990, the economics of agribusiness had changed considerably in Salinas. Consolidation of smaller firms created several larger harvesting and packing companies: Bud Antle Inc. employed 3,000 in vegetable packing; Bruce Church, Inc. employed 1,000 in vegetable picking; Fresh International Corporation and its subsidiaries employed nearly 2,000 in vegetable picking, packing, and preparation; and Nunes Company, Inc. employed 600 in vegetable picking and packing. (Of course, these numbers do not include seasonal migrant labor, which can increase payrolls temporarily by hundreds of people.) By 2000, many local firms had disappeared, having been purchased by larger national firms such as Dole Fresh Vegetable. Employers in the service industries had grown in importance as well, such as Salinas Valley Memorial Hospital and Monterey County government. Tourism now plays in increasing role in the local economy, particularly in nearby local towns such as Monterey, Carmel, and Carmel-by-the-Sea.[11]

Yet the agricultural base has provided residents with a reasonably high standard of living. In 1970, the median household income was about $28,000 (in constant 2000 dollars), which had increased by 74 percent to $48,000 by 2000. But not all households have seen a rise in income; in 1970, roughly 20 percent of families had incomes above the 80th percentile of that national median income, and that percentage had increased slightly to 22 percent by 2000. The percentage of families with incomes below the 20th national percentile stayed about constant at 18 percent over the thirty-year period. However, the percentage of families living in poverty (as measured by the national poverty line) increased from 11 percent in 1970 to about 14 percent in 2000. Thus, Salinas experienced an increasing polarization of income: more households were well off, more households were living in poverty, and the middle class was shrinking.

Even so, residents in the area experienced much greater gains in income over the period than the average for all eighty cities. A large part of the reason for the change in income and for the high income levels is an influx of wealthy residents from the nearby San Francisco Bay Area.

This influx of well-off people meant that the cost of living in Salinas rose considerably; in 1970, the median home in Salinas was valued at about $100,000, already much higher than the average of $70,000 across all eighty metro areas (in constant 2000 dollars). By 2000, the median home value had risen to $264,000, an increase of 277 percent. The cost-of-living index for Salinas indicated that by 2000, the median value of homes averaged about 4.8 times higher than the median income for the city, making purchasing a home unrealistic for many residents. The Salinas area was roughly 200 times more expensive to live in than the average small city based on this calculation. However, home prices rose mostly in the wealthier suburbs of Monterey and Carmel. Renting was more reasonable; the cost-of-living index based on median rental values and monthly median income was only slightly higher—18 percent greater—than the average.

In 2000, the population of Salinas was "minority-majority," although no single racial or ethnic group constituted a majority of the population. In 1970, Salinas was about 88 percent white non-Hispanic, but by 1980, it was about 60 percent white, 26 percent Hispanic, 6 percent black, and 8 percent Asian, Pacific Islander, or Native American. Historically, farmers had used laborers from China, Japan, and (in the 1930s) the Philippines to harvest and process crops. During World War II, The Bracero guest worker program encouraged Mexican workers to come to the United States, and Mexican workers came to Salinas, replacing Asian immigrants and Asian Americans who were put in detention camps during the war. The workers from Mexico added to the long-standing Hispanic population descended from the early Mexican settlers, and the Hispanic population of the city increased greatly over the latter half of the twentieth century. By 2000, Salinas was 40 percent white non-Hispanic, 47 percent Latino/Hispanic, 5 percent black, and 9 percent Asian, Pacific Islander, or Native American. Given the national trends of increasing numbers of Latinos in California and the United States as a whole over the past thirty years, it appears likely that Salinas will become a majority Latino metro area in the next ten years or so (U.S. Census Bureau 1970, 1982, 1993, 2003–2004).

Together, these different ethnic groups create a vibrant cultural landscape. In addition to the long agricultural history of the area, Salinas was the birthplace of author John Steinbeck. Drawing on that legacy as well as the local agricultural and coastal heritage of nearby Monterey, the region has become an important tourism destination over the past several decades. The California Rodeo, which was formalized in Salinas in 1911, and the Steinbeck Festival draw tourists to Salinas proper, while Monterey, Carmel, and Carmel-by-the-Sea (nearby cities within the metro area) have long attracted visitors from near and far.

Like many faster-growing cities, Salinas has a main industry that weathers economic up-turns and downturns well. Agriculture, the main industry of Salinas, serves the city well, but the broader metro area supplements this with a growing service-sector economy based on tourism. Salinas also illustrates the tendency of fast-growing cities to have higher percentages of minorities and immigrants: in 2000, the population of Salinas was 29 percent foreign born, up from 6 percent in 1970. Yet the city faces an uncertain future because of the high cost of living in the area; like many of the cities in the group that experienced rapid growth, home prices in Salinas have risen far faster than incomes.

If Rising Tides Lift All Boats, Does That Mean We Want to Be in Any Boat?

While many factors are important, most people would likely say that income is one of the most important factors in establishing how well they are doing. Cities assess their well-being in a similar way, and this study examines how income is distributed within and across communities. Change in median income offers a way of understanding how the other factors examined in this study—characteristics of residents and economic opportunities, for example—affect people's lives in the eighty cities.

It is often assumed that population growth is good for a city. Population growth should, some say, lead to economic growth because a growing city is likely to be an incubator of entrepreneurship (Madden 2000). Other people suggest that economic growth comes first; they argue that population growth follows from higher income levels or increased employment opportunities. The cities here show that it can be difficult to determine how population and income are related, at least at first glance.

While faster-growing small cities have experienced a greater change relative to their initial income levels in 1970, the slowest-growing cities have consistently had higher levels of income over time (table 2.3). Clearly this relationship must be examined in greater detail, and in subsequent chapters I will use other techniques beyond simple comparison to try to understand the factors that influence the relationship between income levels and population levels.

One might ask if income levels in slower-growing cities are higher because it is more expensive to live in such cities. However, faster-growing places tend to be more expensive to live in. A simple cost-of-living index calculated by dividing the median home value for the metro area by the median household income demonstrates that faster-growing places tend to have higher housing costs. The same calculation based on monthly median income and monthly median rents for the four groups is virtually

TABLE 2.3

Average Median Household Income by Decade by Rate of Population Growth, Eighty Small Metro Areas, 1970–2000

	1970	1980	1990	2000
Slow-growing metro areas	$37,000	$39,800	$38,100	$51,200
Medium-growing metro areas	$34,500	$37,100	$39,400	$49,900
Fast-growing metro areas	$29,200	$35,200	$35,700	$45,900
Explosive-growing metro areas	$27,400	$34,700	$36,100	$46,200

Note: All income calculations are done in constant 2000 dollars based on Consumer Price Index conversion factors provided by the U.S. Bureau of Labor Statistics.

Source: U.S. Census Bureau data from the 1970, 1980, 1990, and 2000 censuses.

identical. As noted in each case study, some places, such as Providence and Salinas, have seen skyrocketing home values, while others, such as Green Bay and Laredo, remain remarkably affordable for many residents. In cities such as Providence, some people who already owned homes in 1970 benefited from increases in home equity, but others suffered because they could not afford to pay increasing property taxes or because they could not afford to buy a home at all.

Cost of living is important, but so too is how equitably income is distributed across a community. In a capitalist economy such as ours, income is not distributed equally. In general people are fine with this. However, extreme levels of income inequality can lead to problems. Communities with only very rich and very poor residents face difficulties in the absence of a strong middle class. These bifurcated places are often very expensive to live in but are also unable (or unwilling) to provide the services low-income residents may need. A more even distribution of income may also indicate that there are jobs for people with a variety of levels of skills and education. Morally, we may also believe that communities should strive for all people to have a decent standard of living as opposed to just the richest few.

One way to assess how equitably income is distributed is to calculate what economists refer to as a 90:10 index of inequality. This measure is a way of looking at how income is distributed in a population. The idea behind it is that if we look at the range of earnings within a given population, we are able to gain a sense of how equitably income is distributed within that group.

To calculate this measure, the income level of the 90th percentile of the range of incomes is divided by the income level at the 10th percentile. So, for example, if in a given community people in the top 90th percentile (i.e., those with earnings that were in the top tenth of the range of all earnings) earned an average of $100,000 and people in the bottom 10th percentile earned an average of $20,000, the 90:10 ratio for that population would be 5. Conversely, if in another community the 90th percentile earned an average of $150,000 and the 10th percentile earned an average of $15,000, the ratio would be 10, and we would think that income is distributed less equally within the second community than the first. This is because there appears to be greater polarization of income between the rich and the poor in the second community. The higher the number on the 90:10 index, the less equally income is distributed within a community.

Sociologists Michael Hout, Claude Fischer, and Jon Stiles (2008) argue that while economic inequality has increased throughout the entire United States since the 1970s, faster-growing small places have experienced much higher rates of increases in inequality than slower-growing small places. The data in this study support that finding (figure 2.9). Faster-growing places appear to be more like the "new economy" because they have more service-sector jobs, but their economies have led to a greater polarization of wealth and poverty than in other cities in this study.

Another issue related to income and its distribution is how much unemployment exists in a place. Like the rest of the nation, unemployment levels in all cities in this study were considerably lower in 1970 than in any year after. While the slowest-growing places experienced the highest levels of unemployment in 1980, this pattern had changed by 2000 (figure 2.10).

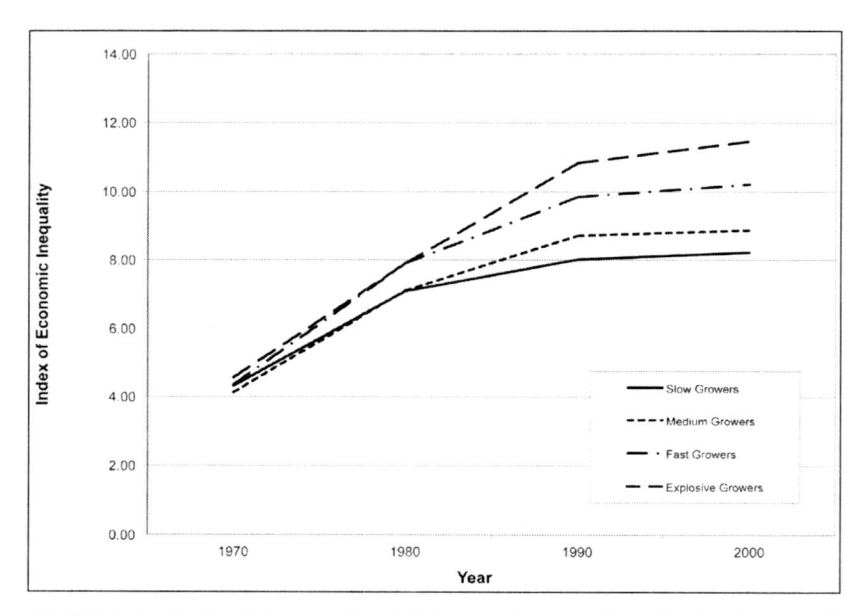

FIGURE 2.9. Median Values on the 90:10 Economic Inequality Index in Eighty Small Metro Areas, 1970–2000

Source: U.S. Census Bureau data from 1970, 1980, 1990, and 2000.

THE DIVERGENT FATES OF SMALL CITIES 65

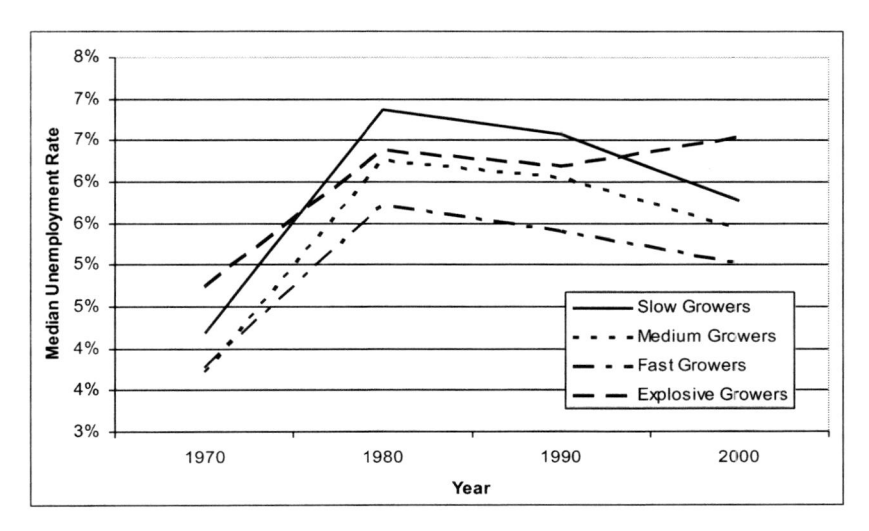

FIGURE 2.10. Median Unemployment Rate in Eighty Small Metro Areas, 1970–2000
Source: U.S. Census Bureau data from 1970, 1980, 1990, and 2000.

Twenty years later, the fastest-growing cities were experiencing the highest levels of unemployment.

For example, Tallahassee experienced very rapid population growth during the period of this study. Unemployment in Tallahassee increased from about 3 percent in 1970 to over 9 percent in 2000, averaging about 5 percent in the intervening years. In 1970, when jobs in both the high- and low-end services sector accounted for about 38 percent of all employment in the metro area, Tallahassee had one of the lowest unemployment rates among all eighty places. It appeared to be on the path to economic prosperity. By 2000, unemployment had increased overall, and employment in service-sector jobs had decreased by about 7 percent even though the number of jobs in the field of government increased slightly. Tallahassee lost new-economy jobs over time, even though it was located in Florida, a state that overall had benefited from regional shifts of both people and businesses during the time period.

The high levels of unemployment in fast-growing places in 2000 may indicate that their economies were unable to participate in the wave of economic expansion in the late 1990s that focused on high-end service industries. Cities that experienced the most rapid rate of population growth were not able to offer enough employment opportunities to all the newcomers attracted to them. Researchers such as Roger Waldinger and Michael Lichter (2003) found that cities that attract an initial group of immigrants often become more popular for future immigrants as people seek out places where a network of compatriots already exists. In this way, population growth can become self-perpetuating. As immigrants make a new city their home, others from their home country are more likely to move there as well.

In the slow growing places, unemployment is likely due to the reduction in manufacturing jobs, while in the explosive-growing cities it is due to large influxes of new (often immigrant) workers who are unable to find jobs. However, it is unclear if similar factors influence domestic migrants to seek out similar locales. While Americans are in general moving less, specific groups (younger, less-educated native-born men and recent immigrants) continue to move both locally and distantly, thus complicating the analysis (Fischer 2002). Both the fastest-growing cities and the slowest-growing ones tend to have higher rates of unemployment, although the rates of unemployment in these cities are likely due to different reasons.

Laredo, Texas, illustrates the kind of opportunities and constraints that accompany very rapid population growth.

Laredo, Texas: Growing, But at What Cost?

Laredo, one of the fastest-growing metro areas among the eighty cities examined, illustrates some of the main determinants of urban change in the United States as well as the unintended and unexpected consequences of rapid population growth. Although Laredo was small throughout much of the nineteenth and twentieth centuries, by 1940 it had almost 40,000 residents, and over the next three decades the population nearly doubled, to almost 73,000. The next thirty years brought explosive growth; by 2000, the metro area population had increased to 193,117, and over 90 percent of that population was living in the center city area (U.S. Census Bureau 1970, 1982, 1993, 2003–2004).

Latino residents are in the majority in Laredo; they constituted 92 percent of the city's population in 1980 and 94 percent in 2000. During that same time, the percentage of the population identified as non-Hispanic white dropped from 8 percent in 1980 to 5 percent in 2000. (Comparable

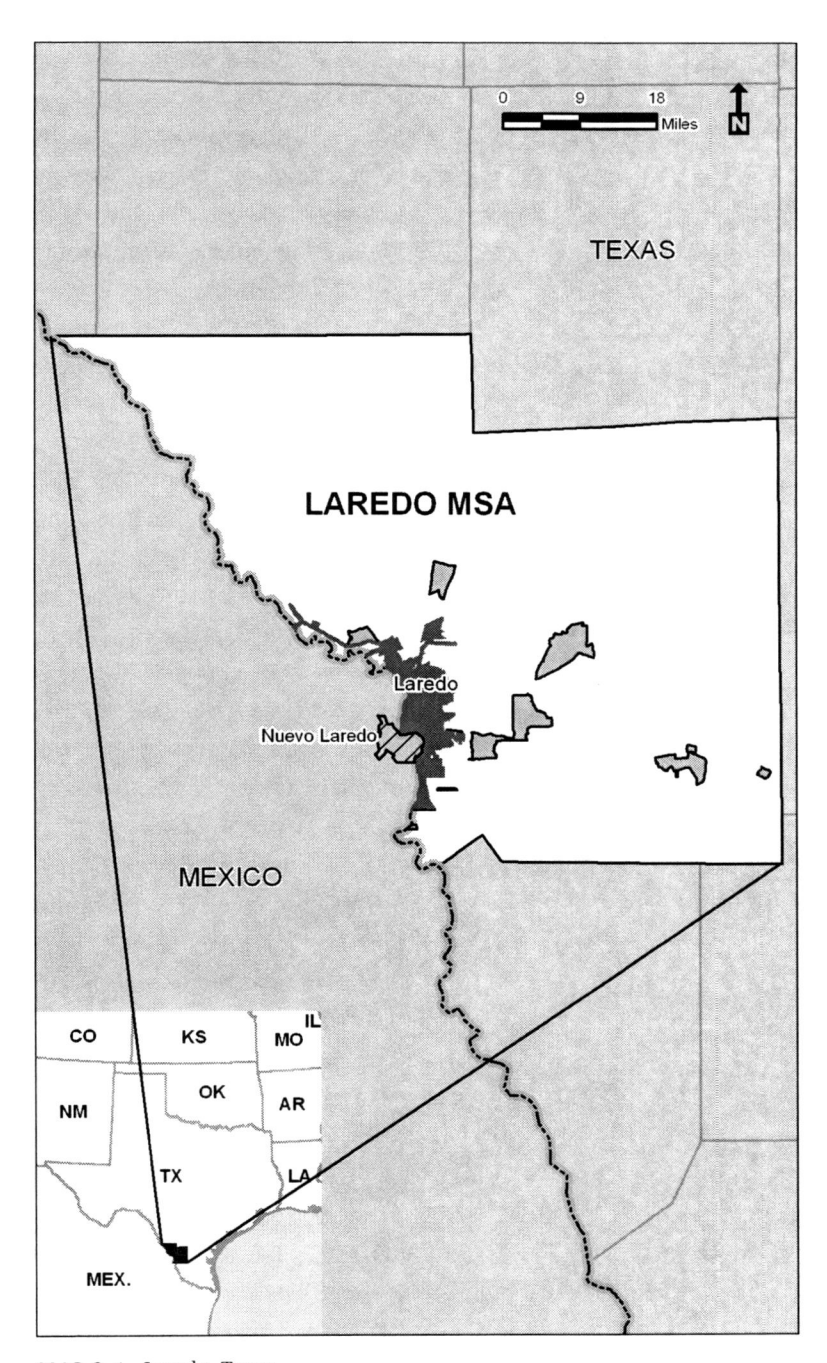

MAP 2.4. Laredo, Texas

1970 data are not available because of changes in how the U.S. Census Bureau collected data on race, but estimations indicate that Laredo was already heavily Hispanic/Latino by that year.) Laredo is one of the most homogenous metro areas in this study in terms of race and ethnicity; only a few northern cities rival it, and those cities are all majority white.

While in the early part of the twentieth century oil and other resource-extraction industries dominated the local economy, by the end of the twentieth century trade and services had moved to center stage. Nuevo Laredo, across the border, is the largest collector of tariffs in Mexico among cities on the border between the United States and Mexico, and every day thousands of people cross one of several bridges that connect the two cities (and nations). In the 1970s and 1980s, local retail businesses, such as the department stores Hachar's, Richter's, and El Rio, had considerable influence in the community as some of the largest local employers. But by the turn of the twenty-first century, these local businesses had disappeared, replaced by Walmart, JCPenny, and several Mexican chain stores. The composition of industries that are the largest employers in Laredo also looked markedly different by 2000. While the Texas Mexican Railway Company remained a key employer in the area, the largest employers were banks and health-care facilities. One manufacturing plant—a tire company—remains in Laredo, but many similar firms have moved across the border.[12]

Like many other cities that grew tremendously, Laredo has had relatively (and sometimes absolutely) high levels of unemployment over the thirty-year period. In 1970, Laredo had an unemployment rate of about 6 percent, higher than the average of a little over 4 percent for all of the cities in this study. Unemployment was only a little higher in 1980, but by 1990, unemployment reached over 11 percent—much higher than the average for all metro areas of 6 percent. By 2000, unemployment had decreased—down to a little over 9 percent—but it remained high compared to the other cities in this study and to the national average.[13]

Even so, real median household income in Laredo increased considerably from 1970 to 2000. In 1970, median household income for the city was $19,000; by 2000, it had increased to $28,000, or about 45 percent in thirty years' time. For all eighty metro areas, mean income growth was only 29 percent, indicating that Laredo far exceeded the average growth rate. Nonetheless, median household income for all areas was $40,000—well above Laredo's. Although the city experienced higher growth in median household income over the three decades compared to other metro areas that started off with similarly low income levels, Laredo residents were more likely to be poor, both compared to the other cities in the study and to the nation as a whole. The earnings of about 37 percent of Laredo's households put them below the federal poverty line during the thirty-year period compared to 14 percent for all places during the same period.[4]

Although median household income remains low in Laredo, housing prices continue to be comparatively affordable, although they are increasing rapidly. In 1970, the median value of a single-family home in Laredo was $36,000; by 2000, it had risen over 100 percent to $74,000. The cost-of-living index for Laredo was 10 percent above the average for all eighty cities. Compared to many other metro areas, a house in Laredo priced only slightly more than twice the median income is more affordable than homes in other markets that had median home values of triple the median household income. In this, Laredo is a bit different than other explosive-growing cities. For those cities, housing was 25 percent more expensive than in small cities with slower rates of growth over the thirty-year period.

Laredo illustrates many of the attributes of cities that have experienced explosive growth in population from 1970 to 2000. Like many cities in this category, Laredo has a high proportion of immigrants: 29 percent of its population is foreign born, compared with an average of 12 percent for cities that experienced very rapid growth and an average of 6 percent for all eighty places in this study. Also like many cities that experienced very rapid growth, in Laredo, a high proportion of the population works in trade and professional services. Yet the future of Laredo and other cities that are growing very rapidly may be uncertain because such cities have higher unemployment levels, lower levels of income, and large disparities between segments of society.

Moving Forward

The story of how well small places are doing is complex. In examining how the eighty cities have changed, it becomes clear that no single story explains everything. However, trends are clear among different cities. What remains to be seen is how well the basic trends described in this chapter hold up when examined in combination with other trends as opposed to in isolation. In the next several chapters, I will look at how various combinations of characteristics of cities influence outcomes such as income and population change.

This chapter has brought to light developments among small places that run counter to conventional understandings of how cities have fared over the past several decades. The population of most of the small cities increased over time, and the cities whose population grew at the fastest rate did so because of urbanization as well as suburbanization. Cities with large populations in 1970 did not grow as much as places that started with smaller populations. This appeared to be due to changing immigration patterns; the older, relatively larger cities had more European immigrants who had arrived before the 1960s, while the smaller places were more attractive to newer immigrants from Asia and the Americas during the three decades of this study. Immigration accounted for much of the population growth among the faster-growing cities from 1970 to 2000.

Small cities also demonstrate different patterns in terms of both population and economic opportunities. Small cities that grew faster tended to have more residents with low levels of education and more jobs in the low-end services sector. The slower-growing cities, in contrast, tended to have more highly educated citizens and more jobs in manufacturing for those with lower levels of education. Overall, this pattern generated higher income levels in slower-growing cities than in faster-growing ones. Many of the slower-growing places were home to Fortune 500 company headquarters, providing evidence that some small cities continue to be important components of the national (and potentially the international) economy. But while the economies of faster-growing places resemble the "new" economy in terms of job opportunities, they were not necessarily better places to live in terms of income or economic inequality levels.

In the next two chapters, I will focus on how people matter and on how the mix of economic opportunities matters. Clearly the people who live in a city and the economic opportunities available to them contribute to changing levels of population. Yet these factors also influence other important measures of success or failure among urban areas, namely changing levels of income and economic inequality.

3

Putting Out the Welcome Mat

How People Affect Small Cities

Brown University in Providence, Rhode Island, is one of the few colleges in the United States where students can major in Portuguese. While Brown is known for having a highly varied and particular undergraduate curriculum, Portuguese is a strong department there because of student interest and because Rhode Island is home to a large number of people from Portugal (including the Azores) and Brazil. Indeed, the existence of a doctoral program in Portuguese and Brazilian Studies indicates just how entrenched the Portuguese-speaking community is in Rhode Island and nearby southern Massachusetts.

Yet Portuguese-speaking countries are only several of a multitude of nations whose citizens have moved to Providence and its surrounds. Although in 2000 only about 4 percent of the population claimed Portuguese descent (and another several percent Brazilian ancestry), over 40 percent of the population spoke a language other than English at home. This included new Latino immigrants (about 30 percent of all households that speak a language other than English) as well as a smaller group of immigrants from Asian or Pacific Island nations (about 6 percent of such households). About 25 percent of Providence's population was born outside the United States; 11 percent had come to the United States since 1990. By 2006, about 29 percent of the city was foreign born.

And while the city is known for its Portuguese and Italian neighborhoods, particularly Federal Hill with its La Pigna sculpture, a symbol of welcome and abundance, hanging over the main street, over one-third of residents identified as Hispanic/Latino by 2006. This change in the demographic composition of Providence has changed the local landscape. Where there used to be Italian groceries there are now bodegas.

In addition to the slightly unusual ethnic composition of the metro area, Providence is home to a large number of institutions of higher education. While all of the small cities in this book have at least one four-year college or university, Providence boasts ten. The most famous are Brown University and Rhode Island School of Design, each of which is influential in the city. Both institutions bring in speakers, offer extension courses, have renowned museums and library collections, and sponsor ongoing projects in collaboration with local communities. Other nearby schools fill the needs of a variety of student groups: the land grant school of the University of Rhode Island offers a much less expensive education and Providence College and others offer private alternatives.

Like many smaller cities, Providence's leaders have embraced the idea of cultivating the "creative class" and the "creative sectors." In the city's June 2009 publication *Creative Providence: A Cultural Plan for the Creative Sector*, city leaders outline their strategies for encouraging the growth of this group (City of Providence 2009). Key goals for the city include "mobiliz[ing] the creative sector by positioning the [city's] department of art, culture and tourism as a leader in creative economic development" and "creat[ing] conditions for creative workers to thrive in Providence" (ibid., 9, 29). Providence has implemented the theories Richard Florida only partially; it seeks to attract and provide support for people involved in the arts instead of trying to stimulate all sorts of creativity as Florida advises in his book *The Creative Class*.

However, Providence has largely succeeded in fostering the creative class. According to census estimates, as of 2005, a little over 40 percent of the city's work force was employed in jobs related to arts and entertainment, education, health care, or social services. (Of course, the data do not reveal how many of those are low-level jobs with low wages and few benefits, compared to high-level ones with better compensation and benefits.) If we add the census category of "professional and scientific management," the percentage of workers in Providence in the creative class exceeds 50 percent. Providence epitomizes the "new economy" of the United States; it is focused on services, many of which are in the creative sector.

Introduction

As Providence illustrates, smaller cities are destinations for a wide variety of people. Smaller cities draw people just as big cities do, and for surprisingly similar reasons. In this chapter, I assess how the characteristics of the people who live in a smaller metro area affect how well that place has fared over time. Scholars have long posited that certain mixtures of people in cities are likely to yield benefits to all and that cities that lack certain social or demographic characteristics are likely to struggle over time.

Scholars of larger cities have provided tools for assessing success or stagnation in smaller metro areas over the latter part of the twentieth century in the United States (Sassen 2001; Florida 2002; Glaeser et al. 1992; Negrey and Zickel 1994; Henderson 1997; Coulson 1999; Eisinger and Smith 2000; Madden 2000; Stanback 2002). A key argument concerning success in metro areas in that time period is that cities needed to have the "right mix" of people. Often, this argument draws on Richard Florida's theory of the ascendance of the creative class, the tolerant and highly educated workers of today's information economy. Other scholars point to immigration as key (Glaeser and Shapiro 2003b), noting that immigrants are now the drivers of population growth in the United States, particularly since the mid-1990s. In this chapter, I examine how well these theories explain how and why smaller metro areas grow or shrink, prosper or stagnate.

In addition, I argue that multiple factors, not just one factor in isolation, should be included in definitions of a city's success or failure. Some scholars privilege population (Henderson 1997; Pack 2002; Glaeser and Shapiro 2003b), some look at income (Savitch et al. 1993; Crihfield and Panggabean 1995; Erickcek and McKinney 2004), and some focus on employment levels (Glaeser et al. 1992; Negrey and Zickel 1994; Henderson 1997). I argue that what makes cities and suburbs successful is what makes them a good place to live, and this tends to be a combination of all of these characteristics. While this is unusual in the academic world, people outside universities who are interested in how cities are faring have developed multifaceted measures.

Eugene McCann (2004b) has looked at "best cities" lists, which use a variety of factors to determine "the best place to live." Although these lists are compiled for popular publications without much regard to scholarly conventions, they present the useful idea that what makes a city livable is a combination of characteristics. Taking a cue from these popular lists, I argue that we must look at the measures of population, income, and inequality in combination to assess success or failure among cities. In this chapter and the next, I look at each of these three outcomes separately to examine how they are related first to social and demographic characteristics and then to economic characteristics. In chapter 5, I bring these three measures together to assess how and why cities are successful or not over time.

Explaining Urban Change

Attempting to understand how metro areas change is a complex affair. How can the success or failure of an urban area be determined? Which attributes, in theory, contribute most strongly to the possibilities of success or failure in metro areas? I argue that no single indicator satisfactorily represents how well or how poorly a metro area has fared. Instead I examine three indicators over the entire thirty-year period to draw conclusions about which characteristics of a metropolitan statistical area most contribute to a place's chances of success or failure, growth or stagnation. These indicators are change in population, changes in median household income, and change in economic inequality. While these are not the only outcome measures available, together they offer a powerful assessment of how people are managing in these cities.

Scholars, policy makers, business leaders, and residents all share concerns about population expansion or decline in their communities. Scholars often use population change as a key indicator of how well a city or metro area is doing (Pack 2002; Vey and Forman 2002; Glaeser and Shapiro 2003b). Population change has direct consequences for people living in metro areas. A rapid increase in population may be welcomed as both an indicator of a healthy economy and as fuel for that economy, but it may also lead to problems. Economists refer to these problems as "externalities" because they are problems related to a change but are not due directly to the change itself. The externalities that might occur include housing shortages, increases in rents and mortgages (which may force some long-term residents out of their homes), strains on social services and educational institutions, and backlash against those who have recently arrived, particularly if the newcomers belong to minority racial or ethnic groups. Yet population decline is also a problem; decreasing population is often a sign (and sometimes a cause) of a sluggish or moribund economy or a lack of cultural amenities and diversity.

Personal income is also commonly used as a proxy for understanding well-being in cities (Mills and McDonald 1992; Savitch et al. 1993; Crihfield and Panggabean 1995; Erickcek and McKinney 2004). Cities with higher levels of income on average are generally thought to be doing better, everything else being equal. But while median household income is a good indicator of the average level of well-being in a city, it does not capture how equitably income is distributed within the population.

To capture how much economic inequality exists in a metro area, I use a measure of income disparity to indicate general levels of inequality in a metro area. The 90:10 economic inequality index described in chapter 2 is used to assess how equitably income is distributed. I do this not just because of a sense of fairness or social justice; extreme income inequality is associated with all sorts of problems. While there is still some debate about how inequality affects growth and much of the evidence comes from transnational comparisons, economists such as Jason Furman and Joseph Stiglitz (1998) of the Federal Reserve show that economic inequality is indeed detrimental to economic growth and thus is worth worrying about regardless of one's political preferences or ideology.[1]

The 90:10 economic inequality measure, however, does not give a good sense of how high or low absolute income levels are, so it must considered in combination with analysis of median household income. Together these three indicators (population, income, and economic inequality) present a more detailed picture of how a metro area has fared over the thirty-year period under examination. Still, knowing which outcomes to examine is only half the story. What factors lead to changes in population, income, and inequality? In chapter 1, I introduced some of the main arguments scholars make about how and why cities change. Here, I revisit these ideas briefly, focusing on how they apply to social and demographic characteristics of smaller metro areas.

I focus on two scholarly frameworks for understanding urban change over time. The first—of which Saskia Sassen (2001) is the prime example—focuses on how economic changes, particularly at the international level, have transformed cities. The second—of which Richard Florida (2002) is the prime example—focuses on how changing social environments have fostered specific responses to the types of economic changes Sassen discusses. Each provides a broad understanding of urban change over the latter part of the twentieth century. Yet the broad-brush strokes these scholars employ obscure what has actually happened in many urban areas and thus misrepresent the experiences of many residents of the United States who live outside the largest urban areas in the country.

These scholars point to specific indicators that influence change. Sassen (2001) and others (Knox and Taylor 1995; Marcuse and van Kempen 2000; Savitch and Kantor 2002) argue that changes in employment—specifically the growth of high-end service jobs in law, accounting, finance, and other related industries—are responsible for the booming economies of world cities. This group of scholars believes that examining the number and types of establishments as well as employment levels will explain why a city is doing well or not. Florida (2005) and those interested in his work (Jenkins, Leicht, and Jaynes 2006; Rausch and Negrey 2006; Scott 2006) look at the human capital that drives employment instead of focusing on employment levels in the areas that Sassen and others see as the engine of growth. For Florida and others, the education levels and diversity of a population are the key requirements for urban growth because having higher levels of both attributes leads to a greater number of "good jobs." From this perspective, it is essential to look at employment, education, and racial diversity as well as the institutions that are related to these characteristics, such as the number of colleges or cultural institutions in an urban area.

Other scholars focus on different factors that may prove equally important in determining how well a metro area fares. Since 1965, immigration has heavily influenced growth in urban areas. In general, smaller urban areas (those with metro populations below one million) have experienced declining populations since 1950, even though they had grown before that period (Crihfield and Panggabean 1995). At the same time, smaller cities became more popular destinations for immigrants during the last thirty years of the twentieth century. Immigrants are still moving to smaller cities, and many are moving to suburbs as readily as to cities (Frey 2005). Similarly, the continued movement of people from the largest cities of the

Northeast and the Midwest to southern and western cities has changed the face of urban America (Ehrlich and Gyourko 2000; Glaeser and Shapiro 2003b). Janet Pack (2002) argues that region is the single strongest variable that explains population change in urban areas over the second half of the twentieth century.

How People Affect Cities

In this chapter, I look at how the characteristics of people and cities affected population, income, and economic inequality over time in the eighty small metro areas of this study. In chapter 4, I turn my attention to the economies of small cities, but in this chapter the focus is on people. As in chapter 2, I have grouped the eighty small metro areas according to how much they have changed. In chapter 2, I grouped cities according to population change. In this chapter, I instead group them by change in income and economic inequality.

In addition, I analyze data on small cities statistically using regression analysis. Technical details about this analysis, along with the results, are found in the appendix. Regression analysis makes it possible to examine how a specific factor affects changes in an outcome measure while taking into account (statistically controlling for) other characteristics of cities. Using these techniques, one can isolate the impact of factors such as immigration or the presence or absence of a Fortune 500 company headquarters on the outcomes under examination.

The three outcome measures are evaluated separately from each other in this chapter and in chapter 4. In chapter 5, all three are put together to form a composite success index. While this index is useful, I assess the three outcomes of population, income, and inequality individually first because not all cities have the same issues or problems. Some small metro areas are concerned about population change more than income change and others are perhaps concerned about growing inequality. By examining them separately first, it is possible to observe the factors that affect each measure specifically; this information might help citizens, community leaders, and policy makers improve their own small places. The policy ideas that stem from this analysis are considered in greater depth in chapter 6.

Population

Chapter 2 looked at how smaller cities had different trajectories of growth from 1970 onward. The slowest-growing cities tended to start out with larger populations in their metro areas but did not gain many more people over time. In contrast, many of the fastest-growing cities, which are often located in the Sunbelt, were comparatively smaller in 1970 but then experienced rapid growth both in their central cities and in their suburbs and other nearby communities. However, chapter 2 examined population change alone without taking into account other factors that influence who moves where in the United States. To best understand how some cities ended up with more people by 2000, it is necessary to examine what characteristics of people, the economy, and the cities themselves are associated with growth or stagnation. In this chapter, I focus on people and cities; in chapter 4, I turn to the economies of metro areas to understand change.

Like the largest cities in the nation, the primary force behind population increases in smaller cities was in-migration of people born outside the United States. Since 1970, immigration has been the key to population change in the nation, and smaller places are not different. Among the ten fastest-growing smaller metro areas, the median change in percentage of the population that is foreign born was over 600 percent! Conversely, among the ten areas that grew slowest (or lost population) over the thirty years, the median change in percentage of the population foreign born was negative 2 percent. Cities that gained many immigrants did not necessarily start out with many; in fact, many of the cities with the largest percentage of immigrants in 1970 gained comparatively fewer over time. These cities did not experience an increase in population.

Duluth, Minnesota, and Youngstown, Ohio, for example, were both among the top ten cities in terms of percent of the population foreign born in 1970. By 2000, both cities had seen a decline in foreign-born residents, dropping from over 4 percent in 1970 to a little over 1 percent in 2000. Why? Most of the foreign-born residents in these cities had come to the United States in the first part of the twentieth century before the National Origins Act of 1924, which limited the number of immigrants from each nation until the Hart-Cellar Act of 1965 removed quotas from U.S. immigration policy. By 1970 the youngest of these immigrants were in their late 40s or early 50s, and by 2000 many had passed away. But because of the economic structure of these cities—as we will see in the next chapter—Duluth and Youngstown were not attractive destinations for immigrants who came to the United States after 1965. In contrast, cities such as Reno, Nevada, and Orlando, Florida, had foreign-born populations of around 1 percent in 1970, but by 2000, they had 14 percent and 12 percent, respectively.

Many of the metro areas that gained population through in-migration of immigrants were in the Southwest, but half of the twenty cities with immigrant populations of over 6 percent (the top quartile of the eighty places in terms of percentage of foreign-born population) were in other regions of the United States. When characteristics of the population and economy are taken into account, cities located in the western region of the country gained more people during the period of this study, so it is not surprising that western cities had large increases in immigration. In addition, as Audrey Singer (2005) of the Brookings Institution notes, more immigrants are bypassing the established "gateway" cities of entry into the United States, such as New York and Los Angeles, and are choosing to move to smaller cities that have not traditionally attracted Central and South American or Asian newcomers. While Salinas, California, has historically drawn immigrants, other cities such as Madison, Wisconsin, and Salt Lake City, Utah, are now attracting immigrants as well. The rate of increase in the number of foreign-born residents in those two cities was 180 percent and over 350 percent, respectively, over the period of this study. Only about 1 percent of the population of Las Vegas, the fastest growing small city (and the fastest growing place in the entire nation in the latter part of the twentieth century overall), was born abroad in 1970. By 2000, over 16 percent of the metro area's population was foreign born.

Las Vegas presents an interesting example of the other key factor associated with population growth among smaller cities: educational attainment. In 1970, less than 2 percent of the population in Las Vegas had a college degree; by 2000, just over 16 percent did. Yet Las Vegas trailed behind the average for all cities—23 percent—in this regard. Instead, the other end of the educational spectrum was better represented. Immigrants from abroad and from other parts of the United States who came to Las Vegas tended to have low levels of education. In fact, in 2000, about one-fifth of the population of Las Vegas had not completed high school. This compared to an average for all cities of about 18 percent that had not completed high school.

Overall, cities that gained people tended to attract both the highly educated (people who had completed college) and the poorly educated (those who had not completed high school), a curious bifurcation at first glance. In the United States as a whole, the percentage of people with at least a high school degree has increased greatly since World War II. In 1940, only 25 percent of the population had completed high school or beyond; by 2000, just over 80 percent of the population had obtained a high school degree or higher.[2] The eighty cities studied here mirror this trend. For all eighty cities, in 2000, an average of about 81 percent of metro area populations had completed high school or more. Indeed, in cities such as Green Bay, the proportion of the population without a high school diploma decreased markedly, from about 42 percent in 1970 to about 14 percent in 2000. At the same time, the proportion of residents in Green Bay with a college degree or higher increased from 5 percent in 1970 to 23 percent in 2000.

Given the general trend of rising levels of education among residents of the United States, why this curious phenomenon of increasing numbers of people with either low levels of education or high levels of education? In large part, the answer lies in the fact that much population growth has been due to immigrants from Central and South America, who generally come to the United States without completing the equivalent of high school. Statistically, taking other factors into account, increases in the percentage change in the population without a high school degree are associated with increases in percentage change in the population. But if we look at the average effect of education and immigration on population over time, the percentage of the population with a college education is influential, while the population without a high school degree is not (statistically).

What this points to is the influence of educational attainment on population growth. Richard Florida (2001) posits that cities with more college-educated people will grow more, but he focuses on the related characteristics of individuals and their preferences rather than on education itself. When Florida's tolerance index is included in the analysis, it is not statistically a predictor of population change in these metro areas. The evidence from the eighty cities in this study does not always completely support his theory. Fast-growing cities do not grow only because increasing numbers of college graduates move to them. In five of the ten fastest-growing metro areas in this study, less than 16 percent of the population had a college degree in 2000. In Laredo, the percentage of college-educated individuals increased considerably but still was only 13 percent in 2000. In contrast, in both Green Bay and Salinas, 23 percent of the population had a college degree, and in Providence the corresponding number was about 24 percent. However, the general trend was that slow-growing cities tended to not gain as many college-educated people on average over time.

While the types of people matter, other characteristics of cities are significant factors in generating population growth. As noted in chapter 1, scholars have tried to determine what things matter most in increasing population. One prominent trend is the shift of population in the nation from northern and eastern cities to southern and western cities. A variety of reasons for this shift have been posited, but an enduring one is that weather is a key factor. In statistical examinations of the influences on population that take into account demographic characteristics, economic characteristics, and city-specific factors such as number of colleges and universities, presence or absence of a Fortune 500 company headquarters, climate, and region, the only city-specific feature that matters is region. While researchers such as Janet Rothenberg Pack (2002) have noted this general trend, some scholars have paid particular attention to how well January and July temperatures predict population change. Surprisingly, colder temperatures in January or warmer temperatures in July do not matter when people choose where to live; the important thing is regional location. Thus, cities such as Colorado Springs, Boise, and Salt Lake City have all experienced high levels of population growth because they are in the West, not because they are particularly warm cities.

Together, immigration, education, and region are the most important factors (outside of economic ones) related to population expansion among small metro areas in the United States. This combination is not very different from what other research has identified as key factors for the largest cities in the United States. What is interesting is that these general trends hold true for smaller metro areas as much as for larger ones. Richard Florida and Saskia Sassen have argued that populations in large cities are growing for different reasons than in smaller cities. The evidence here suggests that population growth in smaller metro areas is driven by similar reasons: immigration and education. Thus the separateness of the experiences of small cities from those of large ones may not be as real or deep as originally thought. Faster-growing cities are "glocal cities" in the sense that they are growing for similar reasons as the global or creative large cities are. When income is examined, similar trends appear, further complicating the division that scholars have argued exists between how and why small and large cities change over time.

Income

As important as population change is for explaining the growth of a city, for many people, income levels are even more important. People hope to live in a prosperous area and to reap the benefits of doing so. When people talk about growth at the local level, they almost always mean both population and economic growth. In the next chapter I examine the economic landscape of smaller cities to understand how it affects income levels in different places and over time; here I focus on how factors related to people and aspects of the cities themselves. Of course, these factors will also come into play in thinking about local economies (in chapter 4). Nonetheless, it is useful to consider how characteristics of people and places are associated with rising or falling incomes in smaller metro areas over time.

One of the challenges government and private sector leaders face as they strive to understand economic growth is whether to be more concerned with absolute levels of income or changes in levels of income. While having income change positively over time is important, so is having a relatively high level of income overall. Laredo, Texas, demonstrates this quandary. Between 1970 and 2000, median household income in Laredo increased by 45 percent. This rate of growth ranked 11th overall out of all eighty cities in this study. Compared to Youngstown, Ohio, or Beaumont, Texas, where median household income shrank by 2 percent and 12 percent, respectively, Laredo residents experienced real growth in purchasing power.

However, the story is not quite so clear cut when absolute levels of income are taken into account. In 1970, the median household income in Laredo was about $19,300 (in constant 2000 dollars); a figure that had increased to $28,200 by 2009.[3] While the United States as a whole saw stagnating levels of real income over this period (Hout and Fischer 2006), Laredo bucked the trend and experienced growth. The national median household income in 1970 was $38,800; for the eighty small metro areas, it was $32,700. By 2000, the median was $42,200 for the nation and $39,200 for the eighty metro areas. By 2009, the national median household income was right around $40,000. Thus, although Laredo's median household income grew over the three decades of this study, the metro area remained much poorer than the nation as a whole.

In contrast, Green Bay experienced only moderate income change; median household income increased by 16 percent from 1970 to 2000, below the average rate of change for all eighty areas (26 percent). In 1970, median household income in Green Bay was $40,000. By 2000, that figure had increased to $46,500, but in 2006, it had declined to $42,100. Although household income in Green Bay increased from 1970 to 2000, income levels did not increase as dramatically as in Laredo. Even so, the average household in Green Bay was more likely to be prosperous compared to the average household in Laredo.

Among the ten cities that ranked highest in terms of rate of growth in median household income in 2000, the average growth rate in median household income from 1970 to 2000 was 40 percent. In the ten cities with the lowest median household income in 2000, the rate of change from 1970 was only 29 percent. In other words, income in cities with the highest median income in 2000 grew at a faster rate since 1970 than income in cities with the lowest median income in 2000. However, income in cities that had high median household income levels in 1970 tended not to increase as much over the thirty-year period, while those with the lowest levels of median household income in 1970 saw far greater increases. This is discussed in greater depth in chapter 4.

While it is clear that economic factors are very influential in determining both median household income levels and the rate at which that measure changes over time, other aspects of residents and the cities they live in are important too. In small cities where the percentage of college graduates increased, income levels were higher and the increase in income was greater over time (figure 3.1). This relationship holds true even when we look at it from a variety of perspectives. Levels of college education in one decade are correlated with future levels of income in smaller places

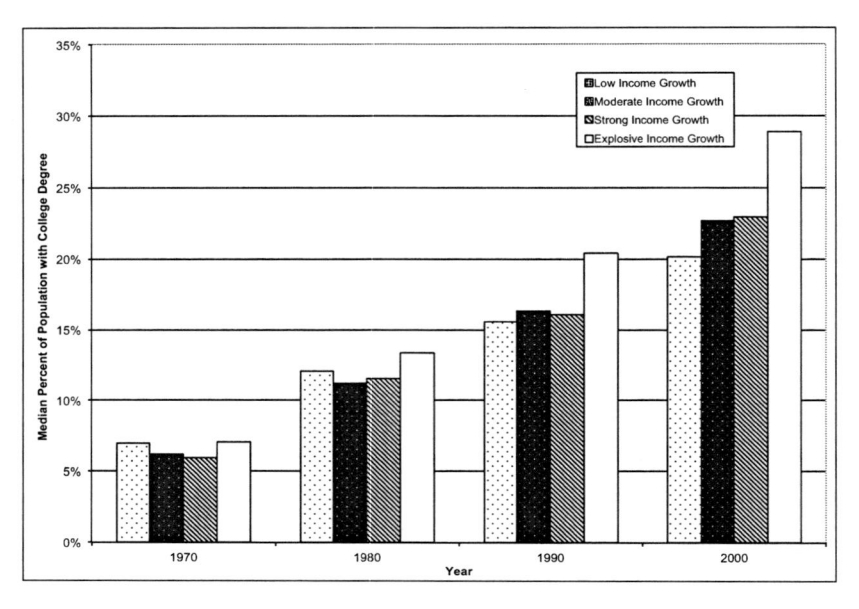

FIGURE 3.1. Median Percentage of Population with a College Degree by Income Growth Group, Eighty Small Metro Areas, 1970–2000

Source: U.S. Census data from 1970, 1980, 1990, and 2000.

in subsequent decades. Even controlling for other factors, an increase in the population that has a college degree by 1 percent is associated with an increase in median household income by about $340. Thus the difference between a metro area where 12 percent of the population has a college degree and a metro area where 22 percent has a college degree is approximately $3,400 in median household income.

Of course, overall, the percentage of the population of the United States who had completed college increased tremendously between 1970 and 2000. In 1970, 11 percent of adults over age 25 had completed college. By 2000, this had climbed to 24 percent (U.S. Census Bureau 2003–2004). The small cities studied here showed similar gains. In 1970, the average among all 80 places was about 6 percent of residents in these smaller metro areas with college degrees, but by 2000, that average had climbed to 23 percent. For those smaller places that were above average in 2000 (i.e., more than 24 percent of their populations had a college degree), median household income stood at $42,200; for those below average, median household income was $37,600. The cities with the highest percentages of college-educated people tended to be home to large state universities; however, the number and type of universities in a city was not a statistically significant factor in rising income levels over time.

If we look instead at how changes in the percentage of the population with various demographic characteristics affect percentage change in income—which allows us to take into account more factors—education is still important. However, when we take into account a variety of demographic characteristics of the population, what matters is the percentage of people who have not completed a high school degree. Cities where the proportion of people who did not complete high school increased tended to see decreases in the percentage change in median household income over time. The percentage change in college-educated people is not a significant factor in this analysis. When we take into account many aspects of the local economy as well as city-specific attributes, percent change in college-educated people does not influence change in income. While this may seem to contradict the findings stated above, it is important to remember that we are looking at two separate but related outcomes: income levels over time and percentage change in income over time. These two indicators are not necessarily influenced by the same factors.

The other important factor that plays a large role in increasing levels of household income in smaller cities is immigration (figure 3.2). Cities where the percentage of immigrants increased in their metro areas also tended to experience increasing levels of income. As with increases in college education, at the national level, the percentage of the population born outside the United States greatly increased between 1970 and 2000. In 1970, about 5 percent of the U.S. population was born outside the country. By 2000, this had increased to 11 percent. On average, the smaller metro areas in this study did not attract as many foreign-born individuals as the nation as a whole. In only thirteen of the eighty metro areas did the size of the foreign-born population exceed 11 percent in 2000, and nine of these cities were in the border states of California, Nevada, and Texas.

However, immigrants in the United States have recently begun to relocate to smaller cities and to cities in states that traditionally have not seen tremendous influxes of people from South and Central America or Asia. In 2000, the size of the foreign-born population in both Salem, Oregon, and Providence, Rhode Island, was about 12 percent. Other places, such

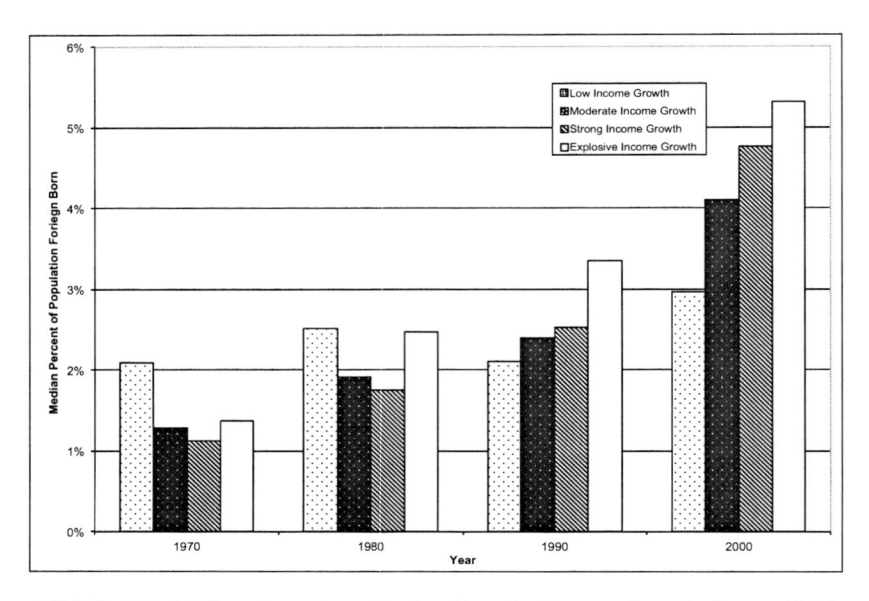

FIGURE 3.2. Median Percentage Foreign Born by Income Growth Group, Eighty Small Metro Areas, 1970–2000

Source: U.S. Census data from 1970, 1980, 1990, and 2000.

as Salt Lake City, Rochester, Minnesota, and Sioux City, Iowa, attracted even larger numbers of immigrants. Some cities that were not attractive to immigrants in 1970 continued to remain unattractive. But others, such as Youngstown, Ohio, and Duluth, Minnesota, experienced dramatic decreases in the percent of foreign-born population by 2000. These cities became less attractive to immigrants over time as older immigrants died and were not replaced.

The cities that experienced declines in percent of population foreign born also experienced decreasing levels of income. In Youngstown, for example, where the foreign-born population decreased by 57 percent over the thirty-year period, median household income decreased by 12 percent. Trenton, New Jersey, in contrast, epitomized the success stories among small places. From 1970 to 2000, Trenton's foreign-born population grew by 136 percent, and its median household income grew by 43 percent to $56,600. The connection between increasing immigration and increasing income levels holds true even when we take into account other factors such as the number of Fortune 500 companies in a metro area, the climate, the number of colleges or universities, and characteristics of the local economy.

Small cities that attract immigrants tend to prosper. But they are not necessarily attractive for the same reasons that global cities are; that is, smaller cities are not necessarily home to large immigrant communities that draw more members from a particular part of the world. Instead, successful small cities offer a mix of employment opportunities that generally offer higher wages than other cities, and that is what attracts immigrants.

Economic Inequality

While economic equality is not necessarily on the minds of most residents of smaller metro areas, the issue is important in many ways. It is difficult to compare how smaller cities fared with the nation as a whole since levels of economic inequality and equality are not often calculated by scholars, government officials, or private organizations, although some researchers have studied it. Sociologists Claude Fischer and Mike Hout (2006) examined trends in the distribution of income over the twentieth century. They found that from 1900 to 1970, the general trend in the United States was one of increasing economic equality. However, after 1970, wealth has become increasingly concentrated in a smaller and smaller portion of the population. The metro areas studied here reflect this trend. From 1970 to 2000, economic inequality (as measured by the 90:10 index described in chapter 2) increased in all of the metro areas of this study. Thus, the question is not whether cities became more equal but which cities did a better job of mitigating the trend toward inequality.

Table 3.1 shows the distribution of metro areas based on how much their levels of economic inequality increased between 1970 and 2000. In 1970, the cities with the lowest levels of economic inequality tended to be in the East and Midwest. Reading, Pennsylvania, was the most economically equal city among the eighty. Conversely, the cities that were least economically equal were in the South. McAllen, Texas, was the least equal metro area in 1970. As time passed, these patterns generally persisted. In 2000, Cedar Rapids, Iowa, was the most equal city, while Gainesville, Florida, was the least economically equal. The most unequal cities were still heavily concentrated in the South; metro areas in Florida, Alabama, Texas, and Louisiana ranked in the top ten least equal places. The top ten cities that were comparatively more equal in 2000 were more geographically diverse; although most of them they were in the Midwest, cities such as Salt Lake City, Colorado Springs, and Boise were also among the group.

TABLE 3.1

Eighty Small Metro Areas Grouped by Percentage Change in 90:10 Economic Inequality Index, 1970–2000

Smallest Increase in Inequality[a]	Medium Increase in Inequality[b]	Large Increase in Inequality[c]	Tremendous Increase in Inequality[d]
Billings, MT	Abilene, TX	Amarillo, TX	Bakersfield, CA
Boise City, ID	Chattanooga, TN	Ann Arbor, MI	Beaumont, TX
Cedar Rapids, IA	Evansville, IN	Baton Rouge, LA	Columbia, MO
Colorado Springs, CO	Fargo, ND	Columbus, GA	Decatur, IL
Columbia, SC	Fort Wayne, IN	Duluth, MN	Eugene, OR
Des Moines, IA	Grand Rapids, MI	Erie, PA	Flint, MI
Fayetteville, NC	Jackson, MS	Fort Smith, AR	Fresno, CA
Green Bay, WI	Las Vegas, NV	Kalamazoo, MI	Gainesville, FL
Huntsville, AL	Lawton, OK	Knoxville, TN	Lafayette, LA
Lincoln, NE	Madison, WI	Lansing, MI	Laredo, TX
Little Rock, AR	Modesto, CA	Lexington, KY	Lubbock, TX
Orlando, FL	Montgomery, AL	Macon, GA	Providence, RI
Rochester, MN	Reno, NV	McAllen, TX	Pueblo, CO
Salem, OR	Roanoke, VA	Mobile, AL	Shreveport, LA
Salinas, CA	Rockford, IL	Peoria, IL	Springfield, MA
Salt Lake City, UT	San Angelo, TX	Reading, PA	Syracuse, NY
Sioux City, IA	South Bend, IN	Richmond, VA	Tallahassee, FL
Sioux Falls, SD	Springfield, IL	Savannah, GA	Trenton, NJ
Springfield, MO	Topeka, KS	Spokane, WA	Waco, TX
Wichita Falls, TX	Tyler, TX	Stockton, CA	Youngstown, OH

Source: U.S. Census data from 1970, 1980, 1990, and 2000

[a] Increases between 71 percent to 105 percent.

[b] Increases between 108 and 124 percent.

[c] Increases between 124 and 146 percent.

[d] Increases between 146 percent and 219 percent.

Two demographic factors influenced levels of economic inequality over time. First, cities that experienced relatively lower declines in the percentage of the population that identified as white experienced smaller increases in economic inequality. Second, cities that had higher percentages of citizens with college degrees over time experienced greater increases in levels of economic inequality. Third, cities that were more tolerant (using Richard Florida's tolerance rank from 2000) saw greater increases, in terms of percentage change, in economic inequality. Finally, cities that had higher average low temperatures in January saw greater increases, in terms of percentage change, in economic inequality.

How do we make sense of these findings? We know that the percentage of whites decreased in all metro areas from 1970 to 2000. Statistical analysis seems to suggest that metro areas that do a better job of retaining white people as other racial groups move in are doing better in terms of economic inequality; that is, the cities with racially diverse populations seem to do better. The role of college graduates is harder to interpret. As chapter 4 will show, higher levels of employment in high-end service jobs (such as law or software development) are tied to lower levels of economic inequality, and these jobs generally require college degrees. Thus it is unclear how these two factors intersect.

However, the influence of tolerance rank on percentage change in economic inequality may offer some ideas. Increasing levels of tolerance, as measured by this one index at least, are tied to an increase in percentage change in economic inequality. The tolerance index, by definition, is related to the percentage of college graduates, and it may be that increasing the number of college graduates, who tend to be more tolerant, somehow restructures metro area economies in ways that make them less equal economically. The final identified factor, higher low temperatures in January, is likely related to the higher levels of economic inequality found in the South.

Conclusion: Welcoming Diversity

Smaller cities that are doing well tend to be doing so because they have a diverse and educated population. While this might not be very surprising (these are the characteristics of growing larger cities), it does present a new way of thinking about how small cities are doing. Successful smaller cities are not the backwaters of larger cities, home to cast-off or residual populations. Rather, smaller cities that are growing, well-off, and more economically equal attract a wide range of people. These places are truly glocal cities, places that are successful without necessarily following the formulas laid out by scholars such as Sassen and Florida.

Richard Florida posits that a very specific type of diversity is required in the twenty-first century for a city to do well. He posits that cities that attract the "creative class" (people who work in creative service-sector jobs), are bohemian, accept difference, and offer all sorts of traditional and nontraditional recreational opportunities are more likely to be economically successful. While it is difficult to measure all of these things, Florida provides a composite index constructed from these ideas. Florida's tolerance index offers a way of discerning whether or not tolerance or some other characteristic of a city is statistically significant in determining growth. (The next chapter looks at the tolerance index in greater depth.)

When Florida's tolerance rank is included in statistical analysis designed to take into account many characteristics of places (see the appendix), it is associated with changes in levels of inequality but not in changes in levels of population or income.[4] In fact, it has a negative effect on levels of inequality; that is, places that score higher on Florida's tolerance rank experienced greater increases in economic inequality over time. Many planners and civic boosters believe that the future prosperity of urban or metro areas can be achieved only by attracting the creative class. However, there appears to be an unsavory externality to this strategy: places that do well in Florida's view do poorly in the eyes of people who want places to be good destinations for all newcomers.

While it is necessary to examine economic characteristics of metro areas to fully understand how and why places change over time, the assessment of the characteristics of the people who live in these places offers much evidence about how people themselves influence success or failure. Successful smaller places—the ones I refer to as glocal places—are attractive to similar types of groups that are attracted to global cities. However, residents of glocal cities are not necessarily part of the creative class, and as chapters 4 and 5 will show, the economies of such cities are not necessarily overly oriented toward what Florida calls the creative economy. Sadly, glocal places draw people not because of tolerance based on the presence of a creative class but for more mundane reasons, primarily economic, that I will examine next.

4

Diversify, Don't Specialize

Salinas, California, originally was known as the Salad Bowl of the World. Today, as you wander through the small city, you realize that while agriculture is still very important, Salinas and its surroundings are home to much more than large agribusiness enterprises. Although in 2005, 19 percent of the city's work force was still employed in agriculture and agriculture is still the largest single employment sector, retail, education, health care, and social services together account for about 30 percent of all employment. The Salinas metro area still reflects this heritage; agricultural firms such as Fresh Express, a salad greens wholesaler, and Taylor Farms, a grower and shipper of agriculture products, are located there. At the same time, the other largest employers in the city are hospitals and social service agencies.

The nearby areas that surround Salinas offer further explanation of how this once slightly sleepy agricultural area became a rather posh getaway for wealthy families from other parts of the state. Pebble Beach and its famous golf course has historically been a playground for the wealthy, and today the resorts in Pebble Beach are some of the largest individual employers in the metro area. But in the last thirty or so years, Monterey, Carmel-by-the-Sea, and other cities nearby have become permanent homes for well-off families rather than just vacation destinations. The economies of Monterey and Carmel-by-the-Sea are still centered on tourism and vacationers; an estimated four million people visit these cities each year (City of Monterey 2012). But what is unusual about these cities among tourist towns is that the median household income of Carmel-by-the-Sea was about $78,000, far above the average in the United States.

Monterey, unlike Salinas, has very few people employed in agriculture, but many of its residents are employed in high-end services jobs such as finance, law, real estate, and health care. The U.S. Navy is one of the largest employers for residents of Monterey and nearby Seaside, particularly the Naval Postgraduate School in Monterey. McGraw-Hill, a large publisher, also employs many in Monterey, as does HSBC, a large multinational bank. Overall, the Salinas metro area houses a diverse economy centered on services and a robust agricultural sector. This helps explain why the area has experienced tremendous increases of people at both ends of the education spectrum—people with college or graduate degrees and people who did not finish high school. Agriculture and tourism provide jobs for the latter group, while health care, finance, and education attract those from the former group.

Introduction

As Salinas shows, smaller metro areas contain complex economies. In this chapter, I examine how the economies of smaller metro area have changed since 1970. When scholars think about how urban economies function, they have generally focused on employment levels within and across economic sectors (Sassen 2001; Savitch and Kantor 2002; Stanback 2002). Employment levels are important indicators of how local economies perform. The national economy has changed over the last several decades; there are fewer jobs in manufacturing industries and more and more jobs in service industries. Manufacturing has not completely disappeared, but the types of things being manufactured in the United States has shifted; many firms that produce such things as durable household goods and automobiles have moved their operations to other countries.

In the 1950s and 1960s, the economy in the United States rested on what might be called old manufacturing—the production of consumer goods such as cars, washing machines, and televisions as well as commercial or industrial goods such as locomotive engines, airplanes, and industrial machinery. In contrast, much manufacturing today is new manufacturing—the production of computer components, advanced robotics, and technical instruments. While old manufacturing has not disappeared from the United States, industries in this category now employ a small fraction of the people they once did, and many of the new jobs in the sector are nonunionized ones with lower pay and benefits than the older jobs they supplanted.

There has also been a geographic redistribution of manufacturing employment within the United States from the Northeast and Midwest to the South primarily. A fair portion of the remaining old manufacturing jobs, such as in the automotive manufacturing facilities of foreign car companies located in the South, do not employ unionized work forces with high earnings. Many domestic manufacturers have left the United States altogether in search of lower labor costs and higher profit margins. Scholars such as Jefferson Cowle (1999) have shown how these types of changes have affected particular smaller cities, but it remains to be seen how such movement has affected smaller metro areas as a group.

At the same time that manufacturing jobs moved or disappeared, jobs in services have increased. The U.S. economy is based on consumption, and much of that consumption is of domestically produced services of all sorts, ranging from haircuts and oil changes to legal work, accounting, and software design. Services can be thought of as being divided into high-end and low-end sectors. Jobs in the high-end service sector include those that generally require a college or graduate degree, such as law, architecture and engineering, or medicine, while most jobs in the low-end service sector are open to most anyone and generally involve customer service or menial tasks. Of course, people with many years of education may work in a company in the low-end services industry in a position high up the ladder, while those with low levels of education and experience may work in a high-end service company doing data entry or as a customer service representative.[1]

A category related to high-end services that many economists examine as distinct are those jobs in the finance, insurance, and real estate (abbreviated FIRE) industries. As Saskia Sassen (2001) notes, these sectors are particularly important in the new services-oriented global economy of the late twentieth century. Sassen discusses how these jobs are bellwethers for economic activity and represent services that are essential to the workings of the high-end service economy. The FIRE sector is most robust in cities that have considerable new economy activity, such as information technology, biotechnology, health sciences, or other sectors. These sectors are commonly seen as the engines of economic growth.

In this chapter, I use these five sectors to assess how the composition of a city's economy affects economic growth or decline. Each of these sectors offers different opportunities for entry into a company or organization, different career paths, and different levels of compensation (both wages and benefits). Often, low-end service firms have many more jobs with low levels of pay and benefits than jobs with high levels of pay and benefits. Companies in the high-end service or FIRE sectors, conversely, tend to have a higher proportion of good-paying jobs that offer many benefits to employees, although they are likely to offer fewer of such jobs. Jobs in these two sectors tend to attract the "creative class" that Richard Florida refers to.

Thomas Stanback (2002) notes that along with the general shift from manufacturing to services, there has been a growing consolidation of firms within sectors in the United States over time. The number of firms within a given economic sector is an important part of the story for understanding local metropolitan economies. The distribution of employment over time makes it possible to examine how these small cities have changed, to see if they have changed in similar ways to the larger national economy, and to assess whether a local economy offers "good" jobs or not. Adding an examination of the number of firms within a sector provides detail to this picture and helps illuminate how that sector has functioned over time. Sectors that have many firms may be growing and competitive, while those with few may be moribund and stagnant. Alternatively, sectors with few employers may be mature and may have captured a specific segment of a local (or national) market and thus may be able to offer steady employment.

Wage levels are often not included in sociological assessments of cities or metro areas. Yet if we want to understand population growth, income growth, and economic inequality, wage levels must be taken into account. As shown below, wage levels have little relationship to population change, but they are influential in terms of median household income and economic inequality levels. Using the three economic indicators (of employment levels in sectors), number of firms within sectors, and average wages by sector provides a clear picture of how local economies function. Such an analysis makes it possible to assess the role of economies as multifaceted systems that function at the local level (even if they are also integrated into the regional, national, and global economies).

In this chapter I look at the effects of economic sectors on the three outcomes discussed in the previous chapters. My analysis uses absolute levels of employment, numbers of firms and wages, and indices that take into account national trends. The next section outlines these indices, called location quotients.

How Cities Measure Up: Location Quotients

One way that economists and other social scientists analyze how local economies compare to national economies is by using what are called location quotients. Location quotients are the ratio of employment in a given sector in a local area to the national level of employment within that sector. For example, a city with a location quotient of 1.0 in manufacturing would have the same percentage of the workforce employed in that sector as the nation as a whole. A location quotient greater than 1.0 indicates that a local area has a higher proportion of employment in that sector than the national average, while a location quotient of less than 1.0 indicates a lower proportion locally. Location quotients are useful for examining how cities fare compared to the national economy. They allow us to assess whether a place is similar to the nation as a whole in terms of employment and provide a way to compare different places using a standard measure.

While traditionally location quotients are used to examine employment levels, they can be constructed based on the number of establishments and wage levels in localities as well. Calculating location quotients based on the number of firms in a sector is useful for understanding how widely developed or concentrated a particular economic sector is in a local area compared to the national economy. Of course, location quotients based on the number of firms in a sector need to be compared to other indicators, including the absolute number of firms in that sector. Even so, we can see how sectors impact local economies by looking at location quotients across time.

For example, if a city has a location quotient of 1.5 in manufacturing, we know that it has many more firms than the national average for that sector. This may lead us to think about whether this means the sector is robust and competitive—because it has generated many firms—or whether it perhaps is in its initial phases of development. Looking at location quotients over time can help us see whether a particular sector is expanding (perhaps due to general growth in the sector) or contracting (perhaps due to competition or consolidation).

Using location quotients for wages offers similar benefits. While wage location quotients must be compared with absolute wage values, they provide a sense of how well paid a sector is in a given city. Wage location quotients may also help us understand if high or low wage levels, compared to other cities and nationally, are driving employment in a sector. We might expect that places with high wage levels compared to the national average would draw people to that metro area who are searching for high-paying jobs in a particular sector. Conversely, low wage levels in a sector or sectors may be the root of high economic inequality as measured in the 90:10 economic inequality index.

Comparing the National and the Local

In chapter 2, we learned a bit about local economies in relation to population growth. In this section we examine them in greater detail. The economies of small cities are tied to regional, national, and global economies. To a certain extent, they mirror these larger economies in the division of workers and firms within and across sectors. But there are some key differences between the eighty small metro areas studied here and the national economy of the United States in general.

As figure 4.1 shows, like the United States as a whole, a majority of people working in small metro areas work in the service industries that are the heart of the contemporary American economy. And like the nation as a whole, small metro areas have seen large increases, on average, in the percentage of their workforces employed in services, particularly high-end services. It is worth noting that these eighty cities have seen decreasing employment in the FIRE sector. As I noted in chapter 2, we can think of services of all types as being the hallmark of the "new economy" and manufacturing as more characteristic of the "old economy." On average, small metro areas are part of the new economy, although subsequent analyses in

DIVERSIFY, DON'T SPECIALIZE 97

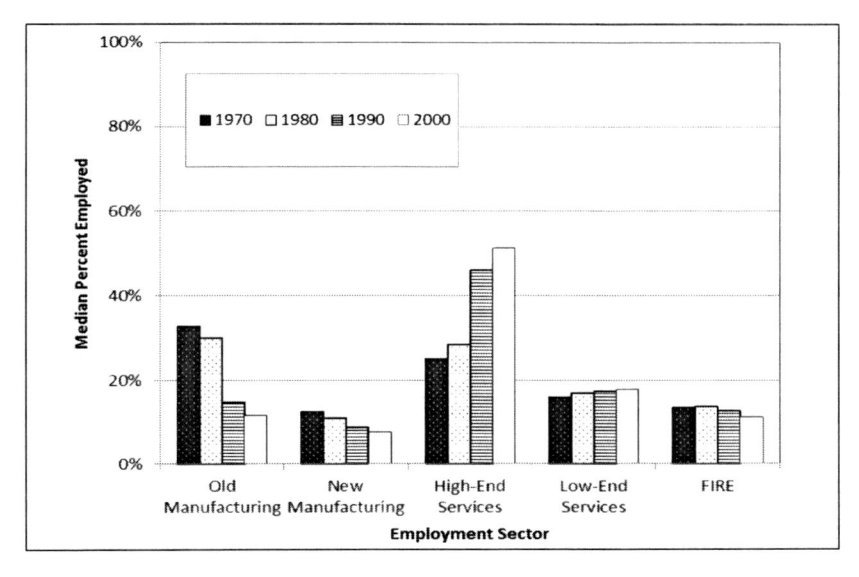

FIGURE 4.1. Median Percentage of Workforce Employed by Sector for Eighty Small Metro Areas, 1970–2000

Source: U.S. Department of Commerce, U.S. Bureau of the Census, County Business Patterns data for 1974, 1979, 1989, 1996 (U.S. Census Bureau 1985, 1986, 1989, 1991, 1998).

this chapter will show that successful places are not necessarily as tied to the new economy as less successful ones.

At the same time, the distribution of firms in each sector indicates that the number of firms generally is commensurate with the percent employed for that sector. It would be striking, for example, if a sector commanded 30 percent of metro-area employment but only accounted for 10 percent of the metro area's firms. Figure 4.2 shows that the new manufacturing and high-end services sectors tend on average to be slightly more concentrated than might be expected from the employment levels for each sector. Conversely, small metro areas tend to have more FIRE firms than might be expected given the employment numbers, and even with decreasing employment, the proportion of firms in this sector stayed roughly the same between 1990 and 2000.

The wage data in Figure 4.3 provide a sense of how these sectors contribute to income levels in small places. Given that high-end service employment was on average the largest sector, it is heartening to see wage increases in that sector across time. However, old and new manufacturing

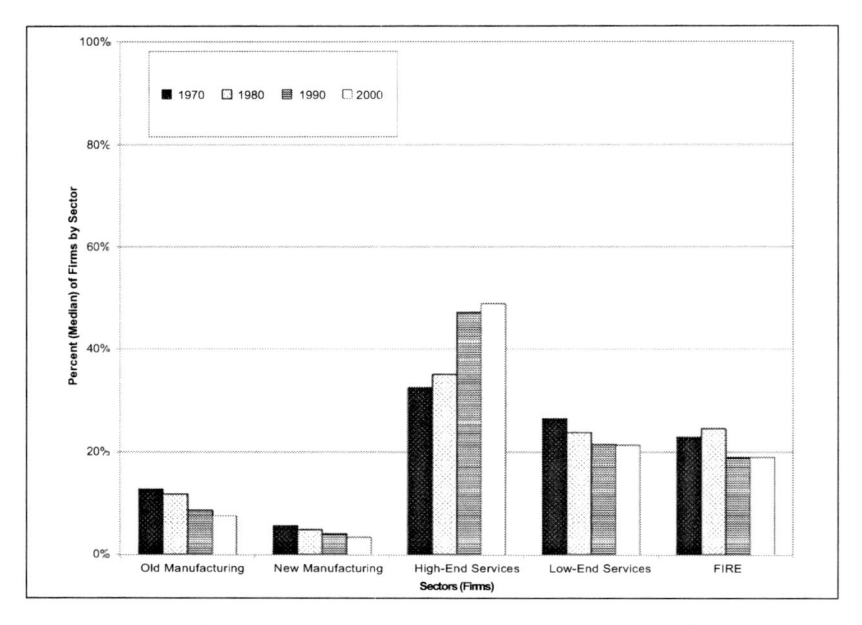

FIGURE 4.2. Median Percentage of Firms by Sector for Eighty Small Metro Areas, 1970–2000

Source: U.S. Department of Commerce, U.S. Bureau of the Census, County Business Patterns data for 1974, 1979, 1989, 1996 (U.S. Census Bureau 1985, 1986, 1989, 1991, 1998).

account for the highest-paid industries across the 80 smaller places. And while low-end service jobs remained roughly flat across time, wages remained quite low, offering these workers a much lower standard of living. However, as FIRE employment shrank, wages increased, indicating that the fewer jobs in that sector offered higher pay than jobs in other sectors.

While the absolute level of employment, number of firms, and average wages within a sector are useful, how small cities stack up to the national economy on these measures provides insight as well. Overall, small metro areas have become more like the nation as a whole over time (figure 4.4). Across all industries, the location quotients for all sectors are approaching 1.0. Small metro areas, on average, have become thus less different from other cities—even global cities—over time. But there are some differences between the economies of more successful small cities and those of the less successful ones.

While old and new manufacturing offer some of the best paid jobs in these smaller places, the two sectors employ fewer workers proportionally. Even

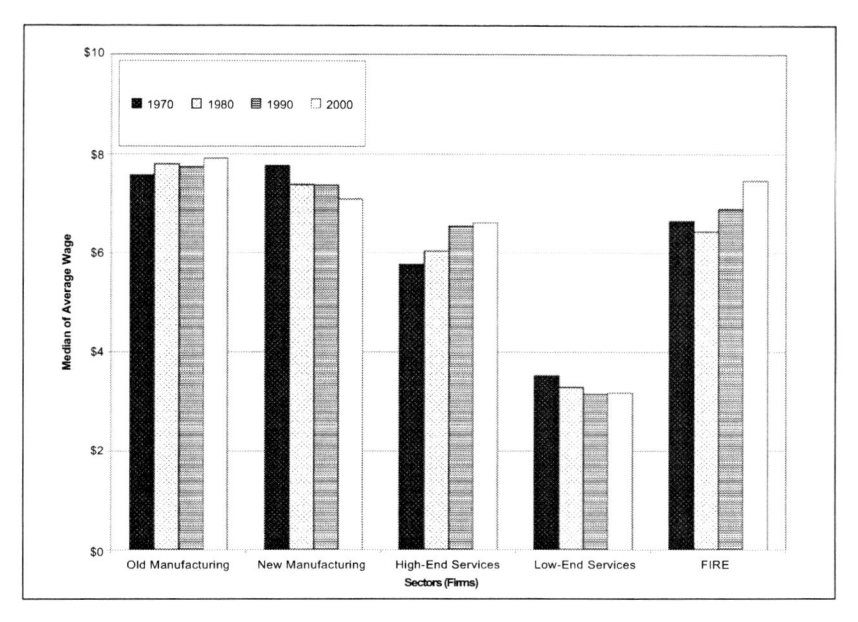

FIGURE 4.3. Median of Average Wages by Sector for Eighty Small Metro Areas, 1970–2000

Source: U.S. Census Bureau, County Business Patterns data for 1974, 1979, 1989, 1989, 1996 (U.S. Census Bureau 1985, 1986, 1989, 1991, 1998).

though manufacturing jobs are generally disappearing, on average in these small places they are not disappearing at the same rate as in the nation as a whole. Similarly striking is a disproportionate concentration of employment in the low-end and high-end services sectors in small cities. While the concentration of service-sector employment fits with the global cities hypothesis that smaller cities provide the back offices for the major cities of the nation, the fact that jobs in this sector exist in small cities compared to the national average complicates the picture. In small metro areas the number of low-end service jobs is decreasing, both absolutely and compared to the nation as a whole. However, the picture for high-end service jobs is quite different. The number of such jobs in small metro areas is increasing at the same time that the location quotient for this variable is decreasing. This means that while there are more jobs in this sector in small cities, the number of such jobs is not increasing at the same rate as they are for the nation as a whole.

The distribution of firms echoes the distribution of employment (figure 4.5). All sectors are more concentrated in fewer firms than the employment

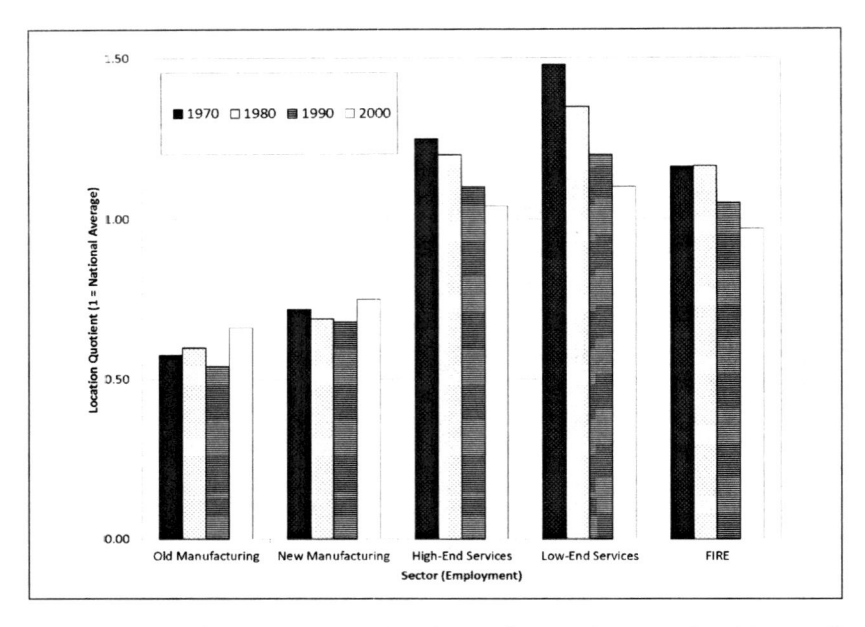

FIGURE 4.4. Median Location Quotient for Employment by Sector for Eighty Small Metro Areas, 1970–2000

Source: County Business Patterns data for 1974, 1979, 1989, 1996 (U.S. Census Bureau 1985, 1986, 1989, 1991, 1998).

numbers would suggest. Yet small places are more like the nation as a whole than might be expected. Contrary to popular conception, these smaller metro areas are not simply sites for the leftover manufacturing centers of the old economy. In fact, the eighty smaller cities of this study have lower levels of employment and fewer firms in manufacturing than the national average. At the same time, they are much like the nation as a whole in terms of the proportion of firms within the three service sectors.

Unfortunately, although the data about employment and numbers of firms show that the eighty small cities are keeping up with the rest of the nation, the wage location quotients show otherwise. The median wage location quotient for each sector is below 1.0, indicating that on average, the pay in small cities is lower than the national average (figure 4.6). The low number of high-paying jobs in the manufacturing sector accounts in part for the low median incomes in small cities. This difference in wages from the national average has the potential to contribute to increasing levels of economic inequality. However, the cost of living is generally lower

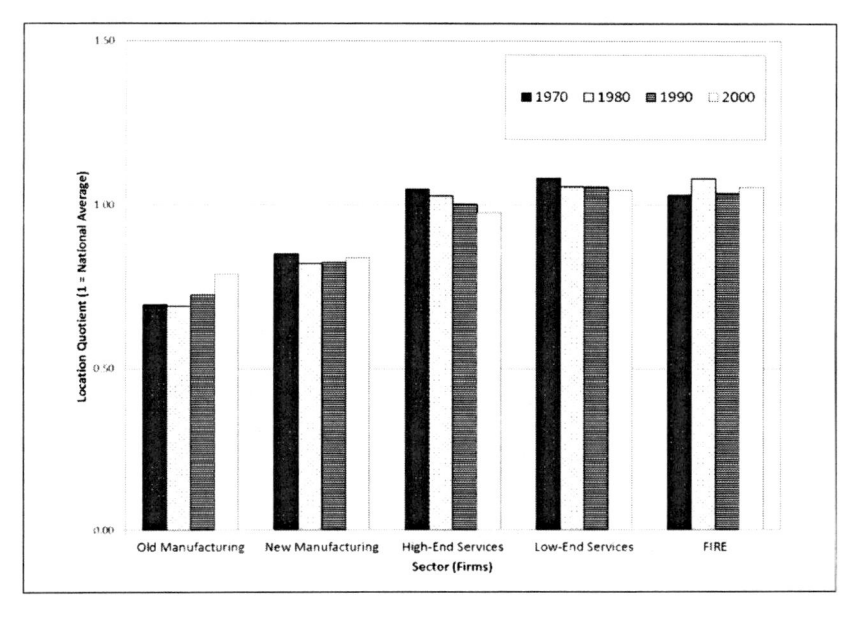

FIGURE 4.5. Median Location Quotient for Number of Firms within Sectors for Eighty Small Metro Areas, 1970–2000

Source: County Business Patterns data for 1974, 1979, 1989, 1996 (U.S. Census Bureau 1985, 1986, 1989, 1991, 1998).

in small cities, so the picture the numbers portray may look worse than the reality on the ground.

The comparatively lower pay for jobs in the high-end services and FIRE sectors may also be a factor in who works in small cities and how attractive such positions are. Employers in these two sectors in small cities may be at a disadvantage when it comes to recruitment. Lower wage levels rather than lack of cultural resources may be stunting the growth of the creative class in smaller places.

Examining the Outcomes: Population, Median Household Income, and Economic Inequality

One of the challenges of trying to understand how local economies affect metro areas over time is trying to decide whether it is more important to look at how characteristics of a city affect outcomes or how changes in a particular sector affect outcomes. Each type of inquiry has benefits.

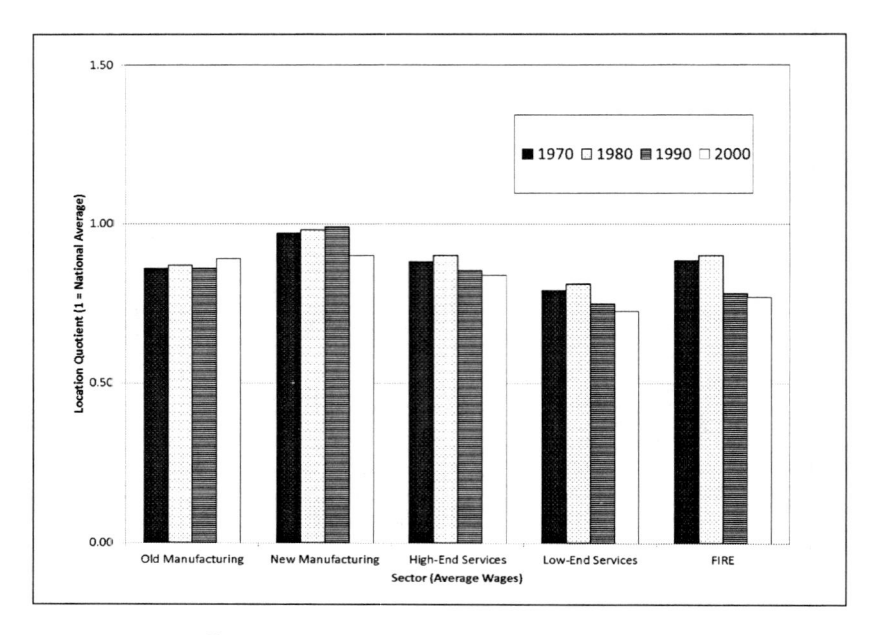

FIGURE 4.6. Median Location Quotient for Wages by Sector for Eighty Small Metro Areas, 1970–2000

Source: County Business Patterns data for 1974, 1979, 1989, 1996 (U.S. Census Bureau 1985, 1986, 1991, 1998).

Examining the general influence of levels of employment, number of firms, and average wages over the thirty-year period of this study provides a sense of how on-the-ground experiences affect population, income, and economic inequality. On the other hand, using the percentage change to look at sectors and other characteristics related to economic changes provides information about how changes in one area affect changes in others.

The main drawback of using these two types of analysis together is that they measure different things—namely, average affect of absolute levels over time versus the influence of the amount of change over time. But if levels of income at particular points in time are examined side by side with percent change in income over time, they offer a way of understanding how economic sectors influence places in ways that are not commonly considered. All of the findings below draw on the statistical models in the appendix. Those who are interested in the technical aspects of the analysis will find more details there.

Population Levels

As noted in chapter 3, some demographic characteristics of small metro areas affect population, but the question remains as to how economic factors affect it as well. A statistical technique called fixed effects regression analysis makes it possible to estimate the average influence of a characteristic of a city on population over time. This technique provides a sense of "what matters" for a growing small metro area. An analysis that considers the absolute levels of employment and wages (in a given year, as opposed to changes in levels across time) and the number of firms in the old manufacturing, new manufacturing, low-end services, high-end services, and FIRE sectors determines that the following are related to increases in population:

- higher employment levels in the FIRE and low-end services sectors
- more firms in the FIRE and high-end services sectors

In contrast, the following are associated with decreasing population levels:

- higher levels of employment in high-end services
- more firms and lower wages in the low-end service sector

This analysis paints a slightly complicated picture of which characteristics are associated with higher populations over time in small cities. Metro areas with diverse economies centered on services are larger than those with more homogeneous economies, but it is interesting to note the particulars of how the service sectors work. Having a high number of jobs and firms in the FIRE sector is associated with larger populations, as is having fewer high-end service jobs spread over a large number of firms. The low-end service sector plays a different role in contributing to higher populations: for that sector, it is important to have a high number of jobs in a relatively low number firms that pay higher wages. Places with many low-paying low-end services firms do not attract as many people.

This suggests that the larger cities among the eighty studied here (and those with growing populations) are more fully integrated into the contemporary services-oriented economy of the United States. Again, this fits with the assertion that the places where population is increasing are the glocal cities, the metro areas that have economies that are more similar to those of larger cities. As the figures in the previous section indicate, on average the metro areas are fairly similar to the national economy in terms of employment levels and number of firms by sector among the service sectors. But while on average smaller metro areas are seeing decreasing levels of employment and firms in the FIRE sector compared to the national norm, the larger (and growing) small cities are finding that growth in these areas helps population growth. When we examine percent change in population levels over time, no economic characteristics are statistically relevant.

Median Household Income Levels

As mentioned in chapter 2, for people living in smaller metro areas, absolute levels of median household income and the rate of income growth are both important. Table 2.3 showed that places with slower population growth tended to have higher levels of income over time. But many other factors influence both the level of income and how much it changes.

One way to consider income change is to group the eighty metro areas into quartiles based on change in income (in constant 2000 dollars) from 1970 to 2000, similar to how they were examined in chapter 2 in terms of population. As Table 4.1 shows, over the thirty years of this study, cities experienced growth in income at different rates. Population size does not dictate whether or not a city will have strong growth in income over time, although the slowest-growing places tended to be slightly larger in 1970 than the other groups. Geography appeared to be a more influential factor; a slightly disproportionate number of cities that experienced slow income growth were located in the Midwest and a slightly larger percentage of southern cities experienced explosive growth.

The smaller metro areas in this study differed in income levels in 1970 and 1980, but by 1990 and 2000 there were no statistical differences between the groups (Table 4.2).[2] It makes sense that the group of cities that experienced the greatest growth in median household income is the group that started out with the lowest level of income. All of these eighty places changed with the currents of the national economy, and it is not surprising that all eighty cities would have fairly similar income levels by 2000; the U.S. economy became more homogenous across regions over this period.

TABLE 4.1
Increase in Median Household Income by Quartile, Eighty Small MSAs, 1970–2000

Low Income Growth[a]	Moderate Income Growth[b]	Strong Income Growth[c]	Explosive Income Growth[d]
Amarillo, TX	Baton Rouge, LA	Abilene, TX	Ann Arbor, MI
Bakersfield, CA	Cedar Rapids, IA	Boise City, ID	Colorado Springs, CO
Beaumont, TX	Chattanooga, TN	Des Moines, IA	Columbia, MO
Billings, MT	Evansville, IN	Fargo, ND	Columbia, SC
Decatur, IL	Fresno, CA	Fort Smith, AR	Columbus, GA
Duluth, MN	Grand Rapids, MI	Knoxville, TN	Fayetteville, NC
Erie, PA	Green Bay, WI	Lansing, MI	Gainesville, FL
Eugene, OR	Huntsville, AL	Little Rock, AR	Jackson, MS
Flint, MI	Lubbock, TX	Macon, GA	Lafayette, LA
Fort Wayne, IN	Mobile, AL	McAllen, TX	Laredo, TX
Kalamazoo, MI	Providence, RI	Modesto, CA	Lawton, OK
Las Vegas, NV	Reading, PA	Montgomery, AL	Lexington, KY
Peoria, IL	Reno, NV	Rochester, MN	Lincoln, NE
Pueblo, CO	Roanoke, VA	Salem, OR	Madison, WI
Rockford, IL	Sioux City, IA	Salt Lake City, UT	Orlando, FL
Shreveport, LA	Spokane, WA	San Angelo, TX	Richmond, VA
South Bend, IN	Springfield, MA	Sioux Falls, SD	Salinas, CA
Springfield, IL	Stockton, CA	Springfield, MO	Savannah, GA
Syracuse, NY	Topeka, KS	Waco, TX	Tallahassee, FL
Youngstown, OH	Tyler, TX	Wichita Falls, TX	Trenton, NJ

[a]Change in income from -12 percent to 13 percent.

[b]Change in income from 13 percent to 21 percent.

[c]Change in income from 21 percent to 33 percent.

[d]Change in income from 34 percent to 132 percent.

For example, as a region, the South has become economically more similar to the rest of the United States since the 1960s (Hout and Fischer 2006).

What factors influenced the different income levels cities experienced and the differing rates of change in income over time? In particular, which aspects of local economies affected income levels the most over time? Looking at what affected both the statistic of median household income

TABLE 4.2
Median Household Income Levels by Growth Quartile, Eighty Small Metro Areas, 1970–2000

	Low Income Growth	Moderate Income Growth	Strong Income Growth	Explosive Income Growth
1970	$37,000	$34,500	$29,200	$27,400
1980	$39,800	$37,000	$35,200	$34,700
1990	$38,100	$39,400	$35,700	$36,100
2000	$37,400	$40,100	$38,300	$39,500

Source: U.S. Census Bureau data from the 1970, 1980, 1990, and 2000 censuses.

for each decade and change in that statistic over time will help answer these questions, as will information about the number of jobs, number of firms, and wage levels in different sectors.

Small cities that experienced greater income growth tended to have the most growth in jobs in the high-end services sector. Overall, metro areas with higher levels of growth in income experienced growth in each of the five economic sectors this study examines (figure 4.7). However, the cities that experienced a large increase in median household income (the 50th to 75th income growth quartile) actually experienced slightly more growth in low-end services and FIRE employment than the cities that experienced the greatest change in median household income. The cities with a medium increase in median household income had slightly higher growth in new manufacturing jobs compared to the other metro areas, but interestingly, this group had nearly the same increase in FIRE employment as did the cities that experienced the greatest increase in median household income.

Figure 4.8 shows how wages were related to changing levels of income for cities. Those places that experienced the smallest change in income saw declines in real wage levels (wage levels adjusted for inflation across time) in three sectors: old manufacturing, new manufacturing, and low-end

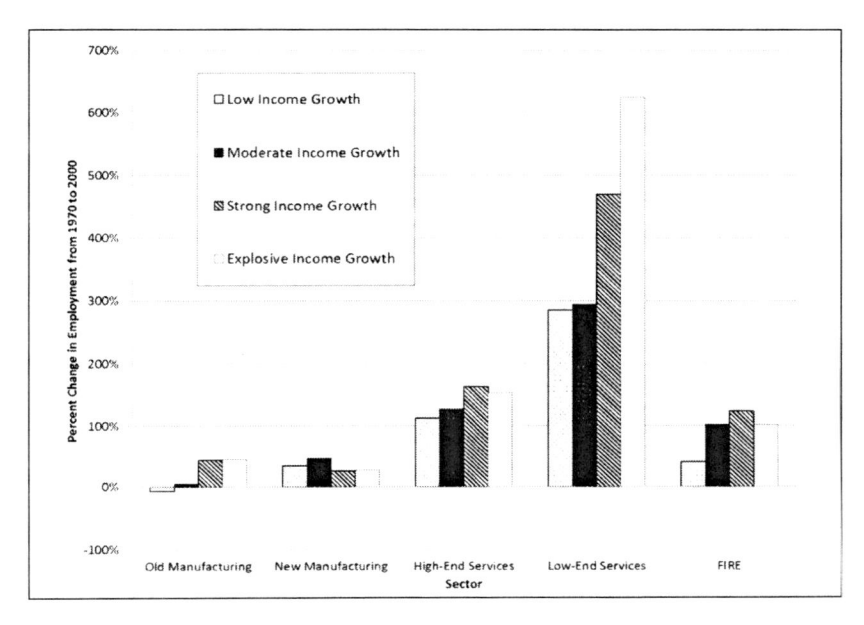

FIGURE 4.7. Percentage Change in Level of Employment by Sector by Level of Change in Median Household Income in Eighty Small Metro Areas, 1970–2000

Source: County Business Patterns data for 1974, 1979, 1989, 1996 (U.S. Census Bureau 1985, 1986, 1991, 1998).

services. Since all four groups experienced declines in wages for low-end services, this is not surprising. But what figure 4.8 really shows is that the twenty cities that experienced the greatest level of positive income change experienced significant increases in wages over the period of this study in the old manufacturing, new manufacturing, and FIRE sectors compared to the other sixty metro areas. Of course, these changes are relative to the group of places studied here; as the location quotient data for wages in figure 4.6 shows, wage levels in all sectors for the small cities in this study remained below national levels throughout the period 1970 to 2000. Each sector showed a location quotient for wages less than 1.0 in each decade.

When all factors that might affect levels of change in income are taken into account, however, the picture is a bit murkier than the data in the figures might imply. Because all cities experienced growth in all areas over time, it is important to try to dissect any differences that might be present beyond the general trends. For example, statistically speaking, old manufacturing employment and average wages in all industries are positively related

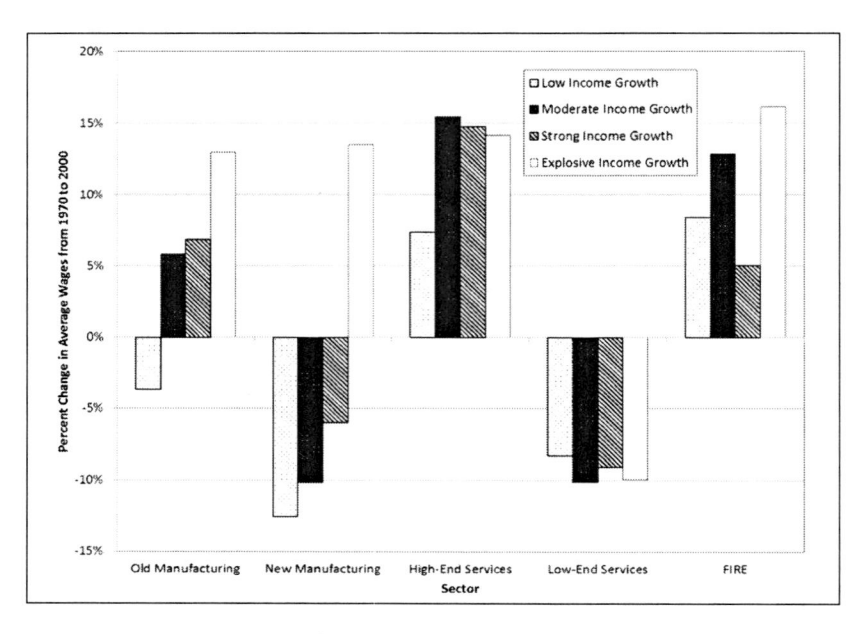

FIGURE 4.8. Average Wages by Sector by Level of Income Change in Eighty Small Metro Areas, 1970–2000

Source: County Business Patterns data for 1974, 1979, 1989, 1996 (U.S. Census Bureau 1985, 1986, 1991, 1998).

to higher absolute levels of income from 1970 to 2000. That is to say, as one might expect, strong economies as measured by rising median household income levels, predictably, are characterized by rising wages.

What is more surprising is the influence of employment in the old manufacturing sector. In the eighty cities in this study, having fewer firms in the old manufacturing sector is linked to greater increases in income levels. This implies that metro areas with more manufacturing jobs among fewer companies—probably places that have well-established and/or consolidated manufacturing sectors—did better over time in terms of income levels. Green Bay's experience of greater consolidation within the paper industry exemplifies this trend. Although there are fewer paper mills and somewhat fewer jobs in that sector today than in 1970, the median household income in Green Bay has remained high because of the strong wages in this industry.

The same trend of fewer firms but more jobs appears to affect income levels positively in the new manufacturing sector as well. In the cities in this study, increases in the number of new manufacturing jobs and decreases in the number of new manufacturing firms are statistically associated with positive income growth over time. Because these analyses are based on two different outcome measures—change in level of income across time versus absolute levels of income across time—this is not necessarily contradictory information. Instead, the analysis indicates that while absolute levels are tied to old manufacturing and wage levels, percent change in income is tied to new manufacturing. Growth in employment in new manufacturing—but among a smaller number of firms—is tied to a larger proportional change in income levels.

Economic Inequality Levels

Economic inequality, like income levels, increased over the thirty-year period of this study. But unlike income, this increase has not benefited people and in fact reflects the unequal distribution of the benefits of rising income levels in smaller places. The roots of economic inequality are difficult to pin down, but examining the distribution of employment and wages in local economies provides some information about how and why inequality levels have changed in smaller places. As mentioned previously, little is known about economic inequality in small places, and even Janice Madden's (2000) comprehensive examination of economic inequality does not use economic data at this level of detail.

As figure 4.9 shows, places with the largest increases in economic inequality had a different distribution of employment over time compared to those that had far smaller increases. (Note that the first bar in the economic inequality charts represents those places that experienced the lowest level of change in economic inequality, and thus can be thought of as doing better.) Places that had large increases in economic inequality tended to experience decreases in employment in the old manufacturing sector and stagnant levels of employment in new manufacturing. In addition, compared to the other cities in this study, they had smaller increases in the other sectors. Places with lower levels of change in economic inequality, on the other hand, saw tremendous increases in high-end services employment and proportionately greater increases (compared to the average for all eighty places) in low-end services and FIRE employment. The main lesson is that diverse metro area economies have lower levels of economic inequality. The more the structure of the economy of a metro

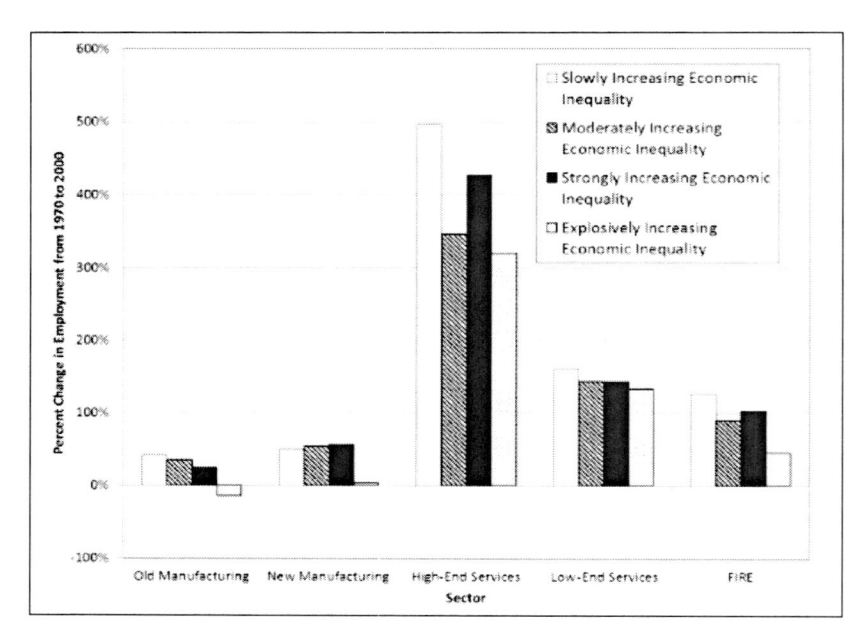

FIGURE 4.9. Changes in Employment by Sector by Change in Economic Inequality Levels in Eighty Small Metro Areas, 1970–2000

Source: County Business Patterns data for 1974, 1979, 1989, 1996 (U.S. Census Bureau 1985, 1986, 1991, 1998).

area looks like the structure of the economy of a large urban center—the more glocal it is—the better it appears able to maintain more moderate levels of economic inequality over time.

Wage levels in the high-end services sector increased more in cities with lower increases in economic inequality (figure 4.10). These slightly more equitable places also saw smaller decreases in wages in the new manufacturing and low-end services sectors compared to places that experienced the largest increases in economic inequality. The metro areas with the largest increases in economic inequality also experienced greater increases in old manufacturing wages, while at the same time they experienced the smallest increases in high-end services. Just as with the figures for increases or decreases in number of jobs in each sector, new-economy metro areas with higher-paying jobs in high-end services tended to have lower increases in economic inequality over time.

When other characteristics of places are taken into account, larger increases in employment in the high-end services sector, in the number of

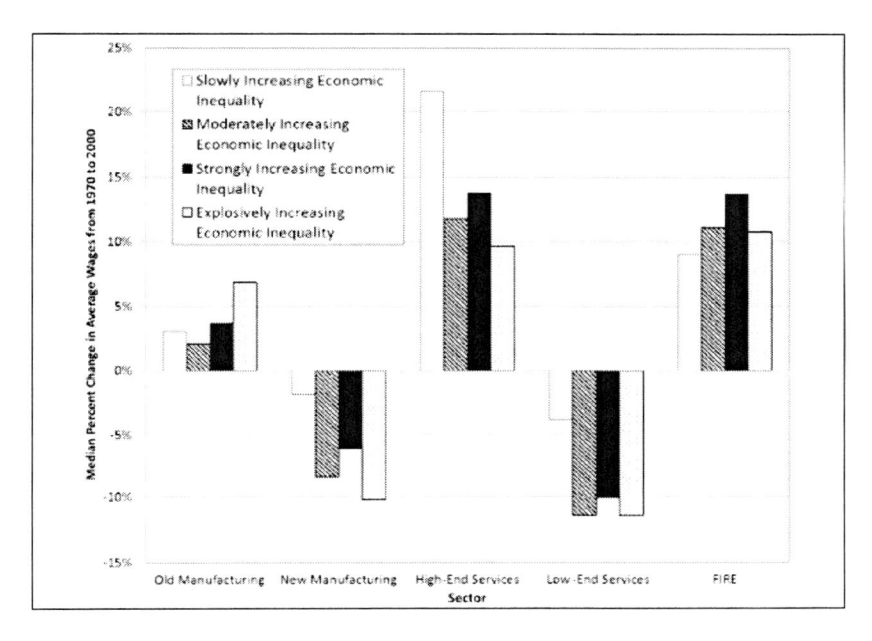

FIGURE 4.10. Median Percentage Change in Average Wages by Sector by Change in Economic Inequality Levels in Eighty Small Metro Areas, 1970–2000

Source: County Business Patterns data for 1974, 1979, 1989, 1996 (U.S. Census Bureau 1985, 1986, 1991, 1998).

firms in the low-end services sector, in wages in the low-end services sector, and in wages in the FIRE sector all were associated with lower levels of economic inequality over time. Conversely, larger numbers of firms in the old and new manufacturing sectors were associated with higher levels of economic inequality over the thirty years. Higher numbers of firms in the high-end services sector were also associated with high levels of inequality, which may mean that a high-end services sector in which firms have consolidated but continue to pay high wages is of greater benefit to a small city than a high-end services sector with a large number of firms that pay low wages. Competition among a large number of high-end services firms may be an indication of a robust sector, but such competition may not necessarily contribute to a metro area economy that benefits everyone. Consolidation within sectors may help reduce economic inequality; the trade-off appears to be that larger firms have the capacity to pay higher wages.

An increasing percentage of change in the number of FIRE-sector firms and in FIRE-sector wages was associated with lower increases in economic inequality. While the influence of high wages in the FIRE sector is heartening—higher salaries in this sector decrease rather than increase levels of economic inequality—the influence of the number of firms on economic inequality is more difficult to interpret.

What's Place Got to Do with It?

Non-economic factors may influence local economies, and scholars have thought about how some non-economic aspects of a city or region, such as climate, might affect that city's prospects. As noted in chapter 1, people have looked at different possible explanations for change in urban areas that are either unrelated to or only loosely related to employment or to the social characteristics of residents.

Scholars have posited a variety of potential influences. In the early 1980s, Glenn Carroll and John Meyer (1983) argued that cities that are state capitals may do better than cities that are not. However, for the eighty small cities in this study, being a state capital had no impact on any of the outcomes measured in this study—population change, change in wages, and economic inequality. Similarly, John Logan and Harvey Molotch (1987) argue that smaller places might do well to specialize in certain sectors such as government or education. But my analysis shows that having a larger number of universities or colleges has no impact on the three outcome measures.

Another possibility that might explain how well a city is doing economically is how close or far a small metro area is to its nearest large neighbor. Small metro areas that are farther away from big cities look a bit different than those that are closer to big metropolises. Places that are farther away from the nearest big city tend to have lower levels of employment in both old and new manufacturing and higher levels of employment in both low- and high-end services and in the FIRE sector. These patterns were stable over the three decades of this study. In particular, the FIRE sector appears to be more robust in cities farther away from nearest big cities; the small cities in this study that were the farthest away from large urban centers had higher location quotients for both employment and number of firms in that sector than did cities that were closer to large cities. Still, when examined in relation to the other characteristics of interest, the distance from a big city did not statistically affect the three outcome measures of population change, change in wages, and change in inequality. Being older and more established might also help places. The effect of having a central city that was populated early on was not statistically significant, nor was the effect of housing a Fortune 500 company headquarters at some point during the thirty-year period.

Some scholars have argued that region is very important for understanding how places in the United States have changed (Pack 2002; Glaeser and Shapiro 2003b). However, when all factors are taken into account, being in a warmer location had no affect on changes in levels of income or population. Being in the western part of the United States was associated with increasing population levels over time, but this included colder places such as Boise and Salt Lake City as well as warm places such as Las Vegas and Modesto, California. In fact, higher average low temperatures in January were significantly associated with an increase in economic inequality over the decades of the study.

Finally, Richard Florida, as mentioned before, argues that tolerance is a very good predictor of how well a city is doing at the end of the twentieth century. For him, tolerance is based on how accepting cities are of gays and lesbians, racial and ethnic minorities, artists, and people with other alternative lifestyles. Florida's tolerance index aggregates these various measures into a single indicator of tolerance for a metro area. For the small cities in this study, the tolerance index is a good predictor of population growth. Cities that are more tolerant tended to grow more. How tolerance affects changes in income levels is less clear; when examined in relation to changes in levels of employment, number of firms, and level of wages, tolerance was not significantly associated with growth in median household income.

Surprisingly, however, a high position on the tolerance index is negatively associated with changes in levels of economic inequality, meaning that places that are more tolerant have higher levels of economic inequality. In addition, places that are more tolerant tended to experience greater growth in economic inequality over time. This measure of tolerance is not (statistically) a strong driver of inequality, but at the same time, since so few characteristics of residents or the economy are statistically associated with levels of economic inequality, this association between high tolerance and increasing inequality is worth noting. While Richard Florida appears to be right about the relationship between tolerance and population growth, it is less clear how it affects income levels in small places.

Conclusion: A Tale of Two Economies, but No Guaranteed Outcomes

The paths that are associated with success in small metro areas—places that have gained population and income while keeping economic inequality in check—are complex. When we look at these three outcome measures independently, each outcome suggests different strategies for maximizing success. In the next chapter, all three of these measures are put together into an aggregate outcome measure to help determine which aspects of small metro areas affect the three measures simultaneously. But we can still learn much based on the evaluation of economic factors.

What it boils down to is that there are two different types of metro areas in this group of eighty smaller places. First, there are those that look more like the new economy, with greater than expected employment in the service sector. Laredo, Texas, is a prime example. In 2000, Laredo had much higher employment in high-end and low-end services and in FIRE-sector jobs. In fact, Laredo ranks among the top ten cities in this study when location quotients are examined; Laredo has the ninth-highest index for FIRE-sector employment (at 1.47) and the sixth-highest index for high-end services employment (at 1.29). Salinas, California, is somewhat similar, although it has disproportionately greater employment in low-end services. Salinas was third highest in this area, with a location quotient of 1.91.

These new economy cities also have disproportionately low levels of employment in the old and new manufacturing sectors. Salinas ranked near the bottom in old manufacturing (with a location quotient of 0.05). Laredo, likewise, ranked even lower at second, with a location quotient for that sector of 0.03. These trends are apparent when we look at cities that have the highest location quotients in FIRE, high-end services, and low-end services employment. Four of the small cities in the top ten for high-end services employment, for example, were in the bottom ten for old manufacturing.

The flip side of this, of course, is that there are still many old economy cities that are much stronger in manufacturing than in services employment. Green Bay, Wisconsin, exemplifies this pattern. Green Bay ranked second in old manufacturing (with a location quotient of 2.11) while ranking 71st (with a location quotient of 0.75) in low-end services and 74th (with a location quotient of 0.76) in high-end service employment. Three of the other nine top-ranked cities in old manufacturing were also highly ranked in the new manufacturing sector. At the same time, metro areas that ranked lowest in old manufacturing were also likely to rank lowest in new manufacturing (five of the bottom ten were ranked in the bottom ten for both manufacturing sectors).

The story of the division between the new and old economies is not new. However, what is more surprising is that the new economy cities are not necessarily better off in terms of population, income, or economic inequality levels than old economy cities. New economy cities such as Laredo are very good at attracting people. They tend to have had tremendous population growth between 1970 and 2000; the ten cities with the highest location quotients in the services sector, a key element of the new economy, grew on average by 111 percent compared to only 28 percent for the ten metro areas with the highest location quotients in old manufacturing employment. But at the same time, the ten cities with the highest levels of employment in old manufacturing had average incomes of $42,000 while the bottom ten had incomes averaging $39,500. Both groups had similar percentages of change in economic inequality over time, although the cities that had high levels of old manufacturing had lower levels on the 90:10 index in 2010.

These patterns hold true when we examine the top and bottom ten places related to employment in the FIRE sector. The places with much higher employment in this sector tended to gain more population, but not income. The average income levels for each group—the bottom and the top—were nearly identical at about $42,000. Economic inequality increased slightly less for cities with the lowest levels of employment in the FIRE sector. Low-end services employment rankings mirror this situation. Cities with the highest levels of low-end services employment gained more people but had lower income levels and larger increases in economic inequality over time compared to metro areas with the lowest levels of employment in low-end services.

5

Balancing It All

Paths of Success or Failure for Small Metro Areas

"As I walked out in the streets of Laredo, as I walked out in Laredo one day, I spied a young cowboy, all wrapped in white linen, wrapped up in white linen and cold as the clay." So goes the "Streets of Laredo" (otherwise called "The Cowboy's Lament"), the song about the small Texas city. Laredo is no longer a cowboy town; today it is a bustling, internationally oriented small city. The port of Laredo is ranked as the fourth busiest in the nation; an estimated $94 billion of trade passes through it each year (López and Phillips 2006). In addition to goods, thousands of people travel back and forth between Laredo and Nuevo Laredo in Mexico every day. Estimates indicate that nearly a quarter of a million people walk back and forth between the two countries every three months (Lopez and Phillips 2006).

Laredo is an interesting hybrid of Anglo and Latino culture, which is not surprising given its location on the border. While the city hosts a jalapeño festival and the local state university has a Ballet Folklorico, it also hosts celebrations that are likely to be found in any part of the nation, such as the month-long celebration of George Washington's birthday with dinners, balls, and fund-raising events. This amalgamation of cultures is particularly strong in Laredo and is likely a precursor of the increasing influence of the growing Latino population throughout the United States.

As one walks through downtown Laredo, its small-town roots are still apparent. But it is no longer small. Laredo has grown in population tremendously since 1970. Most of the growth has happened within the city limits rather than in nearby or outlying areas. Laredo has also experienced a tremendous increase, percentage wise, in its median household income level. In 1970, median household income was about $23,400; this figure had increased to about $33,000 by 2006 (in constant 2006 dollars). At the same time, economic inequality grew considerably during the study decades, increasing by 145 percent (putting in the 75th percentile for all eighty places). And although the official percentage of the metro area population living in poverty declined from 44 percent in 1969 to 30 percent in 2006, it still remains quite high.

Laredo thus presents the mix of positive and negative outcomes that makes it difficult to assess how places have changed and even more difficult to pin down why. If we examined population growth only, we might conclude that Laredo has done well; its population has increased by 165 percent since 1970. And if we were to focus solely on change in income over time, it would also look successful. But once we consider absolute income levels as opposed to percent change in income (in 2000, Laredo was second to last; only McAllen, Texas, had lower household income among the cities in this study) and levels of economic inequality, the picture becomes murkier. Laredo's story, and stories of other cities like it, points to the central question of this book: How should we assess success or failure among cities, particularly the small cities examined here? In this chapter, I combine the three outcome measures of population, income, and inequality into a single index as one way to capture multiple dimensions of change that affect people's everyday lives in small cities across the United States.

Introduction

Smaller metro areas in the United States have, as shown in previous chapters, taken a variety of trajectories between 1970 and 2000. In this chapter, I analyze the three important measures (population, income and economic inequality levels) combined into a single outcome to show what actually matters for a city and its suburbs in order to assess success in a holistic way. This examination builds upon those completed in chapters three and four, which looked at the three components of the outcome separately.

A wide array of scholars, researchers, pundits, and advocates have generated visions of a successful city, but quantifying success or failure is still a challenge. One of the most common ways to quantify success is to measure population growth. As noted previously, population growth is an exceedingly important criterion for success for government officials and business leaders. Scholars also continue to use population growth to determine if a place is doing well or poorly (Glaeser et al. 1992; Pack 2002).

Yet this emphasis on population growth does not present a very nuanced vision of success, and current thinking among city planners, community activists, and scholars questions whether rapid population growth is a net positive for a community. Critics such as the New Urbanists, a group of city planners and scholars who argue for recreating small towns (Duany, Plater-Zybeck, and Speck 2000; Kelbaugh 2002), and James Howard Kunstler (1993, 1996) offer an alternative vision of urban development and change that emphasizes livability by keeping municipalities small and more townlike. And while moderate population growth is not trendy in contemporary urban scholarship, scholars in the 1970s found that it can be better for an urban area than unbridled population growth (Haworth, Long, and Rasmussen 1978; Getz 1979). While I do not focus on "livability" as a concept in this book, I take note of the importance of moderate population growth.

I present an alternative way of measuring success or stagnation in metro areas. My analysis combines population change with change in income, the absolute level of income (as opposed to percent change in income levels), and the level of economic inequality for each metro area. Combining these indicators presents a more nuanced and sensitive outcome measure for assessing how well a place is doing. Social science is full of aggregated measures of this type, but few scholars use such an indexical measure. Although other people might decide to construct this measure differently or include other indicators as part of a predictive outcome, the measure I use here presents a solid first step toward using a multifaceted indicator to understand urban change.[1] My hope is that it will spark farther debate among scholars, policy makers, community leaders, and citizens about what matters most for understanding success or failure in metro areas.

The Success Index

Throughout this book I have argued that we need to take into account multiple factors in assessing the success or failure of a metro area. Previous scholarship has examined population (Henderson 1997; Pack 2002;

Vey and Forman 2002; Glaeser and Shapiro 2003) or income (Glaeser et al. 1992; Savitch et al. 1993; Crihfield and Panggabean 1995) separately as ways of determining growth or success. Yet examining changes in one or the other of these two variables in isolation misses the interrelatedness of income and population change and overlooks the fact that both affect how well a city is doing.[2] We need to think about both the consequences of population growth and who the economy helps.

People do not want to move to places with low income levels and poorly performing economies. But it is very difficult to pin down whether population growth precedes or follows economic growth in urban areas. Cities are successful when their populations grow at a reasonable pace and when they have high levels of income that are increasing over time. Rapid population growth may lead to negative externalities and may or may not be tied to economic growth, as the analysis below indicates. In addition, growth that leads to greater economic inequality benefits only the financially well off in a community. The presence of a sizable middle class generally is associated with a diverse economy, which Vernon Henderson (1997), a scholar who has focused on urban change, argues is essential for growth in medium-sized cities.

I therefore propose an outcome indicator composed of all three measures I have focused on in this book—population change, change in median household income, and change in the economic inequality index. I call this composite measure the success index. The first measure, population change, is key because it is a proxy for how desirable a place is for outsiders to move to and for residents to stay in. Yet very rapid population growth may not be best for a metro area. Therefore, I stipulate that a growth rate that is near the mean of population growth for the nation is most favorable. Places that grow very little or places that grow too much are not as successful as places that have moderate growth because of the externalities associated with shrinkage or exceptional growth in a short period of time. Cities that barely grow or shrink clearly are not attractive to either residents or outsiders, and places that grow uncontrollably face problems such as high levels of unemployment, traffic congestion, or overwhelmed school systems. A moderate level of population growth may be a strong indicator that a place is desirable to outsiders but has escaped some of the difficulties associated with rapid growth or population loss.

Median household income levels are an important indicator of both the economy (i.e., employment opportunities, spending power, etc.) and quality of life of a city (Diener and Biswas-Diener 2002). While money may not necessarily buy happiness, people living in lower-income areas face many problems that others in more well-off areas do not: poor physical and mental health, poor-quality housing, and poor schools, to name a few (Danzinger and Gottschalk 1995). Higher levels of median household income indicate a higher overall standard of living. But change in income levels is also important as an indicator of a growing and prosperous economy.[3] Change in income alone is an insufficient measure; the places with the lowest levels of median household income generally experienced the greatest percentage change (see chapter 4). Yet having higher levels of income over the thirty-year period does not indicate success either; a city can have higher levels of median household income compared to other cities but little or no income growth—in other words, a stagnating economy. In particular, stagnant levels of income change but higher absolute levels of income may be an indication of growing economic inequality as a metro area loses economic diversity and vitality, both of which are important for success.

I argue that economic inequality is also important in determining the success or failure of a metro area. Comparing levels of economic inequality across cities or metropolitan areas has not been central to the study of cities and metro areas, even though the effects of economic inequality have been shown to be highly detrimental to people's quality of life (Wilson 1996; Levy 1998). Economic inequality has long been the subject of sociological inquiry, and it has been escalating in the United States over the latter part of the twentieth century (Boushey and Weller 2005; Hout and Fischer 2006). By combining a measure of economic inequality with the two other outcome measures of population growth and income levels, I have calculated a success rating for each city for the end of each ten-year period in my study.

Not all of these factors are of equal weight in determining the success index of a metro area. I weight the three attributes differently, using a straightforward formula to construct the success index. Because tremendous population growth may be just as detrimental to a metro area as population loss, I do not use the statistic of raw change in population per decade. Instead, I use a measure of the difference between a particular metro area's ten-year growth rate and the mean growth rate of all of the metro areas. I then add this measure to the percentage change in income weighted by the absolute median household income level at the end of the ten-year period. Finally, I add the change in economic inequality to the measure, but only at 50 percent of its original value. I modify the value of economic inequality because it seems likely that population change and income change are more strongly related to the well-being of a metro area than economic inequality. In large part this assumption stems from the analysis in previous chapters that shows that it is difficult to determine what factors influence economic inequality over time and place.

The exact formula for this success index, as calculated per decade, is as follows:

$$\text{Success Index} = [(\text{IncChange} * \text{IncAbs}) + \text{PopChange}) + (\text{IneqChange} * 0.50)]$$

where

IncChange = Rank of the percentage change in median household income over the decade

IncAbs = Rank of the (mathematical) absolute value of median household income at the end of the decade

PopChange = Mathematical absolute value of the difference between the calculated percent change in population over the decade from the national mean population change of the decade

IneqChange = Rank of percentage change in the 90:10 measure of economic inequality for the decade

Success Index = Rank of result of formula, in which higher scores indicate greater success

This formula creates a success index rank for each metro area for the 1980, 1990, and 2000 census decades (1970 is not included because the rank is based on ten-year change).[4]

How the Success Index Rankings of Metro Areas Change

How can the distribution of how metro areas have changed based on their success index rankings be examined over time? First, I look at the distribution of metro areas in 2000 to see where places stood at the close of the twentieth century. Table 5.1 shows the rankings for 2000, where 1 is lowest on the success index (worse) and 80 is highest (better). Second, I look at the cities that have changed the most over the thirty-year period. These places give some insight into the processes that affect success or failure most significantly over time. Third, I look more closely at the four case-study metro areas—Green Bay, Wisconsin; Laredo, Texas; Providence, Rhode Island; and Salinas, California—to provide a more in-depth examination of how the experiences of particular metro areas have shaped and been shaped by their success or stagnation over the three decades of this study.

The results of an examination of social, demographic, and economic characteristics in combination are somewhat similar to the analysis found

TABLE 5.1
Success Index Rank of the Eighty Small Metro Areas in 2000

Stagnating	Mixed Outcomes	Doing Well	Successful
1 McAllen, TX	21 Springfield, MO	41 Knoxville, TN	61 Springfield, IL
2 Bakersfield, CA	22 Stockton, CA	42 Orlando, FL	62 Lexington, KY
3 Laredo, TX	23 Columbus, GA	43 Fayetteville, NC	63 Savannah, GA
4 Lubbock, TX	24 Amarillo, TX	44 Tyler, TX	64 Rockford, IL
5 Fresno, CA	25 Roanoke, VA	45 Sioux City, IA	65 Lincoln, NE
6 Gainesville, FL	26 Beaumont, TX	46 Spokane, WA	66 Peoria, IL
7 Springfield, MA	27 Erie, PA	47 Trenton, NJ	67 Salem, OR
8 San Angelo, TX	28 Mobile, AL	48 Chattanooga, TN	68 Reno, NV
9 Syracuse, NY	29 Flint, MI		69 Boise City, ID
10 Lafayette, LA	30 Huntsville, AL	49 Columbia, MO	70 Rochester, MN
11 Pueblo, CO	31 Tallahassee, FL	50 Kalamazoo, MI	71 Cedar Rapids, IA
12 Fort Smith, AR	32 Columbia, SC	51 Fargo, ND	72 Sioux Falls, SD
13 Providence, RI	33 Duluth, MN	52 Baton Rouge, LA	73 Salinas, CA
14 Shreveport, LA	34 Youngstown, OH	53 Lansing, MI	74 Grand Rapids, MI
15 Abilene, TX		54 Las Vegas, NV	
16 Decatur, IL	35 Topeka, KS	55 South Bend, IN	75 Colorado Springs, CO
17 Wichita Falls, TX	36 Macon, GA	56 Reading, PA	
18 Modesto, CA	37 Billings, MT	57 Jackson, MS	76 Green Bay, WI
19 Lawton, OK	38 Fort Wayne, IN	58 Richmond, VA	77 Des Moines, IA
20 Waco, TX	39 Montgomery, AL	59 Evansville, IN	78 Salt Lake City, UT
	40 Eugene, OR	60 Little Rock, AR	79 Ann Arbor, MI
			80 Madison, WI

in chapters 3 and 4. When the attributes of urban areas are assessed in relation to the success index over time, the percentage of the population that is white, the percentage of the population that is foreign born, and the percentage of the population with a college degree are all positively associated with change in the success index. Cities that have more people who identify as white, more immigrants, and more college-educated individuals experienced increased success. As chapter 3 indicated, who lives in a small metro area matters.

Table 5.1 shows the success index rank of each of the eighty cities in this study. In the top group—the metro areas that can be seen as success stories—an average of 27 percent of the population had college degrees or advanced degrees. This contrasts with the cities with the lowest rank on the success index—the stagnating metro areas—where an average of only 20 percent of the population had college degrees or advanced degrees. This is likely related to the fact that the metro areas in the top 50 percent on the success index in 2000 were home to more colleges and universities than those in the bottom 50 percent. But having a large educational sector was no guarantee of high ranking on the index; both Springfield, Massachusetts, with eleven institutions of higher education, and Providence, Rhode Island, with seven, were in the stagnant group in 2000. Three of the cities in the bottom twenty rankings do not have any four-year colleges or universities in their metro areas, while ten only have one. In contrast, among the cities who ranked high on the success index, sixteen have two or more colleges or universities. The stories for immigration and race are similar, although the stagnant group had higher levels of foreign-born residents on average, mostly because many of the places were located in Texas.

The economic factors that influence rank on the success index are far fewer in this type of analysis. Employment levels are not statistically associated with success index rank, and measures of the number of firms by sector or wages by sector are not significant either. The only economic indicators that proved to be statistically significant were the number of FIRE-sector establishments and wage levels in the FIRE sector. The analysis indicates that although the number of FIRE-sector establishments is negatively related to status rank, meaning that a more concentrated FIRE sector is associated with greater success, the actual statistical relationship is small. Conversely, wages in the FIRE sector are more strongly related to success rank, and an increase of one dollar in the average wage would lead over time to a metro area's moving up three places in the rankings.

The twenty successful metro areas in 2000 were more likely to have been urbanized earlier than the other sixty cities, to be a state capital, and to be home to a Fortune 500 company headquarters. The relationship between number of firms and wage levels in the FIRE sector is curious. Changes in the number of firms in that sector did not match changes in wage levels. In fact, the top twenty metro areas in 2000 had a smaller rate of growth in the number of firms in the FIRE sector and a higher rate of change in wages in that sector. Cities such as Laredo, conversely, which saw a tremendous increase (200 percent) in the number of FIRE firms since 1970 experienced only a 20 percent increase in average wages in all sectors over the same time period. The twenty top-ranking places on the success index experienced much lower levels of growth in FIRE-sector firms than Laredo did, but each of these cities saw increases of at least 40 percent in wages across all sectors.

While many places in the South and West experienced population booms from 1970 to 2000, these growth spurts did not necessarily translate into a high ranking on the success index. Twelve of the twenty bottom-ranked metro areas are in the South and only two southern cities are in the top twenty. In contrast, thirteen of the top twenty metro areas are in the Midwest. Even though region is a strong predictor of population change nationally, it is not destiny for small cities when a multifaceted outcome is considered.

Table 5.2 shows the metro areas that experienced the greatest change on the success index from 1980 to 2000.[5] While eight of the ten downwardly mobile metro areas started out in the top half of the status rankings in 1980, by the end of the century, nine out of ten were in the bottom half. All but one (Green Bay) of the upwardly mobile cities were in the bottom third in 1980, but by 2000 all had breached the halfway mark and seven were in the top third of the distribution. Las Vegas's large gain in the rankings is due to its tremendous population growth, which hurtled it from the very bottom to the middle. But while looking at population alone would have made Las Vegas seem amazingly successful, taking into account income and economic inequality levels puts Las Vegas in the middle, as moderately successful.

More downwardly mobile metro areas are located in the South, while more upwardly mobile metro areas are located in the Midwest, further indicating that region is not destiny for smaller cities. Metro areas whose

TABLE 5.2
Small Metro Areas That Experienced the Biggest Change in Success Index Rank, 1980–2000

Downwardly Mobile Metro Areas			Upwardly Mobile Metro Areas		
Metro Area	1980 Rank	2000 Rank	Metro Area	1980 Rank	2000 Rank
Bakersfield, CA	37	2	Youngstown, OH	5	34
Lubbock, TX	34	4	Fayetteville, NC	9	43
Fresno, CA	56	5	Columbia, MO	2	49
Shreveport, LA	48	14	Las Vegas, NV	1	54
Amarillo, TX	62	24	South Bend, IN	24	55
Beaumont, TX	76	26	Reading, PA	19	56
Duluth, MN	67	33	Savannah, GA	22	63
Topeka, KS	66	35	Rockford, IL	23	64
Billings, MT	72	37	Grand Rapids, MI	13	74
Lansing, MI	79	53	Green Bay, WI	32	76

ranking declined are not remarkable in population size or median household income levels, except that their average median income was lower in 2000 than it was in 1980. Cities that moved down in ranking on the success index, however, had decreasing income and increasing inequality over time compared to the sample as a whole. Beaumont, Lubbock, and Shreveport all had 90:10 income inequality indices in 2000 that were much higher than the average for all small cities. At the same time, metro areas whose ranking increased tended to grow considerably larger than average among eighty cities and experienced greater-than-average increases in median household income. They also had greater-than-average increases in median household income and lower-than-average increases in economic inequality.

Some differences are readily apparent among the cities whose success index ranking increased the most and those whose ranking decreased the most. Demographically, the two groups did not differ much; they were very similar in terms of racial composition, levels of immigration, and educational attainment. The top ten had much higher location quotients in the old and new manufacturing sectors, while the bottom ten beat the top ten in all three service-sector categories: low-end services, high-end services, and FIRE services. This result echoes the findings in chapter 4. Six of the cities that advanced the most in ranking on the success index were home to Fortune 500 company headquarters, compared to only three of the cities ranked in the bottom ten. Finally, the ten cities whose ranking increased the most had higher wages across all sectors; median wages in those cities approached the national average in manufacturing and were higher than the average for the eighty cities in the service sectors.

While these twenty small metro areas cannot offer exact recipes for positive transformation or ways of avoiding negative changes, they offer further evidence that betting on the new economy may not be the only or the best way for small metro areas to succeed. Small cities that have diverse economies, particularly those with manufacturing sectors, do better over time using the success index as a metric of change. The case-study metro areas provide more details about this finding, and they are examined in greater detail in the next section.

Case Studies

While the metro areas that have changed the most over the period provide general knowledge of how and why metro areas have succeeded or stagnated, I examine the case studies here to provide greater detail and insight into how success or stagnation has played out at the local level. The four cases—Green Bay, Wisconsin; Laredo, Texas; Providence, Rhode Island; and Salinas, California—have been discussed throughout the previous chapters. Here I examine their different paths of success or stagnation, focusing on how local conditions served to enable or constrain their growth from 1970 to 2000.

As table 5.3 shows, the four case-study cities have had disparate fates. While Green Bay has experienced steadily increasing success, Providence has had considerable volatility. Laredo has seen positive gains yet remains at the bottom of the distribution on the success index even though it has seen tremendous growth in population and income over the period. Finally, Salinas, which started with a lower success index ranking in 1980,

TABLE 5.3
Success Index Rankings of Case Study Metro Areas, 1980–2000

MSA	1980 Rank	1990 Rank	2000 Rank
Green Bay, WI	32	68	76
Laredo, TX	4	1	3
Providence, RI	6	66	13
Salinas, CA	59	76	73

advanced quite high on the success index ranking in the latter part of the period examined.

What the case studies demonstrate most clearly is that while there are tendencies or trajectories among metro areas, multiple recipes for success (or failure) exist. The range of economic opportunities in these four places indicates how different combinations of employment sectors can work for or against success. Although high levels of old manufacturing employment and larger numbers of firms in that sector had negative consequences for the downwardly mobile cities in table 5.2, Green Bay consistently had higher-than-average levels of employment in old manufacturing, although consolidation within the paper industry led to a decrease in the number of firms. Even though employment in old manufacturing declined in Green Bay during the decades of this study, it remained high in comparison to other cities. At the same time, employment in the high-end services and FIRE sectors increased significantly, mostly from growing firms such as AMS (an insurance firm) and Humana (a managed health care company).

Providence's employment profile looked quite similar to that of Green Bay at the beginning of the period, but the outcome for Providence has not been as consistently favorable. Like Green Bay, Providence had a high percentage of workers in old manufacturing industries in 1970—primarily in the remaining jewelry and light metal-working factories in the area— and actually increased employment in this area over the study decades by adding jobs at firms such as Hasbro (a toy manufacturer) and Textron (a defense contractor and supplier). In Providence, the number of jobs in the high-end service and FIRE sectors decreased, in large part due to consolidation of banks such as Hospital Trust (which was absorbed into ever-larger banks and is currently part of Bank of America). Because of this pattern of consolidation, some corporate headquarters disappeared from the metro area when their companies were absorbed into larger corporations. Providence has also seen a steady increase in immigration over the thirty-year period—by 2000 over 11 percent of the population was foreign born—and a 17 percent increase in the official poverty rate to 11 percent of the population. In comparison, both Laredo and Green Bay experienced decreasing poverty over the same time period. Providence has had dramatically rising economic inequality; its 90:10 income inequality measure nearly doubled between 1970 and 2000. Green Bay's and Salinas's levels stayed nearly flat and Laredo's rose slightly.

Salinas has fared well for slightly different reasons than Green Bay. The city does not have a manufacturing base, but it does have a strong agricultural base that includes Dole Fresh Fruit. Salinas has also maintained a strong base of low-end service-sector jobs. The central city of Salinas was not the principal reason for its relatively high ranking; instead, the metro area, which includes Carmel Valley, Carmel-by-the-Sea, and Monterrey, has seen a dramatic increase in wealthy residents since 1970. These three communities have experienced exceptional growth in the real estate market. Housing prices have skyrocketed as well-off people either moved to the area or purchased second homes in these towns. In Carmel-by-the-Sea, for example, median home prices (in constant dollars) increased from $178,000 in 1970 to $877,000 in 2010, compared with Salinas, which had a median home price of $115,615 in 1970 and $227,000 in 2010. Although the proportion of households with high incomes increased over the decades of the study, Salinas (the metro area) has managed to maintain lower levels of economic inequality throughout the time period. It experienced only a 24 percent increase in the 90:10 income inequality measure (the sample average from the same time period was 28 percent) and maintained a comparatively low absolute value.

Laredo, the final case-study metro area, has had the least successful experience during the thirty-year period. Laredo saw tremendous growth in terms of population and median household income. Between 1970 and 2000, the population increased by 165 percent and income increased by 45 percent. Both of these statistics were greater than the sample averages of 55 percent for population change and 26 percent for increase in median household income. In addition, inequality increased more quickly in Laredo than in the sample cities as a whole; Laredo's 90:10 income inequality index increased 20 percent more than the average of the entire group of metro areas. But the main reason for Laredo's low rank on the success index is its median household income; in 1970, the median household income was $19,100 and in 2000 it was $28,100. These levels were considerably lower than the sample averages of $34,500 and $39,600 (in constant 2000 dollars) in 1970 and 2000, respectively. It is therefore no surprise that 44 percent of the population in Laredo was living below the poverty line in 1970 and 31 percent in 2000.

Why did people continue to move to Laredo if the economic situation of the metro area was not nearly as positive as in other cities? One of the main reasons for Laredo's continued population growth is its proximity to the Mexican border; Laredo is the largest import-export center along the border between the United States and Mexico (City of Laredo 2006). And while this influx of trade brings jobs (the location quotient for employment in the low-end services sector in 2000 was 1.68), it does not bring many high-paying ones. In 2000, the location quotient for wages in employment in the low-end services sector was 0.72, indicating that wages in Laredo are well below the national average in this sector. So while Laredo has capitalized on its status as an import-export trade center, this has not translated into a high standard of living for most residents.

The four case-study metro areas present differing paths that have led to varying degrees of success as measured by the success index. The influx of immigrants to Laredo did not translate into success for the city. There were few economic opportunities for new residents that offered good wages. For Providence, a relatively high income level was not enough to mask increasing inequality and the loss of jobs in the high-end services and FIRE sectors over the thirty-year period. Salinas grew for very different reasons over the time period; the combination of an increase in the number of wealthy residents in the metro area and a diverse employment base translated into a fairly high score for Salinas on the success index. Finally, Green Bay maintained manufacturing jobs and added jobs in the high-end service sector at the same time that it maintained high income levels and low levels of inequality. This combination led to steady and impressive improvements in its success ranking over time.

Conclusion: Success Index and the Glocal City

Trying to measure success when it comes to cities and their surrounding regions is difficult. In this chapter, I have suggested a way of thinking about success that is multifaceted, nuanced, and takes into account not only population growth but also income growth, income levels, and levels of economic inequality. This success index captures a cluster of attributes of a metro area in an attempt to set multidimensional criteria for judging success or failure. Of course, this is not the only way to measure success, but my hope is that by offering this composite outcome we can move beyond unidimensional assessments of success and failure among metro areas both large and small.

The answer to what helps a metro area achieve success remains complex, but the analysis in this chapter points to some of the important trends in small cities that have led to success or stagnation during the latter third of the twentieth century. The statistical analysis shows that characteristics of the local economy and population affect the success of a city and its surroundings. More successful places tend to differ from less successful ones in terms of other factors as well. More of cities that ranked higher on the success index house colleges and universities and are home to large corporate headquarters, for example. Yet these characteristics are mediated by local circumstances. The four case studies show that national and international trends in the economy—such as consolidation within industries—affect local economies differently and that there are multiple ways of achieving success.

The main factors in predicting success over time are related to who lives in a metro area. The statistical analysis that showed that metro areas with higher numbers of people identified as white (non-Hispanic) actually translates roughly to increased racial diversity. The idea is not that stagnating metro areas need to "import" white people, which is a ludicrous proposition. Rather, this suggests cultivating a diverse community, one that maintains more of a racial and ethnic balance in its population. The positive association of higher numbers of foreign-born individuals and a high ranking on the success index also points to the importance of racial diversity. Given that the majority of immigrants who came to smaller cities were from Central or South America, places need to be open to a diverse group of newcomers.

Cities that have more people with college degrees also were more successful over time. This finding seems to support Richard Florida's assertion that the creative class boosts growth in a metro area. However, Florida's tolerance index is not statistically related to more success over time and was negatively related to success in 2000 (the only year for which we have data for tolerance). The other issue with Florida's creative class hypothesis is that while the FIRE sector is somewhat influential in relation to success rank, the other economic sector that should be positively associated with a high rank on the success index, according to Florida—high-end services—is not. So it may be that human capital, as discussed in chapter 2, rather than tolerance, as Florida asserts, matters more for small cities. This finding echoes other research done by Stephen Rausch and Cynthia Negrey (2006), who also question the creative class theory of urban success.

Additionally, the twenty metro areas with the highest scores on the success index are farther away from the nearest big metro area (the median distance was about 177 miles) compared to the twenty cities with the lowest scores, which were located a median distance of about 136 miles from the nearest large city. This suggests that successful glocal small cities may be the biggest game around, so to speak, and may draw people to them who might have moved to a larger metropolis instead if they lived closer to it. Data on which people move from city to city are very difficult to come by, so I do not want to overstate this finding. But the finding points to the possibility that glocal cities are the centers of the hinterland that surrounds them, much as Christaller (1933/1966) argued long ago, although for different reasons and using different data.

Part of being a glocal metro area is having an economy that mirrors the larger metro areas of the nation on a smaller scale. Over 50 percent of the twenty cities with the highest scores on the success index in 2000 were home to a Fortune 500 company headquarters, while only 25 percent of the twenty cities with the lowest scores had such companies. Perhaps part of being farther from a large metro area helped the smaller glocal cities that were home to a larger number of Fortune 500 company headquarters over time. The evidence from glocal small cities, which were poised for greater success at the end of the twentieth century, points to some new ways of considering how small cities are doing. The next chapter considers how we should examine metro-area change over time.

6

Small Cities Matter!

How have small cities changed and why? This has been the central question of my analysis. Small cities have been on divergent paths of success and failure since 1970. In the preceding chapters, I examined which factors contribute to stagnation and which ones appear to help small places grow and prosper. Just as important, however, I also put forth an argument about how we should assess urban change, particularly how we can think about success or failure among places large and small. In this chapter, I summarize the main findings from my analysis and offer some ideas about how we might move forward in terms of both policy and scholarship. But first I turn to the central concept of the glocal city.

Glocal Cities

Throughout the book I have argued that successful small metro areas can be thought of as glocal places, or small cities and surrounding environs that look somewhat like the major cities of the world but are not very large in terms of population. Glocal metro areas are characterized by diverse economies but not ones focused solely on the service sector especially high-end services. These places instead have maintained manufacturing jobs that provide decent wages for individuals with lower levels of education, particularly immigrants. At the same time, they also provide jobs in the low-end service sector for workers without a college degree. The population in successful places is a mix of people who have little education and people who have a college education or more, but the college-educated population is not necessarily the creative class that Richard Florida posits.

Glocal places attract college-educated individuals and have healthy FIRE and high-end services sectors. They also are relatively desirable destinations for immigrants. While glocal cities do not have the same absolute numbers of immigrants in their metro areas, they nonetheless have grown through considerable in-migration since 1970. And glocal places did not necessarily start out as destinations for immigrants, as most small places that were not successful actually had higher percentages of their population foreign born in 1970 than did the successful glocal places. In fact, in 1970, most small cities that later ranked low on the success index in 2000 had higher percentages of foreign-born population than the cities that ranked high on the index in 2000.

These successful small metro areas differ from the less successful cities in this study in several other ways. Geography plays a role, but not in the way that some scholars have posited. Glocal places are farther away from larger metro areas, and this may have helped them become the most important and desirable place in their local region. In addition, which national region a place is located in is not nearly as determinative as might be expected. The migration of people and jobs to the West and the South has not guaranteed success in small metro areas in those regions. In addition, many glocal cities are located in the Midwest.

Glocal places also tend to be centers in other ways as well. They have more colleges and universities in their metro areas than do cities that ranked low on the success index. They have also historically been home to a larger number of Fortune 500 company headquarters since 1970 than cities that ranked lower. Being glocal means being an important player within a smaller geographic region and reaping the results. Together, these characteristics generate a picture of cities that have remained vibrant over time because of a diverse population and a diverse economy. The key finding of this study is that small cities that do best are the ones that don't specialize economically and don't try to follow the latest economic trends. The most successful small cities in this study did not attempt to embrace the new economy, for example. Instead, successful glocal cities appear to balance the old and new economies while keeping up with general trends related to human capital. These ideas can be translated into some policy ideas and into ways of understanding how we should thank about urban change in the United States.

What Have We Learned?

The policy ideas I lay out here cover a broad range of topics and are very general Leaders and citizens alike will have to determine the specific needs of their localities in order to best determine the possible policy solutions available to them. As this book shows, cities and suburbs have a wide variety of experiences. Indeed, an advantage of this study is that it reveals a much wider diversity of trajectories than do studies that focus on a handful of places. In addition, people in metro areas will need to reconcile the competing needs of central cities versus suburbs and will have to determine the best balance between policies that benefit one over the other. Nonetheless, I offer these policy possibilities in the hope that smaller metro areas can work toward greater success in the future.

This section is divided into two parts. The first half examines the contributions this book makes to our empirical understandings of how small cities change. It also offers some ideas about the types of policies that leaders (public or private) in small cities might consider for making their small metro areas more successful. The second part discusses the new ideas this book offers about how we might study urban America. In this section, I reiterate how the approach of this book differs from other work in the field of urban studies. I also indicate how some of the ways places are studied here might be useful for studying urban places in general so that we can generate stronger understandings of how U.S. metro areas have changed over time.

Policy and Theoretical Contributions

In this book I have considered how urban areas have changed over time. In chapters 2 through 5, I examined how population, income, and economic inequality have changed and sought to determine the characteristics of metro areas that most strongly influence these changes. In this section, I bring together the findings from those chapters to offer some general observations about how small places have changed. I also focus on what sorts of policies might logically stem from these findings. However, because I am a sociologist and not a city planner, community leader, or government official in a particular small metro area, these policy ideas are merely meant to be seeds. I offer them in the hope that they will help leaders of all types think about ways they can nurture success in their own small cities.

Region Is Not Destiny

Popular and scholarly opinion holds that region is one of the strongest factors in determining where people lived and where jobs flourished in the latter part of the twentieth century. In *Growth and Convergence in Metropolitan America,* Janet Rothenberg Pack (2002) argues that region is the single strongest explanation for population growth in metro areas across the United States since 1960. Edward Glaeser and Jesse Shapiro (2003a), who examined trends in the 1990s, also argued that region dictates growth. Even historic population flows, such as the Great Migration of African Americans from the Deep South the Northeast and Midwest had reversed by the 1990s (Frey 2005). All of these scholars argue, based on data for all metro areas in the United States, that the West and the South have grown at the expense of the Northeast and the Midwest.

While region may tell us a great deal about population growth and economic change in a large metro area, it is not as useful for understanding the smaller cities of the nation. The analysis in chapter 4 showed that region was influential only in terms of population change: western metro areas were more likely to gain population compared to the rest of the nation. But region was not statistically related to median household income or economic inequality; small cities in other regions than the West did better on both of these measures. And the examination of the combination of the three outcomes of population, income, and economic inequality in chapter 5 showed that the role of region appeared to be the opposite of what previous research might have led us to expect.

In fact, cities in the Midwest tended to rank higher on the success index than cities from other regions of the nation. More midwestern small metro areas had higher success index rankings in 2000 than metro areas from the other regions. Proportionally, the Midwest and the West were overrepresented, while the Northeast and South were underrepresented.

Although in 2000, the northeastern small cities were not clustered at the bottom of the index, southern cities accounted for twelve of the twenty bottom-ranked cities.

This leads to two suggestions. First, the national dynamics of the movement of people and jobs from one region to another may not affect small cities to the same extent as they affect larger ones.[1] The statistics for employment and other economic measures in smaller metro areas included in this book are converging with national averages, but they remain slightly different. In particular, given the tendency of firms in small cities to offer lower wages in all sectors than the national average, small cities may not have the same allure as larger places in the South and the West. Also, smaller places grew because of immigration, but the immigrants were primarily those with lower levels of education who were in search of jobs in the manufacturing sector. Thus, the places that did well, using the success index, were those that drew people while maintaining decent wages, and that was often accomplished through jobs in the manufacturing and low-end services sectors.

Second, studying population change in isolation may overstate the role of region. While Pack (2002) shows that region is important, she also argues that population should not be the only outcome we assess. When the variables of median income and economic inequality levels are considered by themselves (that is, not in conjunction with other variables), region is less important for smaller cities. And when these two outcomes are considered in conjunction with population levels, the role of region may even be opposite of what would be expected.

The other question is why businesses have been drawn to the South (and to a lesser extent to the West). While climate is often cited, it is not a strong factor in terms of the outcomes measured in this book. Many companies move to take advantage of labor and environmental laws that are less stringent in the South than in the Midwest or Northeast. These laws were designed in large part to lure companies to the region. But if we consider the outcomes of population, income, and economic inequality, either separately or together, the payoff for low pay and environmental degradation apparently is not that great. Southern small cities tend not to be doing as well as cities in other regions of the nation. Thus, planners and policy makers in other regions may want to think twice before following in the footsteps of southern cities.

Small Cities Tend to Be Like Big Cities—and Are Becoming More So Over Time

Smaller metro areas are thought to be different from larger ones. Saskia Sassen (2001) and other scholars interested in global cities have postulated a hierarchy among urban places. Large global cities, such as New York and Tokyo, are at the top, home to the largest and most important economies. These global cities are centered on high-end services and dominate the economic landscape both nationally and internationally. In addition, they are often more connected to one another than to their hinterlands. Global cities are also characterized by disproportionately high levels of employment in the high-end services and FIRE sectors.

Below these global cities in the hierarchy are what might be thought of as the "almost-global cities," the somewhat smaller cities that still are large centers of population and employment, such as San Francisco, Vancouver, or Buenos Aires. These are important cities for their nations, but they lack the global reach of the truly global cities. Below these places in the world's urban hierarchy, the global cities perspective becomes a bit murky but suggests that the urban areas at lower levels are homes to tertiary services that support the global and almost-global cities. According to the global cities theory, smaller cities are not economic centers in their own right but rather exist for the benefit of the global cities.

The data presented in chapter 4 complicate this story of urban hierarchy. While small metro areas were home to a disproportionate number of jobs in the low-end services sector—because, it was presumed, they provided back-office and support services for the global cities—this proportion has been decreasing over time. Smaller metro areas also housed more than the national average of jobs in the high-end and FIRE services sectors, even though the number of firms in these two sectors was close to the national average. While the global cities of the world indeed stand out in international networks of global capital, the data in this study suggests that it is not clear that the small cities of the world are simply the backwater retainers of surplus labor, dead-end jobs, and less-than-dynamic cultural, social, and economic worlds.

The evidence presented throughout the book shows that small metro areas follow many different paths, some more dynamic than others. Many small cities have experienced growth in the high-end services and FIRE sectors, while others have maintained strong manufacturing sectors. All places experienced growth in the proportion of population with college degrees, and the cities that were doing the best at the end of the twentieth century tended to have more college graduates than those that were ranked lower on the success index. This great diversity of experiences among small cities counters the presumption that they have similar economies focused on low-end services and are destined to die off with the increased globalization of the nation's economy.

Instead, the evidence points to a greater convergence between smaller metro areas and larger ones in terms of local economies. Like larger urban centers, small cities became more attractive for new immigrants after 1970, and like larger cities, small cities had more college-educated residents. Together, these factors indicate that small cities have become more like larger cities. Seventy-five percent of all the cities featured in this book had metro-area populations of less than 500,000 in 2000, illustrating that places could remain small in population but have growing and robust economies.

Small cities are not simply growing into big cities, although some do grow larger. Todd Gardner (2001) shows that many smaller cities in the nineteenth century in the United States grew (in terms of population) into some of the bigger cities of the twentieth century, but they did not necessarily become the biggest. This same trend seems evident at the end of the twentieth century. A few smaller metro areas have become fairly large—Orlando, Las Vegas, and Fresno, for example—while most cities have grown moderately. The key point is that the economic structures of small metro areas are becoming more similar to the structure of the national economy as a whole in terms of employment in sectors, but it is possible for cities to remain small in terms of population and still have growing and robust economies.

This increasing homogenization of local economies (i.e., fewer highly specialized places) raises questions about the applicability of two of the main theories addressed throughout the book: the global cities theory and the creative class theory. Both theories posit that some places are doing better because they are significantly different from other cities. And this may be true to a certain extent; global cities, or exemplars of the creative class economy, may be extreme cases with highly disproportionate employment in certain areas. Yet the fact that the economies of smaller metro areas are starting to look more like the national economy makes it seem likely that most places—which are generally not centers where the creative class lives or centers of global networks—are simply not that different from one another economically or demographically. These similarities may reflect the greater interconnectedness of cities because of technological and economic changes.

This apparent convergence, however, is based on the statistically average small place, not on the particularities of any specific small metro area. The observation that the economies of small cities are becoming more like those of large urban centers, therefore, does not lend itself to an explicit policy perspective. But it does suggest that it might be better for officials and policy makers in small cities to focus on local issues rather than worrying about how much a particular place is like or unlike the national economy. With the likelihood of increased homogenization of small cities over time, it is likely better to spend energy on dealing with local issues than on attempts to make a small place into something similar to a larger place that is viewed as more successful.

New Economy + Old Economy = Success

In chapter 2, I first presented information that questioned the extent to which focusing exclusively on the new economy based primarily on services benefits small metro areas. As subsequent chapters showed, the new economy (particularly the high-end services sector) offers some benefits to small cities, but successful cities generally had strong manufacturing sectors as well. In fact, greater concentration in the manufacturing sector, including higher levels of employment, a larger-than-average number of firms, and higher wages in that sector, is positively associated with increased levels of population and income and lower levels of economic inequality.

The most successful small cities in 2000 did not forsake the new economy, however. Instead, they maintained a diverse economy. As table 6.1 shows, the most successful cities on the success index ranking had proportionately greater employment in the new manufacturing, low-end services, and FIRE sectors while maintaining fairly high employment in the old manufacturing sector. The most successful cities had the lowest proportion of employment in high-end services. These findings contrast with what the creative class hypothesis suggests—that high levels of employment in the high-end services sector should be associated with greater success.

TABLE 6.1
Median Location Quotients by Success Index Quartiles in 2000

	Stagnating Places	Mixed Outcomes	Doing Well	Success Stories
Old manufacturing employment	0.66	0.85	0.60	0.66
New manufacturing employment	0.70	0.61	0.65	0.76
Low-end services employment	1.04	0.95	0.98	1.07
High-end services employment	1.10	1.10	1.04	1.01
FIRE employment	0.89	0.84	0.97	0.97

Source: Dept. of Commerce, Bureau of the Census, County Business Patterns data, various years.

For small cities, a focus on services at the expense of other sectors may not lead to greater success. Among the stagnant metro areas, 87 percent of the work force was in the service sectors and only 11 percent worked in manufacturing. In contrast, in small cities in the success stories group, 79 percent of the work force was in the services sector, but a slightly higher proportion of 15 percent worked in manufacturing. Wage levels follow a similar pattern; in 2000, the an average hourly wage in the manufacturing sector of the most successful metro areas was about $8.22; the comparable wage for the stagnating cities was only $6.96. For all of the service sectors combined, the successful cities had an average wage of $5.94 per hour, while stagnating cities had an average hourly wage of $5.17. Cities in the stagnating group do have more jobs in the high-end services and FIRE sectors than cities in the other three groups, but the combination of lower levels of pay and a weak manufacturing base seemed to have prevented these cities from doing well.

The differences between the economies of the groups of places as ranked on the success index are not overly large. On average, the most successful places in 2000 were not exclusively oriented toward manufacturing and the places that have struggled the most were not exclusively focused on the service sector. But these findings suggest that small cities may not want to forsake manufacturing for services as they consider which sectors to foster in their local economies. Places such as Green Bay, which has historically had a strong manufacturing base, recognize the importance of manufacturing and actively encourage new companies in that area.

The policy lesson here might be that blind adherence to the dictums of the new economy is no guarantee of success for a small metro area. Diverse economies rather than specialized ones are likely to be associated with higher populations and income levels and lower levels of economic inequality. Economic development plans, which are often formulated with the idea of attracting members of the creative class, may not yield dividends for small cities if they focus only on luring firms that provide jobs in the high-end services sector. Instead, focusing on making local areas destinations for a variety of types of companies will generate better results for more people across the community.

People Matter

For some time now researchers have been arguing that human capital affects how well cities do over time. The analysis in this book confirms this. For small cities, success, whether it is measured through the success index or by using one of the three outcome measures, is tied to attributes of the people who live there. Who lives in a place is what matters rather than abstract notions about the preferences of a population. Richard Florida argues that tolerance, as measured through the number of artists, gay couples, and other people living alternative lifestyles, is the key to success for cities in the twenty-first century. My findings suggest instead that levels of education, racial composition, and nativity of a population are most closely tied to success for small cities rather than degree of openness to alternative lifestyles.

Small cities that have higher levels of educated people do better over time. This finding fits well with Florida's assertion that what is important is a high degree of tolerance and a strong presence of members of the creative class, but the local economies of successful cities do not necessarily match the expectations set by his conception of a creative economy. Manufacturing is still important for small cities, and the places that are doing the best are those with lower levels of high-end services within the group of eighty cities in this study. If population is the only variable used to measure success, then Florida's tolerance index is a good predictor of growth. Level of tolerance is also a good predictor of success if distribution of employment across sectors is the variable of interest (Florida 2002, 2005). But when levels of income and levels of economic inequality are taken into account, Florida's tolerance measure is not a good predictor of positive change. In fact, increased levels of tolerance are statistically related to increased levels of economic inequality.

Instead, the characteristics of the people—their education levels, racial identities, and nativity—matter more. Places with more immigrants, greater proportions of people identifying as white, and higher levels of foreign-born residents all do better than places with lower levels of all three groups. Although all three groups are related to Florida's concept of tolerance, when we statistically take them into account with the tolerance level, population characteristics matter while tolerance level does not.

But that does not invalidate the thrust of Florida's assertion that cities need to attract educated people. I argue, however, that the emphasis on amenities and tolerance may be displaced. Leaders in small cities might do best to consider how to attract both immigrants and the college-educated without worrying so much about whether their community has enough art galleries, rock-climbing walls, or coffee houses to cater to the creative class. In fact, when the number of Starbucks establishments per metro area is included in the statistical analysis, it is found to be associated with population only (Sperling and Sander 2004). Because Starbucks as a corporation logically targets growing areas, the number of coffee houses is less a leading indicator than a lagging one.

And while it may be troubling to note that increased tolerance is related to increasing levels of economic inequality, is worth thinking about what kind of growth we want for our communities. Tolerance is related to greater employment in high-end services, but the high-end services sector does not offer many good jobs for people with lower levels of education. Places that are doing well have more employment in old and new manufacturing than cities that are doing poorly. Leaders in smaller cities should consider the types of economic opportunities that are tied to various levels of employment. While global cities require many highly educated people for the upper-tier jobs and similar numbers of less educated people for jobs in the low-end services sector, most small cities will never become global cities. Perhaps the lesson is that they should not aspire to do so but instead foster their own path of development, one that emphasizes a varied economy with opportunities for people with all levels of education.

Immigration Matters for Small Places, Too

Since the early 1990s, immigration has been key to the growth of metro areas in the United States. While the rate of immigration from all over the globe increased after the liberalization of U.S. immigration laws in the mid-1960s, migration into the United States reached new records in the 1990s and early 2000s. Demographers noted the movement of immigrants into cities that had not previously drawn large populations from Central and South America or Asia after the 2000 census data was released (Singer 2003). But the importance of immigrants to smaller places such as the eighty studied here was not identified.

The findings presented in this book show that among small cities, immigration matters for small places, and not just in terms of population growth. In-migration of foreign-born people to small cities is clearly consequential for population growth. Six of the cities in this study actually experienced a decrease in the percentage of population foreign born between 1970 and 2000. For four of these six cities, the overall population decreased as well (Decatur, Duluth, Youngstown, and Flint). While percentage change in rate of immigration was not statistically a factor for the entire group of eighty cities in influencing percentage change in population, income, or level of economic inequality, the statistic of the actual number of immigrants by year did influence levels of population and income over time. And most significantly in terms of policy implications, when all three outcomes of population, median income, and level of economic inequality were combined into the success index, increased immigration was associated with greater success over time.

One way of thinking about the importance of immigration is to consider the economies of the metro areas that ranked highest on the success index (see tables 5.1 and 6.1). The most successful places, on average, have more opportunities in the manufacturing and low-end services sectors than do the other places. These are also the sectors most likely to offer positions to immigrants who arrive in the United States with low levels of education. In addition, the places that are doing the best tend to have higher wages in these two sectors, thus making them more attractive to immigrants at the same time as they reduce economic disparities within metro areas.

Leaders in small cities therefore need to think about the types of welcome mats they put out. It is important for small metro areas to be attractive to college-educated people, both native born and foreign born. Yet because the majority of new immigrants coming to the United States have lower levels of education, small cities need to be prepared to make themselves attractive to these newcomers as well, since this group is tied to success for small cities. This means that small communities need to be ready to offer adequate services for newly arrived people, ranging from instruction in English as a second language to social services that are culturally appropriate. These services are often publicly paid for, but the longer-term return on such investment is likely to outweigh the short-term costs. It may also mean welcoming new small businesses that cater to new populations. Places that do not foster an environment that is welcoming to immigrants may find themselves doing poorly as time goes on.

New Ways of Thinking about and Measuring Success

In addition to the empirical findings this book presents, I have also been both implicitly and explicitly making an argument about how we should think about success and failure among urban areas in the United States. These ideas are meant to stimulate debate within the fields of urban studies and urban sociology and help both scholars and students think about how we should study urban, suburban, and rural America.

Comparative and Historical Approaches to Understanding Urban Change
A central tenet of this book is that urban studies research needs to include more comparative examinations of urban areas. While case studies of one

particular city or a small group of cities (usually three or four) provide us with wonderful in-depth knowledge about a neighborhood, community, or city, only comparative studies that draw on larger samples can give us a good picture of how cities of certain types or classes compare. If we want to emphasize how we can generalize from empirical data, we need larger, statistically based analyses to complement the findings of case studies. Most of the extant studies that use large numbers of urban areas tend to look at particular aspects of how cities are changing, in contrast to books like this one that look at a wide variety of factors as a way to assess change.

I also argue that we must historicize our investigations of cities to a greater extent. Although both economists and demographers tend to study change over time, neither discipline emphasizes cross-disciplinary work. Similarly, many case studies contain wonderful histories of specific locales but do not situate them within broader histories of change in urban areas, although they may discuss national trends. It is important to understand historical trajectories of cities, suburbs, and metro areas within the context of urban change in the United States. Empirical examinations of change are often underutilized, and I hope that the findings of this book present a template for how we can think about studying change over time. This type of study realizes the importance of places—be they cities, suburbs, or metro areas—as units of analysis instead of discussing national trends and making assumptions about how particular places fit within these trends. We need to remember that the histories of cities are both particular and part of broader transformations of cities over time and space.

Multiple Indicators of Success or Failure

This historical and comparative analysis needs to be done with an eye towards the indicators that are used to assess change. Too many previous investigations by scholars have privileged single outcomes, such as population or income or employment levels. I argue that we should also assess outcomes using multiple measures. In general people do not judge a city by a single measure, and scholars should not either. Magazines, books, and websites devoted to ranking cities use multiple criteria to do so. However, most of these lists of best cities are created idiosyncratically without regard to evidence-based scholarship that could provide insight into how metro or urban area attributes are related.

I offer a composite success index as one way of assessing change in small metro areas. I do so because of my training in sociology; hence my focus on the intersection of changes in population, income, and economic inequality. But other indices could easily be used to assess change. Many qualitative studies already use multiple indicators, but if we are to be able to generalize from the findings of quantitative studies, it is essential that we develop indexical outcomes to create stronger assessments of urban change over time.

Use of Economic Inequality in Addition to Population and Income Levels

Data about levels of economic inequality are key to my success index. While population and income levels have long been investigated in urban areas, levels of economic inequality have not been the topic of considerable research. Economic inequality, as outlined in chapters 3 and 4, is related to many negative outcomes for both people and cities. Economic inequality has been on the rise in the United States since 1970, and we need to understand why this has happened, understand how it has increased in particular cities, and explore how certain places have done a better job of mitigating it. In-depth case studies of how cities have worked to thwart or lessen economic inequality, such as the work of Alice O'Conner, Chris Tilly, and Lawrence Bobo (2001), which examines economic inequality in four cities in great detail, are a good start. But these case studies need to be situated within broader comparative studies of urban inequality. And while this book focuses primarily on metro areas, investigations that compare levels of inequality in cities to levels of inequality in suburbs should also be undertaken.

Use of Location Quotients

Location quotients have historically been used to compare levels of employment within a particular industry or economic sector in small geographic units with national levels of employment. My work expands on this practice by constructing location quotients based on the number of firms by sector and average wages by sector. While location quotients are useful for comparing particular cities with national trends, they also provide a consistent measure to use when comparing cities with each other, particularly over time.

Study Places of Varying Sizes

Finally, this book is about small places. Small cities are important for many reasons, not least of which is that so many Americans live in them. Small places need to be studied more, and not just the eighty that are this book. Some small cities were excluded from this book because the population in the central city was too small. Others were located too close to other small cities. Others were slightly too large. All of these cities need to be studied to understand how the United States is changing.

But part of studying small places is reaching a greater understanding of particular places as examples of types or strata. Small cities can be grouped for analysis according to population, the way that they have been done here. They also could be grouped based on income, unemployment levels, levels of immigration, or size of particular economic sectors. Studying cities based on common characteristics that divide them into logical groups allows for stronger assessments of how urban areas change. We can imagine the country as composed of various strata of urban, suburban, or rural areas that can be grouped according to their commonalities (or differences). Analysis by group is the perfect complement to the in-depth case study of one or a few places. Through group analysis, we can better understand how representative case studies are.

7

Epilogue

Small Cities after 2000

As the turn of the twenty-first century approached, things looked good in small cities. While not all had participated in the wave of prosperity of the late 1990s, many had booming economies, growing populations, and vibrant social scenes. Las Vegas was the fastest-growing metro area in the entire United States, and most of the small cities studied here had seen greater increases in median household income than had the nation as a whole. Even though there were signs in 2000 that the economy was cooling off, a good number of small cities looked to be in good shape.

Unfortunately, most actually were not. Although we do not yet have enough data for the first decade of the twenty-first century to say for sure, many of the small cities that did well from 1970 to 2000 suddenly found themselves on a rockier course after the year 2000. While certainly the events of 9/11 and the subsequent souring of the U.S. economy did not help, small places experienced problems even though they are somewhat removed from the difficulties larger cities have faced. And the second downturn in the later part of the decade—dubbed "the Great Recession"—hit small cities hard. Las Vegas, for example, stopped growing and saw significant declines in housing prices and other indicators of economic well-being.

Most of the eighty small cities in this book continued to gain population from 2000 to 2008 (the most recent year for which reliable data are available for all cities). But whereas only three small metro areas experienced population declines from 1990 to 2000, nineteen of the small metro areas in this study did so from 2000 to 2008. Among these nineteen cities were Salt Lake City, which experienced a 16 percent decline in population after having grown by 95 percent from 1970 to 2000, and Lexington, Kentucky, which shrank by 6 percent after growing by 55 percent from 1970 to 2000. Thus, small cities that had previously experienced very strong population growth experienced decline, not just small cities that had experienced no or only moderate growth in population.

The story for income levels is even more disheartening. Nearly two-thirds of the eighty small cities experienced declines in median household income from 2000 to 2008. Over half of the metro areas had experienced growth in median household income of at least 25 percent from 1970 to 2000. But from 2000 to 2008, over 70 percent experienced a decline in median income. Places such as Gainesville, Florida, were particularly hard hit; median household income there declined by 10 percent over the eight years. In 1970, median household income (in constant 2000 dollars) in Gainesville was $19,500. That figure had increased to $31,400 by 2000. But by 2008, it had declined to $28,000. While Gainesville is not a terribly expensive place to live, this loss in income across the metro area hit residents hard.

Unemployment was a primary reason for the declining income levels in small metro areas. Among all eighty places, unemployment averaged 6 percent in 2000. By 2008, average unemployment had crept up to 7 percent, and by 2010, it was nearly 9 percent. Overall, for all eighty cities, the average increase in the unemployment level was just over 50 percent from 2000 to 2008. Small metro areas were hit nearly as hard as the nation as a whole in terms of unemployment, although even at the height of the recession in 2010, these places tended to have slightly lower levels of unemployment than the national average.

Immigration, however, continued in many of the cities. Because the national economy and local economies were transitioning toward a greater emphasis on the low-end services sector, there proved to be plenty of jobs for newcomers with lower levels of education. However, the influx of foreign-born migrants lowered median household income levels in smaller places. While immigration provided workers for jobs in the low-end services sector and certainly added to the cultural vibrancy of small cities, the net result of the period was still negative on average: incomes declined. Indeed, many immigrants may have found that their hopes for a better life have not been realized in their new homes, and many have had to adjust their expectations.

A key problem was the housing boom—and subsequent bust—that took place from 2000 to 2010. Las Vegas presents perhaps the strongest example of this problem. Between July 1996 and July 2006, the year that median home prices peaked in Las Vegas, the median home value increased from $106,200 to $292,800, or 125 percent. Yet between July 2006 and December 2010, home values in Los Vegas plummeted 59 percent.[1] During this same time period, the city's population more than doubled. So while there was an overall increase in home values from 1996 to 2010, for the many people who had moved to the area during the housing boom, home values decreased considerably. Only people who had purchased a house before 1999 saw no real decline in home values. All of the people who had flocked to Las Vegas during the early to mid-2000s and purchased homes tended to see their investments lose value significantly and rapidly.

The four case-study metro areas highlighted throughout the book fared only marginally better throughout the period than did Las Vegas. All experienced declines in home values, although not nearly to the same degree; home values decreased by an average of about 5 percent in these four places. But for Green Bay and Salinas, unemployment was a key problem by 2010. The 1990s had been a good decade for both metro areas in terms of employment. In 1990, Green Bay had an unemployment rate of 4.7, and Salinas had a rate of 13.5 percent By 2000, the unemployment rate in Green Bay had decreased to 2.8 percent and in Salinas it had decreased to 9.5 percent.[2] But by the end of 2010, unemployment had increased in these two cities—as in the nation in general—to 6.6 and 16.4 percent, respectively. While Green Bay maintains a stronger employment outlook than the nation as a whole, in large part because of a manufacturing sector that has remained steady, Salinas and its environs saw heavy downturns in jobs in the tourism sector and in other low-end services at the end of the decade. Losses in these areas led to skyrocketing unemployment in the region.

As has been the lesson of this book, however, not all small places faced similar fates during this decade. Laredo experienced more ups and downs than other cities; there, unemployment was high in 1990 (12.7 percent), lower in 2000 (5.2 percent), and slightly higher again in 2010 (8.1 percent).

In Providence, home values decreased slightly from 2000 to 2010, but the city actually experienced an uptick in employment over the decade. Providence did not prosper in the 1990s, but revitalization efforts by the city's colorful mayor, Buddy Cianci, seemed to have yielded results in the 2000s. In the late 1990s, the city's WaterFire sculpture was installed on its three rivers and the Mall of New England opened. These two additions rejuvenated much of the city's moribund downtown. In 1990, Providence had an unemployment rate of 17.3 percent, which had dropped only slightly by the end of the decade to 15.9 percent, but by the end of 2010 the city's unemployment rate had decreased to 10.9 percent, only slightly higher than the national average. As I have noted in previous chapters, Providence seems poised to do well given its economic base in education and health care. Although it did not seem to be able to capitalize on these strengths before 2000, since then, the metro area seems to have done better than average.

Unfortunately, we do not have access yet to complete data for all of the study cities during this period. But data for Providence and Green Bay are available and provide some insight into how local economies changed during the 2000s. In Green Bay, job losses were primarily in the manufacturing sector, which employed 22.6 percent of the labor force in 2000 but only 18.8 percent in 2006, the most recent year for which data are available.[3] Most other sectors stayed roughly the same throughout the period. Employment in the high-end services sector grew by 12 percent from 2000 to 2006 but still accounted for only 6.5 percent of the labor force in 2006. Part of the manufacturing losses can be attributed to the decision of FreshLike, a vegetable packer, to close its Green Bay plant after a labor dispute concerning the housing of migrant laborers. But there was also further consolidation and streamlining in the paper industry during this period, which led to fewer jobs in that area.

Providence also lost jobs in manufacturing; the number of jobs in that sector declined by 26 percent from 2000 to 2006. But the number of jobs in the FIRE and the other professional service sectors grew in the same period; together, they accounted for 32 percent of the labor force by 2006. While in Green Bay the number of jobs in the low-end services sector decreased but were replaced with more jobs in the high-end services sector, in Providence, jobs in the low-end service sector, particularly in entertainment, hospitality, and food-related areas, increased by 14 percent from 2000 to 2006, thus partially offsetting the city's decline in manufacturing. Much of the growth in these areas came from the revitalization of the downtown with its new restaurants, galleries, and the like.

Finally, how have small cities fared on the success index in the first decade of the twenty-first century? A new success index for 2010 cannot yet be calculated, but we can see how the different cities fared in the 2000s based on their ranking in 2000. On average, the cities that ranked highest in 2000 continued to grow and prosper; the top twenty places had the highest median income levels. In 2008, the top twenty places had an average median household income of $42,900, while the bottom twenty had an average median household income of $34,900 (in constant 2008 dollars). The cities that ranked highest on the index in 2000 also continued to grow in terms of population, although cities in the 50th to 75th percentile grew at a slightly greater rate than did the top twenty cities.

In the first decade of the twenty-first century, as in the previous three decades, population change was tied to in-migration of foreign-born individuals. The twenty cities that ranked highest on the success index in 2000 experienced greater influxes of immigrants in the following years than did the twenty cities that ranked lowest in that year, although on average, all four groups of metro areas had positive changes in the percentage of foreign-born population. But unlike in the preceding decade, when the immigrant population in very few cities declined, as of 2008, several metro areas—including the border cities of Laredo and McAllen—had experienced declines in immigrant populations. Some of these declines can likely be linked to changes in federal policies toward immigrants. Cities such as Sioux City, Iowa, that had attracted immigrants to slaughterhouses and meat-packing facilities suddenly became less attractive after raids by federal officials on establishments that employed undocumented workers in mid-2008. Sioux City experienced a 17 percent decline in the percentage of foreign-born population in its metro area from 2000 to 2008.

And as further proof of the increasing diversity of destinations for newcomers to the United States, the places that topped the list of those that gained immigrants from 2000 to 2008 were metro areas that had previously had lower levels of in-migration. Little Rock, Arkansas; Peoria, Illinois; and Chattanooga, Tennessee, all experienced over 100 percent increases in in-migration of immigrants; the percentage of immigrants in these three cities was 7.4, 5.9, and 5.2, respectively. While the percent of immigrants in these cities did not exceed the national average, this level of growth among immigrant communities was profound for each of these places. On the other hand, among the ten places with the highest levels of foreign-born residents in 2000, only one (Ann Arbor, Michigan) was among the metro areas that gained many immigrants from 2000 to 2008.[4] Overall, places that had been attractive to newcomers from abroad before 2000 were less likely to be so after 2000.

Perhaps one reason the cities that ranked the lowest on the success index in 2000 had higher levels of immigration on average in subsequent years was that fact that manufacturing jobs in these cities declined less than in other cities in this study in the 2000s. While the twenty places that ranked highest on the success index in 2000 tended to have higher levels of employment in manufacturing in that year, this group of cities experienced the greatest decline in that sector from 2000 to 2008.[5] Job loss in this sector ranged from 41 to 85 percent for these twenty cities over these eight years. No metro area experienced job growth in manufacturing during this time. Still, cities that tended to have higher levels of employment in that area did not necessarily experience the greatest percentage of change in employment in that sector.

Overall, all economic sectors in many of the small places of this study experienced contraction, following the trend of the downturn in the national economy. It is too soon to know if the Great Recession has had a disproportionate impact on smaller places or if it has affected some small cities more than others. Additionally, the forces of consolidation and homogenization appear likely to continue to affect smaller metro areas. Larger corporations continued to merge with or absorb their competitors in the first decade of the twentieth century, a process that reduced the number of firms per sector for many small places. While the impact of this will not be known until more data from the 2010 U.S. census become available, the likelihood is that greater consolidation is not helping these smaller metro areas.

While smaller places tended not to experience an economic slump at the end of the 1990s that was as severe as that in larger metro areas, this was largely due to their low level of involvement in the information technology sector that prospered during the dot-com bubble of that decade.

But in the first decade of the twenty-first century, small cities may not have been so lucky. Both small and large cities alike appear to have been part of the housing bubble that has wrought so much economic havoc across the nation, and the collapse of that sector has implications for the eighty small cities studied here. From 2000 to 2008, employment in the construction sector decreased in seventy-eight of the eighty cities. The number of jobs in the FIRE sector also decreased in many places. These sectors, which are part of the housing industry, will likely take many years to recover from the record drops in housing values and the oversupply of homes across the nation.

Yet if the findings about small cities in this book demonstrate anything, it is the considerable resilience of smaller metro areas over time. We must remember that of the eighty places examined here, only four lost population overall from 1970 to 2000. Most experienced gains in median household income levels during that period as well, although some of those gains have eroded since 2000. Small cities present vibrant mini-metropolises that are unlike the largest cities of the United States in some ways but are also becoming more like them as time passes. Future examinations of change in small cities will help us understand how the downturn of the late 2000s affected smaller places, but we will likely see continued buoyancy among many of them.

APPENDIX: TECHNICAL INFORMATION ON DATA SOURCES AND STATISTICAL ANALYSES

In this book, I draw upon a wide variety of data sources for the analysis in chapters 2 through 5. I explain in this appendix where the data were collected from and the types of manipulation undertaken to make it suitable for analysis. All tables for the appendix are found on the website www.smallcitiesusa.com.

Metropolitan Statistical Areas

Through the book, I use "metropolitan statistical area" (MSA), "central city" and "suburbs" in reference to the places I am studying. I first outline how MSAs were used and then move onto central cities and suburbs.

I drew a sample of eighty MSAs using U.S. Census FIPS (Federal Information Processing Standards) codes to designate places. I used a standard 1990 metropolitan statistical area (MSA) definition for data over time when possible. The State of the Cities Data Systems (SOCDS) generated by the Department of Housing and Urban Development (U.S. Department of Housing and Urban Development 2006) contains data from 1970, 1980, 1990, 2000 and for certain years from 2001 to 2011 for MSAs using the constant 1990 definition so that data are comparable across years. Unfortunately, the SOCDS data are not comprehensive for all of the variables that I use in my analysis; therefore, some data were collected based on the geography of the MSA definition of the year they were collected (in the case of data collected by the U.S. government). Other data, that were time-invariant, were collected to match the 1990 MSA definitions (e.g., data on the number of educational institutions).

To facilitate analysis over time, I did not use the Core Based Statistical Area (CBSA) geographic definition that the U.S. Census Bureau moved to in 2000. The advantage of the CBSA definition is that it brings together metropolitan and micropolitan geographic areas that formerly had existed under different coding schemes. The main disadvantage of using it is that it is impossible to use for 1970 data.

I coded data for four MSAs using either a PMSA (Primary Metropolitan Statistical Area) or NECMA (New England Central Metropolitan Area) codes, although the data from these places were available in the SOCDS data. These four cities are Trenton, New Jersey; Salem, Oregon; Flint, Michigan; and Ann Arbor, Michigan. While PMSA data may include data for places that are subordinate to a larger central city, the four cities for which I used PMSA data were more than thirty miles from the nearest city with a population of 50 percent of the central city I was examining. Thus, each of these four cities fit my criterion for inclusion in the sample.

To create a better understand the different geographic entities, I include the U.S. Census Bureau's definitions (U.S. Census Bureau 1994):

Metropolitan Statistical Area [MSA]. An MSA consists of one or more counties that contain a city of 50,000 or more inhabitants, or contain an urbanized area (UA) as defined by the Census Bureau and have a total population of at least 100,000 (75,000 in New England). Counties containing the principal concentration of population—the largest city and surrounding densely settled area—are components of the MSA. Additional counties qualify to be included by meeting a specified number of commuters to the counties containing the population concentration and by meeting certain other requirements of metropolitan character, such as a specified minimum population density or percentage of the population that is urban. MSAs in New England are defined in terms of cities and towns, following rules concerning commuting and population density.

Primary Metropolitan Statistical Area [PMSA]. A PMSA is a sub-area of an MSA that has a population of one million or more. PMSAs consist of a large urbanized county or a cluster of counties (or, in New England, cities and towns) that demonstrate strong internal economic and social links as well as close ties with the central core of the MSA. When a PMSA is recognized, the entire area of which it is a component becomes a Consolidated Metropolitan Statistical Area (CMSA). All territory within a CMSA is also part of the associated PMSA.

New England County Metropolitan Area [NECMA]. NECMAs are county-based alternatives to the city- and town-based MSAs and CMSAs for the six New England states. The county composition of a NECMA reflects the geographic extent of the corresponding MSA(s) or CMSA(s). NECMAs are not defined for individual PMSAs.

The cities that used codes other than the MSA FIPS to determine their geographic catchment area were:

Providence-Warwick-Pawtucket, RI	(NECMA FIPS code = 6483)
Springfield, MA	(NECMA FIPS code = 8003)
Trenton, NJ	(PMSA FIPS code = 8480)
Salem, OR	(PMSA FIPS code = 7080)
Flint, MI	(PMSA FIPS code = 2640)
Ann Arbor, MI	(PMSA FIPS code = 440)

Although these six cities are not identical to MSAs in terms of how they are defined, because the geographic circumscription of the metro areas is kept constant across time, the data for these six cities are comparable to the data for MSAs.

Data

Below, I describe how I collected and used each type of data I used in the analysis in this book. Data tables are found on the website www.smallcitiesusa.com. This information is presented in three sections: demographic data, economic data, and geographic data.

Demographic Data

I use a variety of demographic data in this book to assess the impact of demographic changes on metropolitan well-being over time. The majority of the data come from the U.S. Census Bureau, but the data were collected in several different ways.

POPULATION. I used population data for the MSA, the central city, and the central city's suburbs from the SOCDS data.

IMMIGRATION. The data on percentage of foreign-born individuals in an MSA were in the SOCDS data set.

RACE. Race data were retrieved from two sources. Data on the percentage of the population "non-Hispanic white," "non-Hispanic black," "Hispanic, any race," or "other race" from the 1980, 1990, and 2000 Censuses were from the SOCDS data. However, 1970 data on race is not included in the SOCDS data set, and I used data from the 1970 census. Unfortunately, in this year, the Census Bureau used only the categories of "white" and "black," thus making data for that year only partially comparable to the data from subsequent census years.

To combat the compatibility issue, I used only the "white" data from 1970 since I could not determine which races had been included in the "black" category. I then used a regression best fit model based on 1980, 1990, and 2000 data of percentage white to adjust the 1970 number to take into account people of other races.

AGE DISTRIBUTION. Although I did not use age as an independent variable in my analysis, I did use age data to construct the 90:10 income inequality index. I collected age data for 1970 and 1980 by hand from the U.S. census books available at the Bancroft Libraries at the University of California, Berkeley. I collected 1990 census data from the computer file the U.S. Census Bureau published. I collected data for 2000 using the American FactFinder table generator at www.census.gov. I collected data on the percentage of individuals below five years, between eighteen and sixty-five years, and over sixty-five years of age.

EDUCATIONAL ATTAINMENT. Data on the percentage of individuals who did not graduate high school, who graduated high school, who had attended some college, and who had graduated from college were available in the SOCDS data.

Economic Data

Two main sources were used for the economic data in this study: the SOCDS data and the County Business Patterns (CBP) data collected by the U.S. Census Bureau on an annual basis. Because of limitations in access to data, I used CBP data from the years 1974, 1979, 1989, and 1996 in combination with the census data from the years 1970, 1980, 1990, and 2000, respectively. I used the 1974 data because 1969 and 1970 data were not available; 1974 was the first year for which complete data were available. I used CBP data for 1979 and 1989 in conjunction with Census Bureau data for 1980 and 1990, respectively. I used CBP data for 1996 as that was the last year that Standard Industrial Classification (SIC) codes were used prior to the introduction of the North American Industrial Classification System (NAICS) became the standard. The NAICS is more comprehensive than to the SIC system, particularly in relation to new service industries, but some SIC codes do not map to any NAICS codes, and vice versa.

To capture the effects of economic change over time, I used SIC codes for economic data related to employment, number of firms and wage levels. The SOCDS data were already combined into several categories based on SIC codes. I combined data from the CBP data set to create some categories. The 1974 and 1979 CBP data used the 1972 SIC designations and had to be translated to become comparable with the data from the 1989 and 1996 data sets. I combined data to form the general categories of old and new manufacturing sectors, low-end and high-end services sectors, and the FIRE sector. The exact SIC codes that were combined can be found in tables A.1 through A.7 on the website www.smallcitiesusa.com.

All dollar amounts were translated into constant 1999 dollars using the Consumer Price Index. I used conversion factors from the U.S. Department of Labor, Bureau of Labor Statistics, Consumer Price Index website: http://stats.bls.gov/cpi/. County Business Patterns data is at the county level and therefore does not perfectly match the MSA data. However, because all MSAs are counties, CBP data is a reasonably good match, and it provides more economic information than any other available data.

COMBINATIONS OF SICS CODES USED TO CONSTRUCT ECONOMIC SECTORS. I used 1987 SIC codes for the data on economic sectors. To facilitate analysis, I aggregated individual codes into sector groups, and then into general groups. The tables containing the codes as they were combined can be found on the website www.smallcitiesusa.com.

The data from 1974 and 1979 County Business Patterns surveys were originally classified using the 1972 SIC code system. The National Bureau of Economic Research (www.nber.com) provides a file with conversion factors for translating 1972 SIC codes to 1987 SIC codes. This file can be found at http://www.macalester.edu/research/economics/page/haveman/Trade.Resources/Concordances/FromusSIC/sic7287.txt. I used this file to translate the 1974 and 1979 CBP data so that it would be compatible with the 1989 and 1996 data.

EMPLOYMENT LEVELS. I used employment data from two sources: the SOCDS and the CBP data sets. The SOCDS data contained raw counts of the number of individuals employed in a group and the total number of employed individuals in the MSA, central city, or suburbs. The CBP data contained employment information of two types: the total number of employees on payroll in mid-March at all of the firms reporting in the given SIC class, and the number of establishments with employees within given ranges of employees.

ESTABLISHMENT NUMBERS. The CBP data set provided the total number of establishments as well as the number of establishments by number of employees using SIC codes.

AVERAGE WAGE. The CBP data set provided several wage measures. The data set contained the total annual payroll for all establishments using SIC codes. It also provided data on the total payroll for the first quarter for all establishments, again using SIC codes. I calculated the average wage using SIC codes by first converting the payroll dollar amounts to constant 2000 dollars. I then divided the total annual payroll by the number of employees in mid-March. While this may understate or overstate the average wage in some seasonal industries (such as agriculture or construction), this is the best available means of calculating average wages across all eighty MSAs for all four census years.

MEDIAN HOUSEHOLD INCOME. The SOCDS data set contains family income data, but I used household income data throughout the project to better capture the wide variety of households in metropolitan areas. I therefore used median household income from census data for 1970 through 2000.

90:10 INCOME INEQUALITY MEASURE. I constructed the 90:10 income inequality measure using family income data from the four decennial censuses. I created decile levels of income for each census year, interpolating the decile level when necessary, using census data from 1970 through 2000.

HOME AND RENT VALUES. The SOCDS data set contains both median household gross rent as well as the median household owner's value of property for the MSA, central city, and suburbs.

NUMBER OF FORTUNE 500 FIRMS. I collected the number of Fortune 500 firms in an MSA from *Fortune* magazine. Unfortunately, *Fortune* changed its data collection methodology considerably during the period 1970 to 2000, so the counts are not completely comparable across time. Because of this problem, I used only the presence or absence of a Fortune 500 company at any point between 1970 and 2000 in the final analysis. The data come from the following sources:

Fortune, n.d. May 1970: All industrial corporations included, ranked by sales.

Fortune, 5 May 1980: All industrial corporations included, ranked by sales.

Fortune, 2 May 1983: List of top 500 industrial corporations. This is the first year that service industries were separated from industrial (manufacturing) firms.

Fortune, 13 June 1983: List of top 500 service industries, separated into different service industries (refer to table 8c).

Fortune, 23 April 1990: All industrial corporations included, ranked by profits.

Fortune, 4 June 1990: 184–199: All service industries included: diversified service firms, commercial banks, diversified financial companies, savings institutions, life insurance companies, retail companies, transportation companies, and utilities.

Fortune, 18 April 1994: All industrial corporations included. This is the last year that manufacturing and service-sector firms were separated into different lists.

Fortune, 30 May 1994: All service corporations included.

Fortune website, 2000 data: http://money.cnn.com/magazines/fortune/fortune500_archive/full/2000/ All corporations included, regardless of sector.

Complete citations for data sources are found in the bibliography.

Geographic Data

DISTANCE BETWEEN MSA AND NEXT LARGEST MSA. I initially determined the distance between the MSAs and the nearest large city (metro area) initially using the website www.city-data.com, a commercial website that maintains information on cities. Information is gathered by the staff. Each city has an individual page on this site that includes information on demographics, employment, climate, and various other data. Included in this data is a list of nearby cities, both proximate and distant ones. I used the list of cities provided to determine the closest nearby large city. I used Google Maps (maps.google.com) to verify the distance between an MSA in my sample and the nearest large city.

AVERAGE LOW JANUARY AND HIGH JULY TEMPERATURES. Temperatures for January and July were found in *Cities Ranked and Rated*, a guide written by Bert Sperling and Peter Sander (Mr. Sperling helps *Money* magazine generate its "best places to live" lists every year). All MSAs in the United States are listed in the guide.

NUMBER OF COLLEGES AND UNIVERSITIES IN AN MSA. I collected data on the number of colleges or universities in an MSA from *America's Best Colleges, 2006 Edition*. The entries in the publication include the date the institution opened, the types of degrees granted, and number of faculty. The publication lists all institutions (four-year colleges as well as schools that grant graduate degrees) for each state. I compiled a list of all institutions in the MSAs in my sample. Geographic proximity to the central city of the

MSA was checked using Google Maps (maps.google.com) to confirm that each institution located was inside an MSA included in this study.

AGE OF CENTRAL CITY. I constructed two indicators of the age of the central city for each MSA. I created dummy variables for a population over 50,000 by the year 1950 and for a population over 50,000 in the year 1900. To do so, I used U.S. census data from the County Population Census Counts website of the Census Bureau (http://www.census.gov/population/www/censusdata/cencounts.html).

Statistical Analysis

In this book, I use both ordinary least squares (OLS) regression models and fixed effects models. OLS regression models are effective for examining places synchronically, while fixed effects models are more robust when examining places over time. In the OLS models, I regressed variables representing change over time against change in the outcome over time. OLS models allow the inclusion of time-invariant characteristics such as region or number of universities. Fixed effects models, which are used with panel-style data, cannot support these variables robustly. I therefore use fixed effects models to determine how different characteristics influenced the dependent variable over both time and space. I used panel data consisting of observations for each metropolitan area for each census year (1980, 1990 and 2000) to best capture change. This method adequately deals with the dynamic nature of longitudinal cross-sectional data (Halaby 2004).

Following Allison (2005), I use this formula as a general fixed effects model:

$$y_a = \mu_t + \beta x_{ti} + \gamma z_i + \alpha_i + \varepsilon_{it}$$

for i cases across t time observations, in which x is a column vector of variables that vary both over time and place, z is a column vector of variables that vary across place but not over time, μ_t is the intercept, β and γ are row vectors of coefficients, α_i represents all differences between observations that are stable over time, and ε_{it} is a random disturbance term. In this case, I modeled eighty MSAs across census years—the vector x—and controlled for demographic and economic characteristics—the vector z. Fixed effects equations also allow for the differentiation of the influence of time-varying versus time-invariant factors. Most important, fixed effects models account for between-case as well as within-case (metro area) covariance that occurs across time, thereby eliminating potentially large sources of bias (Allison 2005).

All descriptive statistics and regression tables are found on the website that accompanies this book, www.smallcitiesusa.com. On that website, figures B.1 and B.2 present the descriptive statistics for the variables used in the various types of analysis throughout the book. Figures B.3 and B.4 present the correlation matrix for all variables, including the location quotient variables. Figures B.5, B.6, and B.7 are the regression models. Figure B.5 includes the OLS models for chapters 3 and 4, with a separate model for each outcome variables (population change, income change, and change in levels of inequality). Figure B.6 includes the fixed effects regression models that use panel data and also has separate models for all three outcome variables. Figure B.7 contains the fixed effects model I used for chapter 5, which uses the success index as the outcome variable. Note that there is no similar OLS regression for the fixed effects analysis of the success rank.

NOTES

1. INTRODUCTION

1. Aggregate population calculated using 2007 Community Population Survey data accessed via the State of the Cities Data Set (www.socds.huduser.org).

2. I recognize that local economies have always had some connections to larger markets and systems, but I agree with scholars who argue that there has been a shift in the nature of these relations during the twentieth century.

3. While little research has been done since the 1970s on how small cities fit in networks of cities, scholars working in the 1950s, 1960s, and early 1970s did extensive work in the area. These scholars investigated why some places become regional centers. Scholars such as James Vance (1971) noted that certain places prospered and became centers of a hinterland because they were wholesaling centers. These scholars focused on very small places and centered their research on the economic networks that characterized the 1960s. But with the rise of global commerce, just-in-time production and stocking, and "mega marts" such as Walmart, the economic geography of the United States has vastly changed. Thus, I focus more on the scholarship of scholars such as Saskia Sassen who are investigating how recent shifts have affected economic networks in the United States and around the world.

4. From 1970 through 1982, *Fortune* magazine constructed lists of industrial corporations. Starting in 1983, the magazine began to construct lists of service firms as well as industrial firms. In 1993, thirty metro areas had hosted Fortune 500 companies at any time. This trend continued through the 1980s and into the 1990s: in 1990, thirty-three MSAs had Fortune 500 firms, and in 1994, the last year in which *Fortune* separated service firms from industrial firms, twenty-nine MSAs were listed. In 1995 and subsequent years, *Fortune* combined all firms regardless of type, yielding lower numbers than in previous years. I compiled a database from all Fortune 500 lists from 1970, 1980, 1983, 1990, 1994, and 2000. Refer to the appendix for additional details concerning these data.

5. Refer to the appendix for details on tabulation of census data across time. Note that the State of the Cities Data Systems created by the Department of Housing and Urban Development provides data using constant geographic definitions across time.

6. Not only do these criteria exclude large suburbs in large metro areas, they also exclude "multi-nucleated" smaller metro regions (e.g., the Raleigh-Durham region in North Carolina or the Thousand Oaks–Ventura–Oxnard region in California). These multicity regions are interesting and need further research but present fundamentally different stories concerning historical development than do the small cities studied here. Thus, sixteen cities that could have been included using my criterion were excluded. This explains why table 1.1 lists ninety-six cities but only eighty cities are included in the study.

2. THE DIVERGENT FATES OF SMALL CITIES

1. The first group, which I label the "slow growers," includes cities that have shrunk or grown very slowly over the thirty-year period; it contains all of the cities in the first quartile of the distribution of total population change. Thirty-year growth rates in this group ranged from negative 8 percent to positive 17 percent. I refer to the second group as the "medium growers," which are the cities that grew moderately over the thirty-year period; this group contains all of the cities in the second quartile of the distribution of total population change. Thirty-year growth rates ranged from 18 percent to 45 percent. The third group, which I call the "fast growers," includes cities that have grown fairly robustly over the thirty-year period; it contains all of the cities in the third quartile of the distribution of total population change. The fast growers had thirty-year population growth rates ranging from 45 percent to 66 percent. The final group I identify as the "explosive growers," which are those cities that grew tremendously over the thirty-year period. This last group contains all of the cities in the fourth quartile of the distribution of total population change, and the thirty-year growth rates for this quartile ranged from 67 percent to 413 percent.

2. All data are at the metropolitan statistical area (MSA) level of aggregation based on U.S. Census Bureau 1990 constant geographic definitions unless otherwise noted. See the appendix for a discussion of use of data at this level.

3. County Business Patterns Data from 1974, 1980, 1990 and 1996; data were selected from those years for compatibility using SIC codes. See the appendix for a full discussion on why I used data from these years.

4. The differences in the percentage of the population of working age—individuals from 20 to 64—are much smaller between the four quartiles of cities. Only the fast-growing quartile has a notably higher percentage of people in the working-age group—a difference of 2 percent.

5. Many cities in the South experienced an increase in the percentage of African Americans during the decades of this study: Columbus, Georgia went from about 30 percent African American in 1970 to almost 50 percent, while Montgomery, Alabama, went from about 30 percent to about 42 percent.

6. The fastest-growing group of cities has considerably higher percentages of Latino/Hispanic residents on average than the other sixty cities. In 2000, the

average for this group of cities was about 22 percent of the population identified as Latino/Hispanic, compared to less than 8 percent for all the other cities, according to U.S. Census Bureau data.

7. In 1965, Congress passed the Immigration and Nationality Act, which removed racial quotas and allowed people from countries in South and Central America as well as Asia to immigrate to the United States in much larger numbers. Prior to the passage of this law, immigration from these areas was greatly restricted; immigrants from European countries were allowed into the United States, but people from other countries faced severe quotas.

8. Stockton went from having 4 percent of its population foreign born in 1970 to 19 percent in 2000; Fresno similarly went from 3 percent foreign born to 21 percent, according to U.S. Census Bureau.

9. ANOVA analysis based on whether a city has more employment in manufacturing than in professional services yields no significant differences between the two types of places.

10. Data on businesses from the *Million Dollar Directory* by Dun & Bradstreet (New York) from various years. Refer to the appendix for notes on data sources.

11. Data from U.S. Census and County Business Patterns from various years.

12. Factories that deliberately set up in Mexico immediately across the border in order to avoid the more stringent environmental and labor laws in the United States are known as maquiladoras. These enterprises generally import all raw materials, produce a good, and then export the product back to the United States.

13. Data from U.S. Census and County Business Patterns from various years.

14. Ibid.

3. PUTTING OUT THE WELCOME MAT

1. See Janice Madden (2000) for an exception; her book examines metropolitan level economic inequality, but only among the largest metro areas of the United States.

2. U.S. Census data.

3. All income figures in this chapter come from the U.S. Census Bureau's American Community Survey, 2006–2008, and are in constant 2000 dollars.

4. The tolerance rank is used in the OLS regression analysis in which change in population (or change in income levels) are the dependent variables. Note that Florida did not calculate the tolerance rank over time because some of the data needed to construct it is unavailable for years prior to 2000.

4. DIVERSIFY, DON'T SPECIALIZE

1. Employment could also be assessed based on what people actually do in their jobs rather than by the sector of the economy. However, I use it here because

economic sector is associated strongly with other characteristics and other scholars use it.

2. Based on ANOVA results. Differences in 1970: F = 18.19, $p < 0.0001$; differences in 1980: F = 4.99, $p = 0.0033$; differences in 1990: F = 0.90, $p = 0.4441$; differences in 2000: F = 0.79, $p = 0.5036$.

5. BALANCING IT ALL

1. For example, percentage of the population living in poverty or percentage unemployed (or employed) could be included in this type of index.

2. While percentage change in population and percentage change in income from 1970 to 2000 are not correlated, for each census year, income and population are correlated.

3. I recognize that an increasing median income and a large rate of change in the median household income might also come about from a demographic shift in which more higher-income households move to a particular metro area. However, this appears to not regularly be the case among this sample of metro areas, although the case of Salinas (in detail below) does show this possibility.

4. The rank is a somewhat volatile index, but the middle 50 percent of the distribution had a variance of about 20 percent from 1980 to 2000. There were extreme changes in the tails of the distribution, with about 18 percent of metro areas moving about 20 places in the ranking over the period. Nonetheless, because theoretically this rank makes sense based on the importance of the outcome measures and there is little previous scholarship to guide the creation of a multifaceted outcome, I believe it is still a useful index for investigating success and failure among small places.

5. While the top ten and bottom ten from 2000 could have been examined instead, using the ten cities that experienced the most negative change and the most positive change better captures change over time.

6. SMALL CITIES MATTER!

1. The fact that the Northeast contains a disproportionately large number of large metro areas compared to other regions may account for the muted affect of region among the eighty places studied here. Even so, the fact that southern and western places did not live up to the expectations set by previous research on national samples suggests that region is less of an influence than previously thought.

7. EPILOGUE

1. Real estate value data from www.zillow.com, accessed on January 4, 2011.

2. Unemployment data are from the Bureau of Labor Statistics, www.bls.gov.

3. Economic sector data from the U.S. Census Bureau's American Community Survey, 2005 and 2006.

4. The information on Ann Arbor for 2008 is for the city of Ann Arbor, not the metro area. The U.S. Census Bureau continues to change the way data are collected, which includes redefining geographic entities; in 2000, Ann Arbor lost its status as a PMSA, and data are no longer collected at the metro-area level for it.

5. Data are from the American Community Survey. Note that there is not complete comparability between pre-2000 and post-2000 data because of changes in the way the Bureau of Labor Statistics and the U.S. Census Bureau collect information. The manufacturing numbers reported in the epilogue are all according to the NAICS standard employed by these agencies since the late 1990s, but data in previous chapters were based on older STC categorizations (see the appendix for details about the data).

BIBLIOGRAPHY

Adams, Charles, Howard Fleeter, Yul Kim, Mark Freeman, and Imgon Cho. 1996. "Flight from Blight and Metropolitan Suburbanization Revisited." *Urban Affairs Quarterly* 31 (4): 529–543.

Allison, Paul. 2005. *Fixed Effects Regression Methods for Longitudinal Data Using SAS.* Cary, N.C.: SAS Institute Inc.

Berry, Brian. 1967. *Geography of Market Centers and Retail Distribution.* Englewood, N.J.: Prentice Hall.

Bogart, William T. 2006. *Don't Call It Sprawl.* New York: Cambridge University Press.

Boushey, Heather, and Christian Weller. 2005. "What the Numbers Tell Us." In *Inequality Matters: The Growing Economic Divide in America and Its Poisonous Consequences,* edited by James Lardner and David Smith, 27–40. New York: New Press.

Carroll, Glenn, and John Meyer. 1983. "Capital Cities in the American Urban System: The Impact of State Expansion." *American Journal of Sociology* 88 (3): 565–578.

Christaller, Walter. 1933/1966. *Die zentralen Orte in Süddeutschland.* Jena: Gustav Fischer. Translated by Carlisle W. Baskin as *Central Places in Southern Germany.* Englewood, N.J.: Prentice-Hall.

City of Monterey. 2012. "Economic Development Opportunities: Tourism." Available at http://www.monterey.org/en-us/businesstoday/economicdevelopment opportunities.aspx. Retrieved May 16, 2012.

City of Providence. 2009. *Creative Providence: A Cultural Plan for the Creative Sector.* Providence, R.I.: City of Providence. Available at http://cityof.providenceri.com/efile/47. Retrieved December 10, 2010.

City of Salinas. 2006. "Salinas, California: A Great Place to Live, Work, & Visit." Available at http://www.salinas.com. Retrieved February 2, 2006.

Clark, Terry Nichols. 2004. "Gays and Urban Development: How Are They Linked?" *Research in Urban Policy* 9: 221–234.

CNN Money. 2006. "Fortune 500 Database." http://money.cnn.com/magazines/fortune/fortune500_archive/ Retrieved March 27, 2006.

Coulson, N. Edward. 1999. "Sectoral Sources of Metropolitan Growth." *Regional Science and Urban Economics* 29 (6): 723–743.

Cowle, Jefferson. 1999. *Capital Moves: RCAs Seventy-Year Quest for Cheap Labor.* Ithaca, NY: Cornell University Press.

Crihfield, John, and Martin Panggabean. 1995. "Growth and Convergence in U.S. Cities." *Journal of Urban Economics* 38 (2): 138–165.

Danziger, Sheldon, and Peter Gottschalk. 1995. *America Unequal*. Cambridge, Mass.: Harvard University Press.

Davis, Mike. 1992. *City of Quartz: Excavating the Future in Los Angeles*. New York: Vintage Press.

Diener, Ed, and Robert Biswas-Diener. 2002. "Will Money Increase Subjective Well-Being?" *Social Indicators Research* 57: 119–169.

Duany, Andres, Elizabeth Plater-Zyberk, and Jeff Speck. 2000. *Suburban Nation: The Rise of Sprawl and the Decline of the American Dream*. New York: North Point Press.

Dun & Bradstreet. 1980. *Million Dollar Directory*. New York: Dun & Bradstreet.

———. 1990. *Million Dollar Directory*. New York: Dun & Bradstreet.

———. 2000. *Million Dollar Directory*. New York: Dun & Bradstreet.

Egan, Timothy. 2002. "The Nation: Pastoral Poverty; the Seeds of Decline." *New York Times*, 2 November, sec. 4, p.1, col. 1.

Ehrlich, Steven, and Joseph Gyourko. 2000. "Changes in the Scale and Size Distribution of Metropolitan Areas during the Twentieth Century." *Urban Studies* 37 (7): 1063–1077.

Eisinger, Peter and Charles Smith. 2000. "Globalization and Metropolitan Well-Being in the United States." *Social Science Quarterly* 81 (2): 634–644.

Erickeck, George, and Hannah McKinney. 2004. *"Small Cities Blues": Looking for Growth Factors in Small and Medium-Sized Cities*. Upjohn Institute Staff Working Paper No. 04–100. Kalamazoo, Mich.: Upjohn Institute.

Fischer, Claude. 2002. "Ever-More Rooted Americans." *City and Community* 1 (2): 177–198.

Flora, Cornelia, Jan L. Flora, and Susan Fey. 2004. *Rural Communities: Legacy and Change*. Boulder, Colo.: Westview.

Florida, Richard. 2002. *The Rise of the Creative Class: And How It's Transforming Work, Leisure, Community, and Everyday Life*. Cambridge, Mass.: Basic Books.

———. 2005. *Cities and the Creative Class*. New York: Routledge Press.

Fortune. 1970. "The 500 Largest US Industrial Corporations." May, 187–199.

Fortune. 1980. "Fortune's Directory of the 500 Largest Industrial Corporations." May 5, 274–295.

Fortune. 1983a. "The 500." May 2, 227–254.

Fortune. 1983b. "The Service 500." June 13, 153–176.

Fortune. 1990a. "The Fortune 500 Largest Industrials." April 23, 346–366.

Fortune. 1990b. "The Fortune Service 500." June 4, 298–335.

Fortune. 1994a. "A Heck of a Year." April 18, 210–219.

Fortune. 1994b. "The Fortune Service 500." May 30, 200–221.

Frey, William. 2005. *Immigration and Domestic Migration in US Metro Areas: 2000 and 1990 Census Findings by Education and Race*. Report 05–572. Washington, DC: Brookings Institution.

Friedmann, John. 1995. "Appendix: The World City Hypothesis." In *World Cities in a World-System*, edited by Paul Knox and Peter Taylor, 317–331. Cambridge: Cambridge University Press.

Furdell, Kimberly, Harold Wolman, and Edward W. Hill. 2002. "Did Central Cities Come Back? Which Ones, How Far, and Why?" *Journal of Urban Affairs* 27 (3): 283–305.

Furman, Jason, and Joseph Stiglitz. 1998. "Economic Consequences of Income Inequality." *Income Inequality: Issues and Policy Options: A Symposium*, 221–263. Kansas City, Mo.: Federal Reserve Bank of Kansas City.

Gardner, Todd. 2001. "The Slow Wave: The Changing Residential Status of Cities and Suburbs in the United States, 1850–1940." *Journal of Urban History* 27 (3): 293–312.

Garreau, Joel. 1991. *Edge City: Life on the New Frontier*. New York: Anchor Books.

Getz, Malcolm. 1979. "Optimum City Size: Fact or Fancy?" *Law and Contemporary Problems* 43 (2): 197–210.

Glaeser, Edward, and Jesse Shapiro. 2003a. "City Growth: Which Places Grew and Why." In *Redefining Urban and Suburban America: Evidence from Census 2000*, vol. 1, edited by Bruce Katz and Robert E. Lang, 13–32. Washington, DC: Brookings Institution Press.

———. 2003b. "Urban Growth in the 1990s: Is City Living Back?" *Journal of Regional Economic Science* 43 (1): 139–165.

Glaeser, Edward, Hedi Kallal, Jose Scheinkman, and Andrei Shleifer. 1992. "Growth in Cities." *Journal of Political Economy* 100 (6): 1126–1152.

Halaby, Charles. 2004. "Panel Models in Sociological Research: Theory into Practice." *Annual Review of Sociology* 30: 304–344.

Haworth, Charles, James Long, and David Rasmussen. 1978. "Income Distribution, City Size and Urban Growth." *Urban Studies* 15 (1): 1–7.

Hayden, Dolores. 2003. *Building Suburbia: Green Fields and Urban Growth, 1820–2000*. New York: Pantheon Books.

Henderson, Vernon. 1997. "Medium Sized Cities." *Regional Science and Urban Economics* 27 (6): 583–612.

Hout, Michael, Claude Fischer, and Jon Stiles. 2006. "What Americans Had: Differences in Living Standards." In *Century of Difference: How America Changed in the Last One Hundred Years*, 137–161. New York: Russell Sage.

Jackson, Kenneth. 1985. *Crabgrass Frontier: The Suburbanization of the United States*. New York: Oxford University Press.

Jenkins, J. Craig, Kevin Leicht, and Arthur Jaynes. 2006. "Do High Technology Policies Work? High Technology Industry Employment Growth in U.S. Metropolitan Areas, 1988–1998." *Social Forces* 85 (1): 267–296.

Johnson, Kirk. 2009. "For Elderly in Rural Areas, Times Are Distinctly Harder." *New York Times*, 11 December.

Kelbaugh, Douglas. 2002. *Repairing the American Metropolis: Common Place Revisited*. Seattle: University of Washington Press.

Knox, Paul, and Peter Taylor, eds. 1995. *World Cities in a World-System*. Cambridge: Cambridge University Press.

Kunstler, James Howard. 1993. *The Geography of Nowhere: The Rise and Decline of America's Man-Made Landscape*. New York: Touchstone, Simon & Schuster.

Levy, Frank. 1998. *The New Dollars and Dreams: American Incomes and Economic Change*. New York: Russell Sage Foundation.

Logan, John, and Harvey Molotch. 1987. *Urban Fortunes: The Political Economy of Place*. Berkeley: University of California Press.

López, José Joaquín, and Keith R. Phillips. 2006. "Full Steam Ahead for Texas Ports." *Southwest Economy* 6 (November–December). Available at http://dallasfed.org/research/swe/2006/swe0606b.html.

Madden, Janice Fanning. 2000. "Jobs, Cities, and Suburbs in the Global Economy." *Annals of the American Academy of Political and Social Science* 572 (6): 78–89.

Marcuse, Peter, and Ronald van Kempan. 2000. "Conclusion: A Changed Spatial Order." In *Globalizing Cities: A New Spatial Order?* edited by Peter Marcuse and Ronald van Kempan, 249–275. London: Blackwell.

Massey, Douglas, and Nancy Denton. 1991. *American Apartheid: Segregation and the Making of the Underclass*. Cambridge, Mass.: Harvard University Press.

McCann, Eugene J. 2004a. "'Best Places': Interurban Competition, Quality of Life and Popular Media Discourse." *Urban Studies* 41 (10): 1909–1929.

———. 2004b."Urban Political Economy Beyond the 'Global City.'" *Urban Studies* 41 (12).

Mills, Edwin, and John McDonald, eds. 1992. *Sources of Metropolitan Growth*. New Brunswick, N.J.: Center for Urban Policy Research.

Mitchell-Weaver, Clyde, David Miller, and Ronald Deal Jr. 2000. "Multilevel Governance and Metropolitan Regionalism in the USA." *Urban Studies* 37 (5–6): 851–876.

Mollenkopf, John, and Manuel Castells, eds. 1991. *Dual City: Restructuring New York*. New York: Russell Sage Foundation.

Negrey, Cynthia, and Mary Beth Zickel. 1994. "Industrial Shifts and Uneven Development: Patterns of Growth and Decline in U.S. Metropolitan Areas." *Urban Affairs Quarterly* 30 (1): 27–47.

O'Connor, Alice, Chris Tilly, and Lawrence Bobo, eds. 2001. *Urban Inequality: Evidence from Four Cities*. New York: Russell Sage Foundation.

OneSource Database. 2006. http://www.onesource.com/. Retrieved by Gary Peete, Instruction Librarian, Thomas J. Long Business and Economics Library, University of California, Berkeley, on 24 March 2006.

Owens, Eric, Tom Melzer, and Staff of the Princeton Review. 2005. *America's Best Colleges, 2006 Edition*. Washington, DC: U.S. News World Report.

Pack, Janet Rothenberg. 1980. *Regional Growth: Historic Perspective*. Washington, DC: U.S. Advisory Commission on Intergovernmental Relations.

———. 2002. *Growth and Convergence in Metropolitan America*. Washington, DC: Brookings Institution Press.

Portes, Alejandro, and Alex Stepick. 1993. *City on the Edge: The Transformation of Miami.* Berkeley: University of California Press.

Portney, Kent E. 2003. *Taking Sustainable Cities Seriously.* Cambridge, Mass.: MIT Press.

Rausch, Stephen, and Cynthia Negrey. 2006. "Does the Creative Engine Run? A Consideration of the Effect of Creative Class on Economic Strength and Growth." *Journal of Urban Affairs* 28 (5): 473–489.

Robinson, Jennifer. 2002. "Global and World Cities: A View from off the Map." *International Journal of Urban and Regional Research* 26 (3): 531–554.

Rusk, David. 2003. *Cities without Suburbs.* Washington, DC: Woodrow Wilson Center Press.

Sassen, Saskia. 2001. *The Global City: New York, London, Tokyo.* 2nd ed. Princeton, N.J.: Princeton University Press.

Savitch, H. V., and Paul Kantor. 2002. *Cities in the International Marketplace.* Princeton, N.J.: Princeton University Press.

Savitch, H. V., David Collins, Daniel Sanders, and John Markham. 1993. "Ties that Bind: Central Cities, Suburbs, and the New Metropolitan Region." *Economic Development Quarterly* 7 (4): 341–357.

Scott, Allen. 2006. "Creative Cities: Conceptual Issues and Policy Questions." *Journal of Urban Affairs* 28 (1): 1–17.

Scott, Allen, and Edward Soja, eds. 1996. *The City: Los Angeles and Urban Theory at the End of the Twentieth Century.* Berkeley: University of California Press.

Sperling, Bert, and Peter Sander. 2004. *Cities Ranked and Rated.* Hoboken, NJ: Wiley Publishing Inc.

Stanback, Thomas. 2002. *The Transforming Metropolitan Economy.* New Brunswick, N.J.: Center for Urban Policy Research.

Stepick, Alex, and Alejandro Portes. 1993. *City on the Edge: The Transformation of Miami.* Berkeley: University of California Press.

Suro, Roberto, and Audrey Singer. 2003. "Changing Patterns of Latino Growth in Metropolitan America." In *Redefining Urban and Suburban America: Evidence from Census 2000*, edited by Bruce Katz and Robert Lang, 181–210. Washington, DC: Brookings Institution.

United Nations. 2007. *World Urbanization Prospects: The 2005 Revision.* New York: Department of Economic and Social Affairs, Population Division.

U.S. Census Bureau (U.S. Department of Commerce, Bureau of the Census). 1970. Summary Statistic File 4a—Population (Fourth Count). Computer file distributed by the Inter-University Consortium for Political and Social Research (2nd ICPSR version), Ann Arbor, Michigan, 2001. Data drawn from *1970 Census of Population and Housing.* Washington, D.C: U.S. Dept. of Commerce, Bureau of the Census, 1971.

———. 1982. 1980 Census of Population and Housing: Summary Tape File 3a. Computer file distributed by the Inter-University Consortium for Political and Social Research, Ann Arbor, Michigan. Data drawn from. Data drawn from *1980 Census of Population and Housing: Summary Tape File 3a*. Washington, DC: U.S. Department of Commerce, Bureau of the Census.

———. 1985. County Business Patterns, 1974: U.S. Summary, State, and County Data. Computer file distributed by the Inter-University Consortium for Political and Social Research, Ann Arbor, Michigan. Data drawn from *County Business Patterns, 1975*. Washington, DC: U.S. Dept. of Commerce, Bureau of the Census.

———. 1986. County Business Patterns, 1979: U.S. Summary, State, and County Data. Computer file distributed by the Inter-University Consortium for Political and Social Research, Ann Arbor, Michigan. Data drawn from *County Business Patterns, 1979: U.S. Summary, State, and County Data*. Washington, DC: U.S. Dept. of Commerce, Bureau of the Census.

———. 1990. "Population and Geographic Centers" from 1990 Census of Population and Housing, "1990 Population and Housing Unit Counts: United States," (CPH-2). Downloaded from http://www.census.gov/population/www/censusdata/hiscendata.html on March 2, 2007.

———. 1991. County Business Patterns, 1989: U.S. Summary, State, and County Data. Computer file produced by U.S. Department of Commerce, Bureau of the Census. Distributed by the Inter-University Consortium for Political and Social Research, Ann Arbor, Michigan.

———. 1993. *Census of Population and Housing, 1990 (United States)*. Summary Tape File 3a. Computer file generated by the U.S. Department of Commerce, Bureau of the Census. Distributed by the Inter-University Consortium for Political and Social Research, Ann Arbor, Michigan.

———. 1993. *1990 Census of Population and Housing: 1990 Population and Housing Unit Counts: United States (CPH-2)*. Washington, DC: Government Printing Office. Available at http://www.census.gov/population/www/censusdata/hiscendata.html.

———. 1994. *Geographic Areas Reference Manual*. Washington, DC: U.S. Department of Commerce, Bureau of the Census.

———. 1998. County Business Patterns, 1996: U.S. Summary, State, and County Data. Computer file produced by U.S. Department of Commerce, Bureau of the Census. Distributed by the Inter-University Consortium for Political and Social Research, Ann Arbor, Michigan.

———. 2003–2004. *Census of Population and Housing, 2000*. File PHC-3: Population and Housing Unit Counts. Washington, DC: U.S. Dept. of Commerce, Bureau of the Census. Generated using American FactFinder, http://factfinder.census.gov.

———. 2009. American Community Survey (ACS): Public Use Microdata Sample (PUMS), 2008. Distributed by the Inter-University Consortium for Political and Social Research, Ann Arbor, Michigan.

U.S. Department of Housing and Urban Development, Office of Policy Development and Research. 2006. State of the Cities Data Systems. 2006. Available at http://socds.huduser.org/index.html.

Vance, James. 1971. *Merchant's World: The Geography of Wholesaling*. Englewood, N.J.: Prentice-Hall.

Vey, Jennifer, and Benjamin Forman. 2002. *Demographic Change in Medium-Sized Cities: Evidence from the 2000 Census*. Washington, DC: Brookings Institution.

Waldinger, Roger, and Michael Lichter. 2003. *How the Other Half Works: Immigration and the Social Organization of Labor*. Berkeley: University of California Press.

Wilson, William. 1996. *When Work Disappears: The World of the New Urban Poor*. New York: Vintage Books.

Wirth, Louis. 1938/1969. "Urbanism as a Way of Life." In *Classic Essays on the Culture of Cities*, edited by Richard Sennett, 143–169. New York: Appleton Century Crofts. First published in *On Cities and Social Life*, edited by Albert J. Reiss Jr. Chicago: University of Chicago Press, 1938.

INDEX

90:10 Economic Inequality Index, definition of, 63–64

Abilene (Texas): economic inequality, 88*tab*; median household income, 105*tab*; as medium grower, 31*tab*; population, 31*tab*; success index ranking, 122*tab*
AFLAC Insurance (Columbus, Ga.), 53
Akron (Ohio): decline in size, 22*tab*
Amarillo (Tex.): economic inequality, 88*tab*; as fast grower, 31*tab*; median household income, 105*tab*; population, 31*tab*; success index ranking, 122*tab*, 125*tab*
American Family Insurance (Madison, Wis.), 53
American Medical Services (Green Bay, Wis.), 49, 127
Ann Arbor (Mich.): economic inequality, 88*tab*; educational institutions in, 55; as fast grower, 31*tab*; immigration in, 153; median household income, 105*tab*; population, 31*tab*; success index ranking, 122*tab*

Bakersfield (Calif.): economic inequality, 88*tab*; as explosive grower, 31*tab*; median household income, 105*tab*; population, 31*tab*; success index ranking, 122*tab*, 125*tab*
banking, 7
Baton Rouge (La.): economic inequality, 88*tab*; as fast grower, 31*tab*; median household income, 105*tab*; population, 31*tab*; success index ranking, 122*tab*
Beaumont (Tex.): decline in size, 22*tab*; economic inequality, 88*tab*, 125; median household income, 82, 105*tab*; population, 31*tab*; as slow grower, 31*tab*, 36; suburbanization in, 36; success index ranking, 122*tab*, 125*tab*
Berkekey (Calif.), 16
Berry, Brian, 7
Billings (Mont.): economic inequality, 88*tab*; as fast grower, 31*tab*; median household income, 105*tab*; population, 31*tab*; success index ranking, 122*tab*, 125*tab*
Bobo, Lawrence, 146
Bogart, William, 29
Boise (Idaho), 12; economic inequality, 87, 88*tab*; as explosive grower, 31*tab*; immigration in, 45; income levels, 6; jobs available, 6; median household income, 105*tab*; population, 6, 20, 31*tab*, 81, 113; success index ranking, 122*tab*; urbanization in, 36
Boushey, Heather, 120
Brown University, 39, 55, 71, 72
Bruce Church, Inc. (Salinas, Calif.), 59
Bud Antle Inc. (Salinas, Calif.), 59

call centers, 7
Cambridge (Mass.), 16
capital: global, 7; human, 9, 10, 11, 42, 56, 75, 131, 141; state, 11, 57
Carmel (Calif.), 60, 61, 91, 128
Carroll, Glenn, 11, 55, 112
Caterpillar Corporation (Peoria, Ill.), 53
Cedar Rapids (Iowa): decline in size, 22*tab*; economic inequality, 87, 88*tab*; median household income, 105*tab*; population, 31*tab*, 34; as slow grower, 31*tab*; success index ranking, 122*tab*
change: comparative and historical approaches to, 144–145; creative class and, 9–11, 72; demographic, 2; distribution of effects of, 101, 102; due to climate, 81; economic, 2, 76; in economic inequality, 74–77; effect of region in, 77; effect on differing types of small cities, 13; in employment, 75; ethnic, 46, 71, 72; factors leading to, 76; global economic, 6; industrial, 5; in median household income, 74–77; in migration patterns, 5; in patterns of settlement, 4; population, 15*tab*, 74–77; reversal of population living places, 12; in smaller cities, 2, 5–12; success index ranking, 121–126; theories of, 5, 6; understanding, 3; urban, 8, 11, 74–77

Chattanooga (Tenn.): economic inequality, 88*tab*; immigration, 152; median household income, 105*tab*; as medium grower, 31*tab*; population, 31*tab*; success index ranking, 122*tab*
Cherry Semiconductor Corporation (Providence, R.I.), 39
Chicago (Ill.), 2, 4; patterns of settlement, 4
Chicago School of urban sociology, 3–4
Christaller, Walter, 7, 131
Cianci, Buddy, 151
Circuit City Company (Richmond, Va.), 53
cities: diversity of population in, 9, 10, 11; existence in peril, 2; gateway, 45, 79; place-specific attributes of, 11–12; role of people in success of, 9–11; "rustbelt," 30, 35; stagnation in, 2, 9.10; state capitals, 11, 57, 112; universities in, 11. *See also* metro areas
cities, explosive growers: defining, 166*n1*; economic inequality in, 64*fig*; education levels in, 46*fig*; immigration in, 44*fig*; income levels by rate of population growth in, 62*tab*; income levels in, 32; industrial employment in, 54*fig*; population, 33*fig*, 35*fig*; problems with, 119; professional services employment in, 55, 55*fig*; racial composition, 43*fig*; suburbanization and, 36*fig*; unemployment from mass in-migration, 66; unemployment in, 32, 65*fig*
cities, fast growers: adaptation to new economy, 32; cost of living in, 62; defining, 166*n1*; as destinations for immigration, 45; diversity in, 32; domestic in-migration in, 32; economic inequality in, 64, 64*fig*; education levels in, 46*fig*, 70; as glocal cities, 82; housing costs, 62; immigration in, 44, 44*fig*, 45; income levels by rate of population growth in, 62*tab*; industrial employment in, 54*fig*; initially smaller populations in, 78; low-end service sector in, 55; not attracting Fortune 500 firms, 53; population, 33*fig*, 35*fig*; poverty levels in, 64; professional services employment in, 55, 55*fig*; racial composition, 43*fig*; service sector employment in, 64; suburbanization and, 36*fig*; unemployment in, 65*fig*; universities in, 32
cities, global, 7, 137; assumed large populations in, 8; restricted numbers of, 8
cities, glocal. *See* glocal cities
cities, large: immigration and, 4; industrial production and, 4; out-migration from, 6; population, 33; relationships to suburbs, 16. *See also* metro areas
cities, medium growers: defining, 166*n1*; economic inequality in, 64*fig*; education levels in, 46*fig*; immigration in, 44*fig*; income levels by rate of population growth in, 62*tab*; industrial employment in, 54*fig*; in the Midwest, 30, 31*tab*; population, 33*fig*, 35*fig*; racial composition, 30, 43*fig*; in the South, 30, 31*tab*; suburbanization and, 36*fig*; unemployment in, 65*fig*
cities, slow growers: defining, 166*n1*; difficulty in attracting highly educated population, 81; economic inequality in, 64, 64*fig*; education levels in, 46*fig*, 70; Fortune 500 firms in, 70; immigration in, 44*fig*; income levels, 30, 62; income levels by rate of population growth in, 62*tab*; industrial employment in, 54*fig*; initially larger populations in, 78; lack of attractiveness to residents/potential residents, 119; little immigration in, 30; in the Northeast, 30, 31*tab*; not racially diverse, 30; population, 33*fig*, 35*fig*; population age in, 42; professional services employment in, 55, 55*fig*; racial composition, 43*fig*; suburbanization and, 36*fig*; unemployment from loss of manufacturing jobs, 66; unemployment in, 65*fig*
cities, small: affordability of, 46; attracting population to, 41–47; as centers for hinterlands, 3; as centers for national/multinational corporations, 53; changes in, 5–12; combinations of characteristics necessary for success, 71–90; creative class in, 10, 72; defining, 14, 16, 20–21; as destinations, 73; differences in urban life from large cities, 2, 3; differing trajectories of, 27–70; diversity in, 13; diversity of experiences of, 3, 20; economic downturn effects on, 148, 149; economic inequality in, 74–77; economic inequality changes in, 87–89; education, 138; effects of global/national economic change on, 6–9; ethnic changes in, 46, 71, 72; external forces and, 5, 11, 74, 75; Fortune 500 companies in, 11, 53, 165*n4*; growth cycles, 3, 4, 5, 14; growth/decline of, 28, 29, 32–37; higher education in, 55; immigration in, 136, 138; importance of, 132–147; importance of diverse mix of people in, 71–90; importance of diversification for growth in, 89–115; importance of income distribution in, 61–66; importance of presence of universities in, 123; important economic institutions in, 53; income changes in, 82–87; increasing similarity to large cities, 137–139; integration into national economic system, 53; interconnectedness of economies and, 6–9; internal forces in, 5; jobs available, 7; lack of research on, 3, 4; livability of, 118; location quotients,

95–96; loss of manufacturing jobs, 45; lower average wages in, 100, 101; median household income, 74–77, 149; mirroring of economy of large metro areas, 131; multiple indicators of success/failure for, 145–146; as part of global economy, 53; population, 1, 2, 5, 74–77; population change in, 78–82; public policy and, 3; racial composition in, 43, 44; ramifications of mass migrations on, 12; as regional centers, 13, 14, 165n3; relationships to suburbs, 16; relations with global cities, 7, 8, 9; role of immigration in success of, 143–144; rural, 32; sectoral employment in, 52tab; similar characteristics to large or global cities, 9; similarity of employment patterns to average metro areas, 52, 53; size not good predictor of growth, 34; "small-town" feeling in, 3, 14; specialization in tertiary/ancillary services to major cities by, 7; stagnation in, 14; success index rankings, 152 (*see also individual cities*); ties to regional, national, global economies, 96–101; traditional "urban" elements in, 3; trajectories of growth, 13; types of service sector jobs in, 52; unemployment in, 149. See also metro areas
claims-processing centers, 7
Cleveland (Ohio), 4
Colorado Springs (Colo.): economic inequality, 87, 88tab; as explosive grower, 31tab; immigration in, 45; median household income, 105tab; population, 31tab, 81; success index ranking, 122tab
Columbia (Mo.), 31tab, 88tab; as explosive grower, 31tab; median household income, 105tab; success index ranking, 122tab, 125tab
Columbia (S.C.), 31tab; economic inequality, 88tab; as explosive grower, 31tab; median household income, 105tab; success index ranking, 122tab
Columbus (Ga.): African American population, 166n5; economic inequality, 88tab; Fortune 500 firms in, 53; median household income, 105tab; population, 31tab; racial composition in, 45; as slow grower, 31tab; success index ranking, 122tab
Coulson, Edward, 73
Cowle, Jefferson, 53, 93
creative class, 72, 73, 90, 131, 138, 139. See also Florida, Richard
creativity, 9–11
credit card companies, 7
Crihfield, John, 73, 75, 76, 119
cultural: amalgamation, 116; amenities, 75; organizations, 30

Danzinger, Sheldon, 120
Davies, Richard, 32
Davis, Mike, 29
Decatur (Ill.): decline in size, 22tab; economic inequality, 88tab; median household income, 105tab; population, 20, 31tab, 33, 143; as slow grower, 31tab; success index ranking, 122tab
demographic(s): changes, 2; diversity in, 22; trajectories of, 13
Des Moines (Iowa): economic inequality, 88tab; median household income, 105tab; as medium grower, 31tab; population, 31tab; success index ranking, 122tab
de-urbanization, 14
Diener, Ed, 120
diversification: economic inequality and, 109–112; importance for small city growth, 91–115
diversity: attracting creative class and, 10, 11, 72, 90; as attraction to cities, 41; of demographics, 22; of economic activity, 22; ethnic, 42, 43, 71, 72; importance of, 10, 11, 89–90; lack of, 75; population, 76; racial, 30, 76, 130; success/failure over time, 22; tolerance and, 10
Dole Fresh Fruit (Salinas, Calif.), 128
Dole Fresh Vegetables (Salinas, Calif.), 59
Duany, Andres, 118
Duluth (Minn.): decline in size, 22tab; early immigration to, 45; economic inequality, 88tab; immigration, 78, 79, 86; median household income, 105tab; population, 31tab, 33, 143; as slow grower, 31tab; success index ranking, 122tab, 125tab

Eastern Wire Products (Providence, R.I.), 39
economic: changes, 2, 6, 76; development, 30; diversity, 9, 51; expansion/contraction, 6; freedom, 4; growth, 75; integration into national economies, 28; stagnation, 120
economic inequality, 12; changes in, 74–90; changes in levels of by sector, 110fig; combined with population and income to measure small city success, 116–131; demographic factors in, 89; diversification and levels of, 109–112; economic growth and, 30, 75; education levels and, 89; effects of, 120; employment characteristics and, 89; extreme levels of, 63, 75; income levels and, 94; increases in, 64, 109–112; loss of diversity and, 120; problems associated with, 63, 75; race and, 89; role in success of small cities, 146; role of region in, 135; roots of, 109; in success index, 119, 120; tolerance and, 113, 142, 143

economic inequality index, 63, 75, 87, 125, 129
economy: capitalist, 63; creative, 51; effect of employment change on, 75; global, 53, 93; greater integration of local into global/national, 6–9; homogenization of, 138; information, 73; local, 95–96; local ownership and, 28; moribund, 75; national, 28, 34, 53; non-economic factors influencing, 112–114; post-industrial, 6, 7, 8, 9, 13; service-based, 5, 6, 93
economy, industrial, 11
economy, new, 72, 96, 97, 97*fig*, 98–101, 114. *See also* sector, finance, insurance, and real estate; sector, service
economy, old, 29, 51–57, 92, 93, 96, 100, 115, 139. *See also* manufacturing; sector, industrial
economy, service: growth in, 6, 7. *See also* sector, service
education: bilingual, 49; changes in focus, 28; creative class and, 10, 72; employment in, 56, 57; in glocal cities, 133; immigration and, 46, 46*fig*, 47; income levels and, 83, 84, 84*fig*, 85; institutions as sources of jobs, 28; old/new economy requirements for, 51, 52; presence of universities, 11
education levels: economic inequality and, 89; effect on urban growth, 76, 78–82; of immigrants, 79; importance in attracting residents, 80; rising, 80
Egan, Timothy, 7, 32
Ehrlich, Steven, 77
Eisinger, Peter, 73
employment assessment of, 167*n1*; benefits with, 51, 52; changes in, 75; different combinations of sectors in success rates, 127*tab*; distance from large cities and, 112, 113; distribution of, 94, 99, 109; diversification of, 91; in education, 28, 56, 57; in government, 56, 57; human capital and, 75; as indicator of local economic performance, 92; in industrial sector, 54*fig*; location quotients and, 95; manufacturing, 39; non-economic factors and, 112–114; in professional services, 55*fig*. recession-proof, 55; sectors, 96, 97, 97*fig*, 98–101; spatial distribution of opportunities for, 52, 52*tab*, 53; in various sectors, 39, 52*tab*
Erickcek, George, 73, 75
Erie (Pa.), 12; decline in size, 22*tab*; economic inequality, 88*tab*; median household income, 105*tab*; population, 31*tab*; as slow grower, 31*tab*; success index ranking, 122*tab*
Eugene (Ore.): economic inequality, 88*tab*; as fast grower, 31*tab*; median household income, 105*tab*; population, 31*tab*; success index ranking, 122*tab*

Evansville (Ind.): economic inequality, 88*tab*; median household income, 105*tab*; population, 31*tab*; as slow grower, 31*tab*; success index ranking, 122*tab*
exurbs: flight to, 2

Fargo (N.D.): economic inequality, 88*tab*; as fast grower, 31*tab*; median household income, 105*tab*; population, 31*tab*; success index ranking, 122*tab*
Fayetteville (N.C.): economic inequality, 88*tab*; median household income, 105*tab*; as medium grower, 31*tab*; population, 31*tab*; racial composition in, 45; success index ranking, 122*tab*, 125*tab*
Fischer, Claude, 64, 66, 87
Flint (Mich.): decline in size, 22*tab*; economic inequality, 88*tab*; median household income, 105*tab*; population, 20, 31*tab*, 33, 143; as slow grower, 31*tab*; success index ranking, 122*tab*
Flora, Cornelia, 32
Florida, Richard, 9, 10, 29, 41, 51, 55, 72, 73, 76, 80, 81, 89, 90, 94, 113, 114, 131, 133, 141, 142. *See also* creative class; tolerance index
Fort Howard Paper Company (Green Bay, Wis.), 27, 28, 49
Fort Smith (Ark.): economic inequality, 88*tab*; as explosive grower, 31*tab*; median household income, 105*tab*; population, 31*tab*; success index ranking, 122*tab*
Fortune 500 firms, 11, 86, 124, 165*n4*; ancillary businesses and, 53; considered apart from local economy, 53; employment opportunities in, 53; in glocal cities, 133; not attracted to fast growers, 53; in slow growers, 70
Fort Wayne (Ind.): economic inequality, 88*tab*; median household income, 105*tab*; as medium grower, 31*tab*; population, 31*tab*; success index ranking, 122*tab*
Fresh International Corporation (Salinas, Calif.), 59
Fresno (Calif.): economic inequality, 88*tab*; as explosive grower, 31*tab*; immigration in, 167*n8*; income levels, 20, 21; median household income, 105*tab*; population, 20, 31*tab*, population 13; racial composition in, 45; success index ranking, 122*tab*, 125*tab*
Frey, William, 76
Friedmann, John, 7
Furdell, Kimberly, 36
Furman, Jason, 75

Gainesville (Fla.): economic inequality, 87, 88*tab*; as explosive grower, 31*tab*; immigration in, 45; median household

income, 105*tab*, 149; population, 31*tab*; success index ranking, 122*tab*
Gardner, Todd, 3, 138
Garreau, Joel, 2, 12, 16
Georgia Pacific Corporation (Green Bay, Wis.), 27, 49
Glaeser, Edward, 12, 73, 74, 77, 113, 118, 119, 135
global cities theory, 7, 138; inadequate accounting for urban change and growth in, 8
globalization: experiences of, 13
glocal cities, 9, 132–134; creative class and, 10; diversity in, 133; education in, 133; Fortune 500 firms in, 133; geography of, 133; in-migration in, 133; sector combinations in, 132, 133, 134; success index ranking and, 131
Grand Rapids (Mich.), 13; economic inequality, 88*tab*; median household income, 105*tab*; as medium grower, 31*tab*; population, 31*tab*; success index ranking, 122*tab*, 125*tab*
Green Bay (Wis.): agricultural processing in, 47, 49; case study, 47–51, 126, 127; as center city, 14; consolidation of industry in, 108; cost of living in, 49, 50; decline in retail commerce, 50; diversity in, 28; diversity in success/failure comparisons, 23; economic inequality, 88*tab*; economic success of, 11; education levels in, 80, 81; education sector in, 51; FIRE sector employment in, 127; as glocal city, 10, 11; healthcare sector, 49; Hmong community in, 27; home values, 150; immigration in, 23, 27, 49; income levels, 23, 49, 50; income-to-home-price ratio, 50, 63; industrial sector in, 47, 48, 108, 115; lack of white flight in, 49; location quotient, 115; median household income, 83, 105*tab*; as medium grower, 31*tab*; population, 1, 2, 23, 31*tab*, 49; racial composition in, 49; as regional center, 51; rejuvenation efforts, 50; retention of manufacturing in, 47, 48; service sector employment in, 115, 151; standard of living in, 49; success index ranking, 122*tab*, 124, 125*tab*, 127*tab*; unemployment, 50, 150, 151; University of Wisconsin–Green Bay, 27, 28
Green Bay Packers, 27, 47, 50, 51. *See also* professional sports teams
growth, economic: economic inequality and, 30; as goal of all cities, 30; not dependent on population growth, 29, 34; rates of, 35, 61–66; in well-being of small cities, 61–66
growth, population: accompaniments to, 29; income and, 62*tab*; from movement to center cities, 36, 37; rates of, 35, 61–66; self-perpetuating growth in, 66; size not good predictor of, 34; unrelated to economic success, 29; in well-being of small cities, 61–66

Hart-Cellar Act (1965), 78
Hasbro, Inc. (Providence, R.I.), 39, 127
Haworth, Charles, 118
Hayden, Dolores, 16
Henderson, Vernon, 73, 118, 119
Hout, Michael, 64, 83, 87, 120
Humana Healthcare (Green Bay, Wis.), 49, 127
Huntsville (Ala.): economic inequality, 88*tab*; as fast grower, 31*tab*; median household income, 105*tab*; population, 31*tab*; success index ranking, 122*tab*

immigration: before 1965, 45; Asian, 27, 41, 45, 49, 59, 60, 70, 71, 85, 86, 143, 167*n7*; backlash against, 75; changing patterns of, 70; clearing way for future immigrants, 66; decline in certain cities, 85, 86; education levels and, 46, 46*fig*, 47, 79, 80; European, 27, 41, 45, 70, 71; as factor in population increase, 78–79; to fast-growing cities, 45; foreign, 4; gateway cities and, 45, 79; income levels and, 85, 86, 86*fig*, 87; industrial employment and, 46; large cities and, 4; Latino, 27, 31, 41, 44, 45, 47, 49, 60, 61, 70, 71, 80, 85, 86, 143, 166*n6*, 167*n7*; manufacturing and, 4; median household income and, 149; movement to low-end service sector, 45; popular destinations for, 76; population growth and, 44, 45, 70; quotas, 78; relocation to small cities, 85, 86; role in success of small cities, 143–144; seasonal, 59; service sector employment and, 149; from the South to the North, 4; suburbanization and, 76; success index and, 123
Immigration and Nationality Act (1965), 167*n7*
Imperial Knife Company (Providence, R.I.), 39
income: absolute levels *vs.* change in levels of, 82–87; changes in, 74–90; combined with population and economic inequality to measure small city success, 116–131; declines in certain cities, 86, 87; distribution, 61–66, 63, 64, 87; economic factors in determination of, 83; economic inequality levels and, 109, 110, 111, 111*fig*, 112; education levels and, 83, 84, 84*fig*, 85; effect of economies on, 104–109; effect of tolerance on, 113; factors related to changes in levels of, 104–109; immigration levels and, 85, 86, 86*fig*, 87; importance in small city growth, 82–87; income-to-home-price ratio, 40, 50, 60; inequality, 63; levels, 6, 12, 20, 21, 23, 40, 59, 60, 94; levels of employment and,

income (*continued*)
106, 107, 107*fig*; location quotients and, 96; median household income, 168*n3*; personal, 75; polarization of, 63, 64; role of region in, 135; sector, finance, insurance, and real estate and, 123, 124; standard of living and, 120; in success index, 119, 120

Jackson, Kenneth, 3, 6, 11, 12, 16
Jackson (Miss.): economic inequality, 88*tab*; as fast grower, 31*tab*; median household income, 105*tab*; population, 31*tab*; success index ranking, 122*tab*
Jenkins, J. Craig, 10, 75
Johnson, Kirk, 32
Johnson and Wales University, 39

Kalamazoo (Mich.): economic inequality, 88*tab*; median household income, 105*tab*; population, 31*tab*; as slow grower, 31*tab*; success index ranking, 122*tab*
Kelbaugh, Douglas, 118
Knox, Paul, 8, 75
Knoxville (Tenn.): economic inequality, 88*tab*; as fast grower, 31*tab*; median household income, 105*tab*; population, 31*tab*; success index ranking, 122*tab*
Kunstler, James, 118

Lafayette (La.): economic inequality, 88*tab*; median household income, 105*tab*; as medium grower, 31*tab*; population, 31*tab*; success index ranking, 122*tab*
Lansing (Mich.): economic inequality, 88*tab*; median household income, 105*tab*; as medium grower, 31*tab*; population, 31*tab*; success index ranking, 122*tab*, 125*tab*
Laredo (Tex.): case study, 66–69, 126, 128, 129; cost of living in, 69; as cultural hybrid, 116; diversity in success/failure comparisons, 23; economic growth, 20; economic inequality, 12, 69, 88*tab*, 117, 129; education levels in, 81; ethnic distribution in, 66, 68; as explosive grower, 31*tab*; extraction industry in, 68; as fast grower, 66; FIRE-sector employment in, 114; home values, 150; immigration in, 69, 129, 152; import-export center, 129; income levels, 12, 20, 68, 69; income-to-home-price ratio, 63, 69; industrial sector employment, 114; location quotient in, 114, 129; median household income, 82, 83, 105*tab*, 117, 128, 129; population, 1, 2, 12, 31*tab* 66, 116, 128, 129; poverty in, 69, 117, 129; poverty rate in, 128; professional services in, 69; racial homogeneity in, 68; sector, finance, insurance, and real estate firms in, 124; service sector in, 68, 114; success index ranking, 122*tab*, 127*tab*, 129; unemployment, 150; unemployment in, 68
Las Vegas (Nev.), 13; economic inequality, 88*tab*; education levels in, 79, 80; as explosive grower, 31*tab*; home values, 150; median household income, 105*tab*; population, 13, 20, 31*tab*, 113; success index ranking, 122*tab*, 124, 125*tab*
Lawton (Okla.): decline in size, 22*tab*; economic inequality, 88*tab*; median household income, 105*tab*; population, 31*tab*; as slow grower, 31*tab*; success index ranking, 122*tab*
Levy, Frank, 120
Lexington (Ky.): economic inequality, 88*tab*; as fast grower, 31*tab*; median household income, 105*tab*; population, 31*tab*, 149; success index ranking, 122*tab*
Lichter, Michael, 66
Lincoln (Neb.): economic inequality, 88*tab*; educational institutions in, 56; as fast grower, 31*tab*; median household income, 105*tab*; population, 31*tab*; success index ranking, 122*tab*
Little Rock (Ark.), 12; economic inequality, 88*tab*; as fast grower, 31*tab*; immigration, 152; median household income, 105*tab*; population, 31*tab*; success index ranking, 122*tab*
location quotients, 95–96, 114, 146; definition, 95; for distribution of firms within sectors, 99, 100, 101*fig*; for employment by sector, 98, 99, 100*fig*
Logan, John, 55, 112
Lopez, Jose, 116
Los Angeles (Calif.), 2, 79
Lubbock (Tex.): economic inequality, 88*tab*, 125; median household income, 105*tab*; as medium grower, 31*tab*; population, 31*tab*; success index ranking, 122*tab*, 125*tab*

Macon (Ga.): economic inequality, 88*tab*; median household income, 105*tab*; as medium grower, 31*tab*; population, 31*tab*; success index ranking, 122*tab*
Madden, Janice, 61, 73, 109, 167*n1*
Madison (Wis.), 12; economic inequality, 88*tab*; educational institutions in, 56; as fast grower, 31*tab*; median household income, 105*tab*; population, 31*tab*; success index ranking, 122*tab*
manufacturing: decline in, 6, 7; Fordist, 9; immigration and, 4; increase in, 4; new, 96, 97, 97*fig*, 98–101, 99, 99*fig*, 100, 100*fig*, 101*fig*, 109, 110, 110*fig*, 111, 112. *See also* sector, industrial
maquiladoras, 167*n12*
Marcuse, Peter, 75

McAllen (Tex.): economic inequality, 87, 88*tab*, 117; as explosive grower, 31*tab*; immigration, 152; median household income, 105*tab*, 117; population, 31*tab*; success index ranking, 122*tab*

McCann, Eugene, 8, 11, 73

metro areas: case studies, 37–41, 47–51; changes in population over decades, 21*tab*, 22*tab*; complex economies in, 92; definition, 2–3; geographical distribution of population, 11; growth as mantra for, 29; immigration rates in, 44, 45; importance of diversification in employment in, 91–115; importance of presence of universities in, 123; importance of stable base of permanent residents, 29, 30; increasing similarities between large and small, 137–139; measuring success/stagnation in, 116–131; paths to success/failure in, 116–131; by region, 17*tab*; ties to regional, national, global economies, 96–101; types of, 114–115. *See also* cities

Metropolitan Statistical Areas (MSAs), 3, 155–157; creative class and economic strength in, 9–11

Meyer, John, 112

Midwest (region): economic inequality, 87; glocal cities in, 133; growth cycle, 12; medium growers in, 30, 31*tab*; migration from, 20; slowest growth in, 20; slow growers in, 30, 31*tab*; small cities as regional centers in, 3; small cities in, 17*tab*; success index rankings for, 135, 136; upwardly mobile metro areas in, 124

migration: African American movement from South, 11, 135; community benefits from, 29; geographical distribution of population and, 11; from Northeast/Midwest to South and West, 11, 12, 20, 81; rural-urban, 11

Milwaukee (Wis.), 4

Mitchell-Weaver, Clyde, 14

Mobile (Ala.): economic inequality, 88*tab*; median household income, 105*tab*; as medium grower, 31*tab*; population, 31*tab*; success index ranking, 122*tab*

Modesto (Calif.): economic inequality, 88*tab*; as explosive grower, 31*tab*; median household income, 105*tab*; population, 31*tab*, 113; success index ranking, 122*tab*

Mollenkopf, John, 2

Molotch, Harvey, 112

Monterey (Calif.), 60, 61, 91, 92, 128

Montgomery (Ala.): African American population, 166*n5*; economic inequality, 88*tab*; as fast grower, 31*tab*; median household income, 105*tab*; population, 31*tab*; success index ranking, 122*tab*

National Origins Act (1924), 78

Negrey, Cynthia, 7, 10, 73, 75, 131

New Urbanists, 118

New York (N.Y.), 2, 4, 79, 137

Northeast (region): disproportionate number of large cities in, 168*n1*; economic inequality, 87; growth cycle, 12; migration from, 20; slow growers in, 30, 31*tab*; small cities in, 17*tab*; success index rankings for, 135, 136

Nunes Company, Inc. (Salinas, Calif.), 59

O'Conner, Alice, 146

Orlando (Fla.), 13; economic inequality, 88*tab*; as explosive grower, 31*tab*; median household income, 105*tab*; population, 13, 31*tab*; success index ranking, 122*tab*

Pack, Janet, 11, 12, 14, 20, 73, 74, 77, 81, 113, 118, 135, 136

Packerland Packing Company (Green Bay, Wis.), 27

Pebble Beach Golf Club, 91

Peoria (Ill.): decline in size, 22*tab*; economic inequality, 88*tab*; immigration, 152; median household income, 105*tab*; population, 31*tab*; as slow grower, 31*tab*; success index ranking, 122*tab*

policy, public, 3, 134–147; debates on, 5; emphasis on market-driven solutions to problems, 5

population, 1, 2; accompaniments to growth of, 29; age distribution and, 42; center shift, 12; in central cities, 14, 16, 20–21; changes in, 15*tab*, 32–37, 77–90; characteristics of, 41–47; characteristics of associated with growth/stagnation, 77–90; combined with income and economic inequality to measure small city success, 116–131; declining, 75, 76; differing constellations related to differing outcomes for cities, 42; distributions, 42; diversity as advantage, 29; diversity in, 42, 76; education and, 46, 46*fig*, 47, 123; effect of education and immigration on, 78–82; ethnic composition, 123; factors related to increase/decrease in, 103–104; growth not related to economic success, 21; human capital and, 42; immigration and, 44, 45; importance of region in growth of, 135–136; importance of region to changes in, 77; increases, 70; increases linked to immigration, 78–79; influence on city's success, 41, 42; levels over time, 20; migration from the Northeast and, 81; rates of change, 34; settlement patterns, 3; in slow growth areas, 42; success index and, 119, 120, 124; working age, 166*n4*. *See also* growth, population; immigration

Portes, Alejandro, 2
Portney, Kent, 29
post-industrialization, 6, 7, 8, 9, 13
poverty levels, 59, 64, 69, 117, 128, 129, 168*n1*
professional sports teams: Green Bay Packers, 27, 47, 50, 51; Orlando Magic, 47
Providence College, 39, 72
Providence (R.I.), 12; case study, 37–41, 126, 127, 128; as center city, 14; changes in demographic composition of, 71, 72; cultural institutions, 39; demographic path, 40. 41; diversity in success/failure comparisons, 23; economic inequality, 88*tab*, 128; educational institutions in, 55, 72; educational sector in, 39; education levels in, 81; Federal Hill, 71; financial sector in, 39, 40; FIRE sector employment in, 127; fostering creative sector in. 72; home prices, 40; home values in, 151; immigration in, 40, 41, 71, 85, 128; income levels, 23, 40; income-to-home-price ratio, 40, 63; industrial employment in, 39; mass out-migration in, 37; median household income, 105*tab*; population, 23, 31*tab*, 34, 37; poverty rate in, 128; racial composition, 40; relocation of manufacturing to the South, 37; retail closures in, 37; revitalization efforts, 40, 151; service sector employment in, 39, 72, 127; as slow grower, 31*tab*; standard of living in, 40; suburbs of, 37; success index ranking, 122*tab*, 127*tab*; tourism in, 40, 72; unemployment, 39, 151; universities in, 39, 123
Pueblo (Colo.): decline in size, 22*tab*; economic inequality, 88*tab*; median household income, 105*tab*; as medium grower, 31*tab*; population, 13, 31*tab*, 34; success index ranking, 122*tab*

Rausch, Stephen, 10, 75, 131
Reading (Pa.): economic inequality, 87, 88*tab*; median household income, 105*tab*; as medium grower, 31*tab*; population, 31*tab*; success index ranking, 122*tab*, 125*tab*
Reno (Nev.): economic inequality, 88*tab*; as explosive grower, 31*tab*; immigration in, 79; median household income, 105*tab*; population, 31*tab*; success index ranking, 122*tab*
Rhode Island School of Design, 39, 72
Richmond (Va.): economic inequality, 88*tab*; as fast grower, 31*tab*; population, 31*tab*; success index ranking, 122*tab*
Roanoke (Va.): economic inequality, 88*tab*; median household income, 105*tab*; as medium grower, 31*tab*; population, 31*tab*; success index ranking, 122*tab*

Robinson, Jennifer, 5, 8
Rochester (Minn.): economic inequality, 88*tab*; as fast grower, 31*tab*; immigration in, 86; median household income, 105*tab*; population, 31*tab*; racial composition in, 42; success index ranking, 122*tab*
Rockford (Ill.), 88*tab*; median household income, 105*tab*; as medium grower, 31*tab*; population, 31*tab*; success index ranking, 122*tab*, 125*tab*
Rusk, David, 3

Salem (Ore.), 88*tab*; as explosive grower, 31*tab*; immigration, 85; median household income, 105*tab*; population, 31*tab*; success index ranking, 122*tab*
Salinas (Calif.): agribusiness in, 59; agricultural employment in, 57, 59, 128; case study, 57–61, 126; cost of living, 60; decline of farm businesses in, 59; diversification in, 91; diversity in success/failure comparisons, 23; economic inequality, 59, 60, 88*tab*, 128; education levels in, 81; ethnic composition, 60, 61; as fast grower, 31*tab*; healthcare services in, 59; home values, 150; immigration in, 23, 79; income levels, 23, 59, 60; income-to-home-price ratio, 60, 63; industrial sector employment, 114; location quotient in, 114; median household income, 105*tab*; population, 1, 2, 23, 31*tab*, 57; poverty levels in, 59; service sector in, 59, 61, 114; standard of living, 59; success index ranking, 122*tab*, 127*tab*; tourism and, 59, 91, 92; unemployment, 150
Salt Lake City (Utah): decline in public sector employment, 57; economic inequality, 87, 88*tab*; as explosive grower, 31*tab*; immigration in, 86; median household income, 105*tab*; population, 13, 31*tab*, 81, 113, 149; success index ranking, 122*tab*
San Angelo (Tex.): economic inequality, 88*tab*; as fast grower, 31*tab*; median household income, 105*tab*; population, 13, 31*tab*; success index ranking, 122*tab*
Sassen, Saskia, 2, 7, 8, 29, 51, 73, 75, 76, 81, 92, 93, 137, 165*n3*
Savannah (Ga.): economic inequality, 88*tab*; median household income, 105*tab*; as medium grower, 31*tab*; population, 31*tab*; success index ranking, 122*tab*, 125*tab*
Savitch, H.V., 7, 73, 75, 92, 119
Schelling, Thomas, 43, 44
Scott, Allen, 2, 10, 75
sector, creative, 72. *See also* creative class
sector, finance, insurance, and real estate (FIRE), 7, 93, 94; average wages in, 97,

98, 99*fig*; change in employment by change in economic inequality levels, 109, 110, 110*fig*, 111, 112; change in levels of employment and, 106, 107, 107*fig*; factors related to increase/decrease in population, 103–104; location quotient for distribution of firms within sectors, 99, 100, 101*fig*; location quotient for employment by sector, 98, 99, 100*fig*; percentage of firms in, 97, 98*fig*; percentage of workforce employed in, 52*tab*, 96, 97, 97*fig*, 98–101; success index ranking and, 123, 131; wages and, 123, 124

sector, industrial: average wages in, 97, 98, 99*fig*; change in employment by change in economic inequality levels, 109, 110, 110*fig*, 111, 112; change in levels of employment and, 106, 107, 107*fig*; combined with service sector for success, 139–141; consolidation of firms in, 94, 127, 128; declining employment in, 92, 93; employment in, 54–56; fewer firms but more jobs in, 108; increases in income levels in, 108; location quotient for distribution of firms within sectors, 99, 100, 101*fig*; location quotient for employment by sector, 98, 99, 100*fig*; as old economy, 29, 51–57, 92, 93; percentage of firms in, 97, 98*fig*; percentage of workforce employed in, 52*tab*, 96, 97, 97*fig*, 98–101; in Providence, 37; redistribution of employment in to the South, 93; shifts in, 92; unemployment in, 66

sector, service, 34; average wages in, 97, 98, 99*fig*; as bellwether for economic activity, 93; change in employment by change in economic inequality levels, 109, 110, 110*fig*, 111, 112; change in levels of employment and, 106, 107, 107*fig*; combined with industrial sector for success, 139–141; economy shift to, 9; education, 56, 57; factors related to increase/decrease in population, 103–104; government employment in, 56, 57; high-end, 9, 10, 41, 51, 53, 65, 75, 76, 89, 93, 96, 97, 97*fig*, 98–101, 98*fig*, 99, 99*fig*, 100, 100*fig*, 101*fig*, 106, 107, 107*fig*, 109, 110, 110*fig*, 111, 112, 127, 131, 142, 151; increase in employment in, 93; increasing importance of, 56; location quotient for distribution of firms within sectors, 99, 100, 101*fig*; location quotient for employment by sector, 98, 99, 100*fig*; low-end, 9, 45, 52, 70, 93, 96, 97, 97*fig*, 98–101, 98*fig*, 99, 99*fig*, 100, 100*fig*, 101*fig*, 106, 107, 107*fig*, 109, 110, 110*fig*, 111, 112, 144; as new economy, 29, 51–57; percentage of firms in, 97, 98*fig*; percentage of workforce employed in,

52*tab*, 96, 97, 97*fig*, 98–101; producer services in, 51; professional, 54–56

Shapiro, Jesse, 12, 73, 74, 77, 113, 118, 119, 135

Shreveport (La.): decline in size, 22*tab*; economic inequality, 88*tab*, 125; median household income, 105*tab*; as medium grower, 31*tab*; success index ranking, 122*tab*, 125*tab*

Singer, Audrey, 45, 79, 143

Sioux City (Iowa): decline in size, 22*tab*; economic inequality, 88*tab*; immigration in, 86, 152; median household income, 105*tab*; population, 13, 31*tab*; as slow grower, 31*tab*; success index ranking, 122*tab*

Sioux Falls (S.D.): as fast grower, 31*tab*; median household income, 105*tab*; in the Midwest, 30, 31*tab*; population, 31*tab*; success index ranking, 122*tab*

South Bend (Ind.): economic inequality, 88*tab*; median household income, 105*tab*; population, 31*tab*; as slow grower, 31*tab*; success index ranking, 122*tab*, 125*tab*

South (region): African American population, 166n5; downwardly mobile metro areas in, 124; economic inequality, 87; fastest growth in, 20; growth cycle, 12; lax labor laws in, 12, 37; medium growers in, 30, 31*tab*; migration to, 20; redistribution of employment from the Northeast to, 93; small cities in, 17*tab*; success index rankings for, 135, 136; weather and climate, 12; zoning laws in, 12

Spokane (Wash.): economic inequality, 88*tab*; as fast grower, 31*tab*; median household income, 105*tab*; population, 31*tab*; success index ranking, 122*tab*

Springfield (Ill.): economic inequality, 88*tab*; median household income, 105*tab*; as medium grower, 31*tab*; population, 31*tab*; success index ranking, 122*tab*

Springfield (Mass.): decline in size, 22*tab*; economic inequality, 88*tab*; educational institutions in, 55; median household income, 105*tab*; population, 31*tab*; as slow grower, 31*tab*; success index ranking, 122*tab*; universities in, 39, 123

Springfield (Mo.): economic inequality, 88*tab*; as explosive grower, 31*tab*; median household income, 105*tab*; population, 31*tab*; success index ranking, 122*tab*

Stanback, Thomas, 14, 73, 92, 94

Starbucks, 142

Stiles, Jon, 64

INDEX

Stockton (Calif.): economic inequality, 88*tab*; as explosive grower, 31*tab*; immigration in, 167*n*8; median household income, 105*tab*; population, 31*tab*; racial composition in, 45; success index ranking, 122*tab*
suburbanization, 36, 70; effect of World Wars on, 11; geographical distribution of population and, 11; reasons for, 12
suburbs, 36*fig*; flight to, 2; growth in, 35; migration to, 6
success index, 119–131; changes in ranking, 124, 125, 125*tab*, 126; components of, 119; economic inequality in, 119; education and, 131; equation for, 121; Fortune 500 firms and, 124; glocal cities and, 130–131; immigration and, 123; median household income in, 119; population and, 119, 124, 130; presence of universities and, 123; racial diversity and, 130; ranking metro areas change by, 121–126; sector, finance, insurance, and real estate establishments in, 123; service sector and, 131; state capitals and, 124
Syracuse (N.Y.): decline in size, 22*tab*; economic inequality, 88*tab*; median household income, 105*tab*; population, 31*tab*, 34; as slow grower, 31*tab*; success index ranking, 122*tab*

Tallahassee (Fla.): economic inequality, 88*tab*; as explosive grower, 31*tab*; government employment in, 65*fig*; median household income, 105*tab*; population, 31*tab*, 65*fig*; racial composition, 45; service sector employment in, 65*fig*; success index ranking, 122*tab*; unemployment in, 65*fig*
Texas Mexican Railway Company (Laredo, Tex.), 68
Textron, Inc. (Providence, R.I.), 39
Tilly, Chris, 146
tolerance: economic inequality and, 113, 142, 143; as key to success, 141; not associated with income growth, 113
tolerance index, 10, 80, 89, 90, 113, 131, 142, 167*n*4; population growth and, 113. *See also* Florida, Richard
Topeka (Kans.): decline in size, 22*tab*; economic inequality, 88*tab*; median household income, 105*tab*; population, 31*tab*; as slow grower, 31*tab*; success index ranking, 122*tab*, 125*tab*
Trenton (N.J.): economic inequality, 88*tab*; median household income, 86, 105*tab*; population, 31*tab*; as slow grower, 31*tab*; success index ranking, 122*tab*
Tyler (Tex.), 88*tab*; as explosive grower, 31*tab*; median household income, 105*tab*; population, 31*tab*; success index ranking, 122*tab*

unemployment: declines in median household income and, 149; in explosive growers, 32, 65*fig*; in fast growers, 65, 65*fig*; in medium growers, 65*fig*; from reduction in manufacturing jobs, 66; in slow growers, 64, 65*fig*
United States: de-urbanization in, 14; economic geography of, 165*n*3; median household income, 83; patterns of settlement in, 4; racial composition in, 42, 43; suburbanization in, 36; urbanization of, 4, 36
universities: success index and, 123; urban cultural life and, 39. *See also under individual cities*
University of Michigan, 55
University of Rhode Island, 39, 72
University of Wisconsin–Green Bay, 51, 55
urbanization, 36, 70, 124; early increase in, 6
urban life: alternative lifestyles in, 113; changes in, 74–77; growth ethic and, 30; nuances of, 3; public policy and, 3

Vance, James, 7, 165*n*3
Vey, Jennifer, 45, 74, 119

Waco (Tex.): economic inequality, 88*tab*; median household income, 105*tab*; as medium grower, 31*tab*; population, 31*tab*; success index ranking, 122*tab*
wages. *See* income
Waldinger, Roger, 66
Watercity Park (Providence, R.I.), 40
weather: business relocation and, 136; economic inequality and, 89; effect on population changes, 81; influence on local economies, 112; no effect on income or population change, 113
West (region): fastest growth in, 20; growth cycle, 12; immigration in, 79; lax labor laws in, 12; migration to, 20; small cities in, 3, 17*tab*; success index rankings for, 135, 136; weather and climate, 12; zoning laws in, 12
Wichita Falls (Tex.), 105*tab*; economic inequality, 88*tab*; population, 31*tab*; as slow grower, 31*tab*; success index ranking, 122*tab*
Wilson, William, 120
Wirth, Louis, 3
world cities hypothesis, 7

Youngstown (Ohio): decline in size, 22*tab*; early immigration to, 45; economic inequality, 88*tab*; immigration in, 78, 79, 86; income levels, 6; jobs available, 6; median household income, 82, 86, 105*tab*; population, 6, 31*tab*, 33, 34, 143; as slow grower, 31*tab*; success index ranking, 122*tab*, 125*tab*

ABOUT THE AUTHOR

JON R. NORMAN is assistant professor in the department of sociology and the graduate program in urban affairs and public policy at Loyola University Chicago. He received his Ph.D. from the University of California, Berkeley. Dr. Norman's research centers on understanding collective problem solving related to large-scale changes, mostly related to urban settings. He has also written about how smaller institutions adapt to change in the areas of religion and culture. His work has appeared in *Sociological Focus, Afterschool Matters, Method and Theory in Religion,* and the *Journal of Religion & Society.*